SAGE FOCUS EDITIONS

1. **POLICE AND SOCIETY**, edited by David H. Bayley
2. **WHY NATIONS ACT**, edited by Maurice A. East, Stephen A. Salmore, and Charles F. Hermann
3. **EVALUATION RESEARCH METHODS**, edited by Leonard Rutman
4. **SOCIAL SCIENTISTS AS ADVOCATES**, edited by George H. Weber and George J. McCall
5. **DYNAMICS OF GROUP DECISIONS**, edited by Hermann Brandstätter, James H. Davis, and Heinz Schuler
6. **NATURAL ORDER**, edited by Barry Barnes and Steven Shapin
7. **CONFLICT AND CONTROL**, edited by Arthur J. Vidich and Ronald M. Glassman
8. **CONTROVERSY**, edited by Dorothy Nelkin
9. **BATTERED WOMEN**, edited by Donna M. Moore
10. **CRIMINOLOGY**, edited by Edward Sagarin
11. **TO AUGUR WELL**, edited by J. David Singer and Michael D. Wallace
12. **IMPROVING EVALUATIONS**, edited by Lois-ellin Datta and Robert Perloff
13. **IMAGES OF INFORMATION**, edited by Jon Wagner
14. **CHURCHES AND POLITICS IN LATIN AMERICA**, edited by Daniel H. Levine
15. **EDUCATIONAL TESTING AND EVALUATION**, edited by Eva L. Baker and Edys S. Quellmalz
16. **IMPROVING POLICY ANALYSIS**, edited by Stuart S. Nagel
17. **POWER STRUCTURE RESEARCH**, edited by G. William Domhoff
18. **AGING AND SOCIETY**, edited by Edgar F. Borgatta and Neil G. McCluskey
19. **CENTRE AND PERIPHERY**, edited by Jean Gottmann
20. **THE ELECTORATE RECONSIDERED**, edited by John C. Pierce and John L. Sullivan
21. **THE BLACK WOMAN**, edited by La Frances Rodgers-Rose
22. **MAKING BUREAUCRACIES WORK**, edited by Carol H. Weiss and Allen H. Barton
23. **RADICAL CRIMINOLOGY**, edited by James A. Inciardi
24. **DUAL-CAREER COUPLES**, edited by Fran Pepitone-Rockwell
25. **POLICY IMPLEMENTATION**, edited by John Brigham and Don W. Brown
26. **CONTEMPORARY BLACK THOUGHT**, edited by Molefi Kete Asante and Abdulai S. Vandi
27. **HISTORY AND CRIME**, edited by James A. Inciardi and Charles E. Faupel
28. **THE FUTURE OF EDUCATION**, edited by Kathryn Cirincione-Coles
29. **IMPROVING SCHOOLS**, edited by Rolf Lehming and Michael Kane
30. **KNOWLEDGE AND POWER IN A GLOBAL SOCIETY**, edited by William M. Evan
31. **BLACK MEN**, edited by Lawrence E. Gary
32. **MAJOR CRIMINAL JUSTICE SYSTEMS**, edited by George F. Cole, Stanislaw J. Frankowski, and Marc G. Gertz
33. **ANALYZING ELECTORAL HISTORY**, edited by Jerome M. Clubb, William H. Flanigan, and Nancy H. Zingale
34. **ASSESSING MARRIAGE**, edited by Erik E. Filsinger and Robert A. Lewis
35. **THE KNOWLEDGE CYCLE**, edited by Robert F. Rich
36. **IMPACTS OF RACISM ON WHITE AMERICANS**, edited by Benjamin P. Bowser and Raymond G. Hunt
37. **WORLD SYSTEM STRUCTURE**, edited by W. Ladd Hollist and James N. Rosenau
38. **WOMEN AND WORLD CHANGE**, edited by Naomi Black and Ann B. Cottrell

WOMEN and WORLD CHANGE

Equity Issues in Development

Edited by
NAOMI BLACK
and ANN BAKER COTTRELL

SAGE PUBLICATIONS Beverly Hills London

For information address:

SAGE Publications, Inc.
275 South Beverly Drive
Beverly Hills, California 90212

SAGE Publications Ltd
28 Banner Street
London EC1Y 8QE, England

Printed in the United States of America

Library of Congress Cataloging in Publication Data

Main entry under title:

Women and world change.

(Sage focus editions; 38)
Outgrowth of a workshop on women and development given during the 1980 annual meeting of the Comparative Interdisciplinary Studies Society.
Includes bibliographies.
1. Women—Congresses. 2. Social change—Congresses. 3. Economic development—Congresses. 4. Underdeveloped areas—Women—Congresses. I. Black, Naomi. II. Cottrell, Ann Baker.
HQ1106.W65 305.4'2 81-9249
ISBN 0-8039-1700-7 AACR2
ISBN 0-8039-1701-5 (pbk.)

FIRST PRINTING

CONTENTS

EDITORS' PREFACE

This book began at a one-day workshop on women and development, which we organized for the 1980 annual meeting of the Comparative Interdisciplinary Studies Society, an affiliate of the International Studies Association. In these sessions ten papers and commentaries related case material to theories of development. Additional case material from a variety of geographical locations, levels of development, and periods of history has been added for this volume.

Our belief was, and is, that national development cannot be understood without attention to the role of women in relation to social change on all continents, in both fully and less industrialized economies, and in the past as well as the present. Thus, *Women and World Change* purposely includes materials concerning the First, Second, and Third Worlds, as well as historical and contemporary case studies. Rather than group chapters according to geographical area or level of development, we focus on the following themes: a feminist critique of development theories (Parts I and IV), ways the world economic system affects women (Part II), how governmental social policies affect women while largely disregarding their actual situation (Part III), and women's collective efforts to influence policy (Part IV).

We could have organized this volume in other ways, for most of the chapters include material appropriate to several sections. Those in Parts III and IV indirectly show the impact of change on women. The essays in Part II set forth women's responses as individuals and in families, supplementing the group activities reported in Part IV. Part III also contains material on women's collective role as agents of change.

Along with these central themes, the parts provide the bases for a number of generalizations that we would like to emphasize here. Many of them are original; all of them are important. In the first chapter Thelma McCormack extends the current feminist critique of social science to development theory, discussing a number of theoretical approaches. She concludes that they all accept continuing inequality between the sexes in both attitudes and social structures. Even the newest notions about development with equity fail to consider equity for women. Adequate development theory mus include more careful consideration of proper goals for change, and facilitate the collective action of women as agents of change. McCormack ends with a plea for affirmative action to redistribute access to such crucial areas as education, occupational choice, mobility, and participation in decision-making. The first chapter thus epitomizes the book's approach. It is selectively analytic rather than exhaustive. It draws on the recent case material accumulated by feminist scholars, and on a range of interdisciplinary analyses of the relationship between theory and policy. Parts II, III, and IV follow logically, documenting inequality, analyzing the impact of policy based on the criticized theory, and describing the collective initiatives of women.

Part II, "The Impact of Change on Women," shows that governments in widely differing cultural and economic contexts have adopted development theory's recommendations for promoting economic growth. The resulting rationalization and consolidation of resources produces similar consequences for women, in spite of substantial differences in national goals. Rae Blumberg demonstrates this in Third World countries' attempts to produce cash crops for export. Janet Salaff shows the effects of attempts to make Singapore's workforce attractive to investors in multinational industry. Lynn Bolles shows what happened when Jamaica faced the problem of meeting requirements of international lending agencies, and Nanciellen Davis discusses the impact on women when the Canadian government encouraged modernization of the fishing industry in the depressed Maritimes area. In all cases, whether or not economic growth occurs, women seem to lose status relative to men and to be virtually absent from groups planning for change. Women seem to be the most disadvantaged in those least developed nations where they have lost their traditional role in subsistence agriculture without acquiring any new functions in the growing cash economy.

On a worldwide basis, women seem to change less than men as a result of participation in the formal economy. Although they may gain a degree of independence and increased power in the family, they tend to retain family-centered values along with traditional expenditure patterns different from men's. Part II also demonstrates the crucial importance of family support for women's economic activity. Aid comes mainly from other women and is provided in an astonishingly varied range of ways, including the very different versions of the extended family described in Singapore and Jamaica.

Finally, section II casts doubt on the accepted notions of development as a progression from traditional to modern. The articles in this section show that women are constantly adapting to change, but with basic values and preferences essentially unaffected. Their lives move back and forth across the boundaries of public and private, formal and informal, traditional and modern. The appropriate model cannot possibly be linear and one-directional.

Part III, "Social Policies Affecting Women," examines policies adopted by very different modernizing regimes. Katherine Newman discusses colonial governments and the indigenous successor regimes in sub-Saharan Africa. Barbara Jancar analyzes authoritarian Marxist regimes in the Soviet Union, its satellites, and China. Finally, Mary Ruggie compares Sweden's "societal corporatism" with Britain's "liberal welfarism." These chapters also present the range of social policies relevant to the situation of women: fundamental policies not perceived as related to women (land tenure); the package of policies used to change women's situation (legal and economic rights, protective legislation, and legislation related to reproduction); and specific policies seen as central to women's economic and social role (day care). None of the policies discussed was formulated out of a concern for women. None of them involved any substantial consideration of women's point of view. The only partial exception is day-care policy in Sweden, which representatives of women's organizations were involved in planning. Even in Sweden the situation of women was of less concern than overall employment policies and the welfare of children. Ironically enough, as articles in other sections of the book suggest, by and large women would agree in putting such priorities first.

The instrumental nature of policy affecting women is most blatant in the socialist planned economies. Here governments are overtly committed to equity for women. However, considerations of economic growth have repeatedly produced pronatalist policies backed by the revival of traditional attitudes. As all the chapters in Part III demonstrate, women respond selectively to change, resisting it if they perceive it as harmful to their own situations or to the situations of their families, but welcoming it under other circumstances. Legislative enactments seem to have only limited and indirect impact on their preferences for economic independence or reproductive autonomy. Provision or absence of day care seems to make little difference to how many women work for pay; in the absence of available contraceptive devices women have recourse to illegal abortions, and the traditional

African family survives even when its basis in shared land tenure is eliminated.

Part IV, "Women as Agents of Social Change," moves from consideration of women's individual or family adaptation or resistance to a discussion of situations where women's mutual support has become relatively systematic and activist. As the chapters in this section suggest, women's organizations are far more widespread and varied than is generally realized. The groups discussed range from the very small *comité feminino* in a Peruvian village described by Susan Bourque and Kay Warren, to the national and international networks of the great suffrage and women's rights organizations in India that Barbara Ramusack describes. The French group discussed by Naomi Black falls somewhere between in size and longevity. While such groups have had some impact on social policy, their major importance seems to lie in the way they serve as instruments of social mobilization for their members. As Ann Cottrell shows, the American Women's Liberation Movement of the late 1960s was the first explicitly to identify consciousness-raising as a major technique for women's unity and progress. The other chapters in the section are able to demonstrate how more traditional and less self-consciously feminist groups have been able to increase their members' awareness of shared problems and goals.

The essays in Part IV also direct attention to the complex interaction between ideologies and women's collective action. In almost all the cases discussed, the women in question remained fairly committed to family concerns and quite traditional values. The reigning ideologies uniformly failed to provide for women playing a role in decision-making. Yet woman were able to use diverse systems of belief as a basis for collective initiatives: populist modernization in Peru, anticolonial nationalism in India, social Catholicism in France, and participatory democracy in the United States. Without exception the groups managed to make their own concerns lead to public action, using the argument that the policy issues in question were important to all. This was true even of the narrowest sort of "parish pump" approach, or the most undeniably "female" questions. Thus, Peruvian women had as their first project the provision of public toilets for the village, while Indian women were concerned with the sexual experiences of young girls. Translated into the consequences of reduced disease and healthy babies, such campaigns could be seen to produce community goods as well as the alleviation of women's lot. In a similar fashion, the newest women's groups discussed here, constituting the revived women's movement in the United States, extrapolated arguments from the civil rights and peace movements to generate a policy goal for women in public life.

The key would seem to be the felt need that brings women together around issues related to their own specific experience. Almost any ideology can then be adjusted to serve as a justification.

Naomi Black
Ann Baker Cottrell

ACKNOWLEDGMENTS

We would like to express our appreciation to our editors, Don Cottrell and S. P. Rosenbaum. Thelma McCormack also played more than a contributor's role. Any errors, of judgment or otherwise, are of course our responsibility.

PART I
INTRODUCTION

1

DEVELOPMENT WITH EQUITY FOR WOMEN

THELMA McCORMACK

In reviewing the history of recent political and social changes in Africa, Latin America, Asia, and the Middle East, one observation stands out. Women's grievances have been part of the revolutionary spirit; women's aspirations have been included in the various manifestos; women have been among the guerrilla fighters and charismatic leaders of nationalist movements, yet the feminist momentum has seldom been sustained. New regimes praise the contributions of women, celebrate their acts of courage, reaffirm the party's commitment to full liberation, but introduce only minimal or, at best, expedient reforms that coincide with the political and economic goals of new governments. Even Allende's Chile, now mourned by democratic socialists throughout the world, was unwilling to tempt fate by placing additional strain on the traditional roles or prejudices of men (Chaney, 1974). Thus, the old sexual divisions of labor in the household, factory, and field persist with only slight modification; wage and educational differentials reappear, although the occupations and curricula may be different, and the special needs or goals of women slip down on national agendas, designated as less urgent, items that can be—and usually are—postponed. Meanwhile, something approaching a zero-sum game occurs when the consequences of changes with higher priorities create new and unanticipated vulnerabilities for women.

Militant Third World women (Davin, 1976; Stacey, 1979; Stiehm, 1976) who expect more may be surprised by the broken promises, but the scenario is a familiar one to women elsewhere. In Eastern Europe, where Marxist rhetoric resounded with concepts of social justice and denunciations of decadent bourgeois lifestyles, Soviet practice turned out to be selective and conditional (Scott, 1974; Jancar, 1974): equality for women only if it was congruent with other objectives and only if it did not interfere with the important work of male elites. In a strange reinterpretation of Engels's claim for primitive matriarchy a Czech executive is quoted as saying, "Matriarchies exist only in primitive society" (Scott, 1974: 14.)

Equity for women has been promised by political leaders and revolutionary ideologues almost everywhere at some time, but it has been achieved nowhere. The unfinished agendas are far from identical, yet sexual inequality in social, political, and economic life is worldwide. Indeed, it is so ubiquitous that some scholars have begun to wonder if it is realistic to expect total democratization of male-female relationships in the early or middle stages of modernization. Sex roles, either because they are so adaptive or because they are so intractable, may be the last part of a social system to change, a withering away that belongs in some future, not yet realized "postmodern society" (Lapidus, 1974).

Be that as it may, it is the paradox of inequality in modern and emerging countries, in states pledged to economic or political democracy or both, that constitutes the focus of a growing number of feminist studies. This new research has been, in part, descriptive accounts of the hidden contributions of women to history and in cultures unlike our own; it has also been a critical literature showing the damage and distortion imposed by male ethnologists and male development specialists. Here, as in other disciplines, new knowledge and new understandings are being produced by women scholars whose perspective is informed by their own experiences as the second sex. Typical of this new perspective is the question of whether women are better or worse off as a result of modernization, whether "the benefits of modernization have accrued mainly to the male half of society" (Elliott, 1977: 1).

Discussions about the impact of development policies on women often leave out any considerations of a political dimension. Women are seen as objects of change, rather than agents of change, coping rather than initiating, bystanders rather than participants. It is our contention here that the phrase "development with equity for women" refers not just to an end state, not just to a new alignment of social institutions, but to the means, to the action of women in directing their own history insofar as we are able to shape our futures at all. It is not, then, sufficient to be pro-women, to specify reforms that women want or rights to which women are entitled but which would be granted by men; a feminist perspective is *planning* as well as *a plan*.

Many of the discussions about development are so strongly oriented toward the Third World that they neglect women whose lives are trapped in the economically backward enclaves of the First World, in depressed rural areas, or in the wretched inner cities. These women, over 65 years of age and widowed or under 65 and heads of households, live in abject poverty, a condition that is not made more bearable by calling it relative. But in paradigms that emphasize the First World's responsibility to the Third World (as either the oppressors or the benefactors of the latter), these women drop out of the picture.

Yet they are analytically important because they illustrate how a partriarchal system mediates modernization—how marriage, divorce, family life, and a male-controlled welfare system impoverish one set of women and enrich another. Given the same conditions of surplus, the distribution of wealth is a function of social institutions, and when these are built around a principle of male privilege and male authority, women as women do not have any real entitlement to a share; even those who enjoy a high degree of economic security or luxury do not have a firm hold on these resources. Theories of development, then, that are restricted to the economic regions designated officially as the Third World and that do not address the patriarchal character of social institutions are necessarily incomplete.

In the comments that follow we will be examining some of the conceptual problems in constructing a model of development or social change that has at its center the historical denial of equity to women and as its goal the realization of gender equality. As a minimum, the model must satisfy two criteria. First, it must deduce a principle of action that is applicable everywhere but does not interfere with the indigenous programs of women as these vary from one place to another. Parenthetically, it should be pointed out that a principle of action is not a form of justification, for equality is a meta-ethic that validates itself; rather it is a strategy. Second, the model must acknowledge the phenomenon of underdevelopment in all parts of the world, wherever women are both poor and dependent, and wherever they are excluded from full participation in the life of the community either through fear or socialization. We are not here concerned with the origins of patriarchy, whether in biology or social organization (Eichler, 1979) or in some never-never land (Mitchell, 1975) that lies between reproduction and culture.

The first section of this chapter will examine alternative perspectives in development theory: comparative, developmental, systemic. For our purposes, the most desirable perspective, we shall suggest, is one that sensitizes us to the interdependency of women in world systems. The second section will discuss the various ideological orientations—liberal and neo-Marxist—and the extent to which they have in different ways perpetuated male dominance. Particular attention will be given to the concept of modernization itself, a concept that became the twentieth century's version of enlightenment. As we shall note, instead of eliminating patriarchy, it modernized it. In section III we will offer a tentative version of development with equity based on the elimination of either traditional or modernized patriarchy through political action, that is, through affirmative action.

I

"The daily lives of most women in Western and non-Western countries," Iglitzin (1967) writes, "vary only by degree." Still we perceive each other as different, often by as much as 180 degrees. Whichever stand out, the similarities or the differences, and whether differences are regarded invidiously depends on the concepts that structure our observations and the ways data are collected.

The *comparative* perspective scans a broad range of human societies with a view usually to establishing generalizations about social organization. One of its strengths as a method is that it lends itself to approximations of an experimental design without disturbing the normal environment and without the artificiality of the laboratory. Feminist social anthropologists have used the comparative perspective to strengthen the view that the sexual division of labor is anything but uniform, and that the variations in the sex roles of women can better be understood in terms of economy than biology (Friedl, 1975). Other studies have corrected impressions of preliterate women as solely preoccupied with domestic-kinship activity (Reiter, 1975; Hafkin and Bay, 1976). In addition, the new school of feminist anthropologists has revived interest in matriarchy, not with the intention of establishing its primacy, but rather in speculating on it as a viable way of organizing social life (Webster, 1975).

Although this work has provided a greater awareness of human potentiality, of what women have been and what women are capable of becoming, and although it has, as Iglitzin's earlier remark suggests, narrowed the social distance between women wherever they reside, the cumulative impact is a mosaic, a rich sense of diversity, an antidote to narrow-minded, intolerant ethnocentrism, but a perspective that does not necessarily provide a better comprehension of how women relate to each other cross-culturally and cross-nationally. A knowledge of the many patterns of culture opens our minds, but leaves unstated and, of course, unresolved the question of interdependency. It is, however, precisely interdependencies that constitute a basis for group formation and for group consciousness.

The *developmental* perspective provides a more dynamic orientation because it focuses on process, on patterns of change that effect lasting and irreversible structural transformations. If, as Bendix (1967) says, we cannot define modernity, we can examine modernizing and the different routes for arriving there. Although the processes of change are many and difficult to disaggregate, they are not random. The term "development" implies an orderly (not necessarily peaceful) process: (a) a number of analytically distinct processes that operate on each other reciprocally and sequentially; and (b) a scale based on indicators, that allows us to locate certain countries, regions, and groups and refer to them as more or less developed. It goes without saying that: (a) we are speaking of probabilities, not certainties; (b) not all societies are developing, although all societies are adaptive; (c) developing societies can absorb a high degree of ambiguity and inconsistency; and (d) the development process may be arrested at some point.

There is considerable controversy among economists and social historians about "stages" of development. There is also disagreement among anthropologists about evolutionary models of change: to what extent the evolution follows its own logic or can be shaped by purposive human intervention, and whether the process of evolution is, as White (1975) says, "unconscious, blind, bloody, brutal, tropismatic" or is more benign. From a feminist perspective, however, the most serious problem with developmental models is the risk of creating an invidious "we-they" mentality. Nisbet (1971) suggests that it is almost impossible to erase from our minds the memory of nineteenth-century evolutionary doctrines with their barely concealed ethnocentric biases. However much we may try to be objective about development, the myths of progress and teleological development continue to haunt us. And we come to believe that the scales we construct as mere tools, more or less heuristic, are in nature itself.

A we-they mentality is a special liability in trying to construct an international women's perspective. For example, Hafkin and Bay (1976) have pointed out how anthropologists studying women in

Africa imposed Western concerns, like suffrage or divorce, on African studies. Enlightened colonial administrators could then justify their presence as beneficial to women deprived of these rights by their own people. But when the dust of colonialism clears away, the question remains whether Hafkin and Bay believe that concerns like suffrage were inappropriate to African cultures and should not have been raised at all, or that the relative salience given to these issues was wrong. Should women today refrain from passing judgment on the conditions of other women when they involve cruelty, mutilation, and bondage? Within a we-they format, comments made by one group about another are almost inevitably interpreted as culturally uninformed and patronizing. Communication among women becomes that much more difficult.

Conceptual frameworks that are divisive are of special concern to women. Men who study the developing regions of Africa can picture themselves as either proconsuls of empire or detached, value-free social scientists. By listening to male informants and by adopting their constructions of reality, authors of reports may grossly misrepresent women, but not necessarily the power structure. Women informants could provide a more accurate picture of themselves, but one that is of little interest to male political elites. A good example of how the male perspective and the administrative perspective merge is the case described by Van Allen (1976) of the Women's War in Nigeria in 1929. According to official documents it became known as the genderless Aba Riots, and women were seen in these reports as having taken the initiative more by chance than design.

Neither the comparative nor the developmental perspectives by themselves, then, are satisfactory. Efforts to combine them—Eisenstadt's "comparative perspectives on social change" (1968) or Parsons's "evolutionary and comparative perspectives" (1966)—do not resolve the problems noted here. Bendix's (1967) approach, which attempts to examine the spread of modernization (through concepts of diffusion), draws the developing nations together in a communication network, but is, in the last analysis, a better theory of communication and development than it is of worldwide development. However, it provides a transition to a third approach based on the concept of a worldwide system (Inkeles, 1980).

The worldwide *systems* approach postulates the functional interdependency and interconnectedness of women wherever they reside and whatever their position is in the social structure. The "center-periphery" distinction that characterizes the political economy analyses of development is an example of systems analysis, but because it focuses so relentlessly on economic relationships and almost exclusively on exploitative processes at the expense of parallel development and international cooperation, it is too narrow at this juncture for our purposes. Liberal humanistic theories that emphasize international cooperation, with rich nations helping poor ones in a spirit of distributive justice (Eisenstadt, 1966), naively underestimate the degree of geopolitical self-interest behind the rich-nation altruism. What we are proposing instead is a model that is open, one in which both exploitative and cooperative relationships between women are possible,—a model in which there are no preconceptions about the types of relationships that occur and under what circumstances.

Systems analysis regroups units so that the distinction between Third World women and their counterparts in the First or Second Worlds is eliminated. Further, it avoids a divisive mode of thinking by examining linkages between women as senders, receivers, and intermediaries. It leads to the formulation of different kinds of research problems: for example, how sugar prices on the world market affect the earning power of women in the West Indies and the purchasing power of women on welfare in the United States. Conflict and cooperation, continuity and disjuncture, functional equivalence and dysfunctionality, producer and consumer roles are as much a part of the female world system as they are of the male, and the first step in such an analysis is to map the globe. Finally, because the systems approach emphasizes the interdependency of women and the necessity of communication, it provides a context in which women can express judgments without this being misinterpreted as cultural imperialism, meddling in someone else's affairs, or the white woman's burden.

II

Most theories of development have little to say about women (Papanek, 1978); generalized constructs like "the peasant" presumably refer to both men and women, although the empirical studies more often than not look into the fields and see only men (Wolf, 1966). Recent literature attempts to redress the imbalance by distinguishing male and female agricultural workers. Generally speaking, however, it is not men and women who are being differentiated but husbands and wives, the division of labor within a family economy. The studies, then, are not about women but about the family and how the technology of the economy alters the division of labor within the family. An outstanding example is Deere's work on Peruvian women (1979).

Deere's work and work like it owe much to Engels's *Origin of the Family*, more to the Marxist tradition than to family sociology as it developed in the non-Marxist social sciences. Yet, they are similar in the sense that they recognized that family structure was determined by the economy: If the latter changed, the former would change as well. And both saw the family evolving toward greater freedom and equality for women either when women returned to the public sphere (nondomestic economy), or when, as wives and mothers, they become more professional. Neither anticipated that patriarchal relationships would or could exist, much less thrive, in the socialist or nonsocialist future; and neither questioned the family as an institution. Thus, both are flawed, for a feminist perspective must not merely correct traditional academic interpretations of the family; it must also question the viability of the family as an institution. Special considerations must be given to cases like the Israeli kibbutz (Talmon, 1972; Blumberg, 1976), where an agrarian economy functions without the family systems as we have known them. What is gained, then, by substituting a family bias for a male bias is a better accounting system of the economic value of unpaid work carried out by a female spouse or by children; but it is limited by the fact that it is based on the family and not on women for whom family life may one day be a free option.

A second set of problems revolves around the nature of social change, whether it is an internal process or externally imposed, whether it occurs through the erosion of older social arrangements and the aspirations of people for improvement or is the result of conquest or other forms of unwanted, undesired encroachment.

The liberal tradition in the social sciences has been to emphasize the intrinsic desirability of social change that originates freely from widely felt internal needs. Since almost no society is totally isolated from contact with others or from the spread of ideas and fashion, there is also some exogenous influence, but the imported innovations can be incorporated selectively, thus ensuring the maintenance of social cohesion and minimizing disaffection and anomie. Margaret Mead (1974: 24) summarizes the philosophy she and her colleagues held during the 1930s and early 1940s:

> that the thing that anthropologists should do was to protect backward societies or isolated peoples from too rapid change. We thought slow change was better than fast change, that less change was better than more change, that is was a pity to disturb the life of isolated peoples who were reasonably balanced in relationship to the territory they had and the technology they were using.

Mead's solicitude was based on what she and others had observed firsthand, especially during World War II, when the armed forces took over small undisturbed communities and left behind a sordid picture of demoralization. But in their eagerness to protect these societies from traumatic change, the social scientists were also protecting patriarchy as part of a larger pattern that had its own logic. Similarly, Marxists were insensitive to noneconomic relationships; their concern was to protect poor but independent communities from the dependency and uneven economic development that followed when rich nations came bearing gifts of aid and technical assistance. Thus, scholars today confront, on the one hand, a partial vacuum, and on the other, a dual legacy "that women have traditionally been oppressed in Third World societies and that 'development' is the key to changing their situation. The opposing view is that women's status was good in many (not all) Third World societies in the past and that the structure and ideology of male dominance were introduced as corollaries of colonialism" (Leacock, 1979).

Early theories of development had no references to equity. Their focus was on poverty. Typical of this period was Heilbroner's *The Great Ascent* (1963), in which underdevelopment was equated with the poverty of subsistence and stagnant agrarian economies, of persons whose caloric intake was barely enough to maintain life, of people dying needlessly of infectious diseases because they were unable to afford antibiotics, and of adults and undernourished children sleeping on streets for want of housing.

Given these images, it was inconceivable that policies of development, however inept, could worsen the status of either sex; no further impoverishment was possible. Development might not improve their position at once, but it would eventually put a floor under their poverty, raising their standard of living and their self-respect. Heilbroner reproached American aid policy not because it was too much or opportunistically tied with reactionary forces, but because it was too little, too unconcerned, and crippled by the obsession of some members of Congress with Third World socialism. But Heilbroner's hopes, like many others at the time, lay with international agencies providing technical aid and funds that would allow the developing world to start and carry out its own economic scenario. The scenario might be the European pattern or some other, but the test of development policies was the extent to which they eradicated poverty.

Equity, as measured by income distribution within or between countries (Adelman and Morris, 1973) emerged as an issue later and out of an empirical assessment of development policies. "Who benefits from economic development?" Adelman and Morris asked, a question which assumed that someone benefited, if not all persons or all countries. And it is still not clear from discussions whether, despite the same income distribution pyramid, no dent has been made in the poverty of the large masses of population. However, the equity question that many scholars were beginning to raise was not a reflection of disillusionment with the idea, but rather a recognition that certain kinds of policies needed to be thought out better. Strategies intended to increase productivity, for example, often achieved the goal but widened class structure by making rich farmers richer and proletarianizing poor ones (Wharton, 1975).

Income differentials, however, are only part of the stratification system. Measures of occupational structure and intergenerational mobility are needed to arrive at more exact and comprehensive judgments, particularly in the case of women, for if the evidence of advanced societies can be used it suggests that the differential impact of economic growth for men and women is found primarily in the occupation-wage structure and in the opportunities for mobility, with education—access, length, and type—serving as the intervening variable.

Some of the feminist critics of development policies disregard the poverty problem and focus instead on property, the marginalization of women in the larger economy and the loss of control by women over the means of production. Mullings (1976: 249-250) summarizes this view:

> Women, then, find themselves in a commodity economy where their traditional productive role has been devalued and where they have limited access to the new means of production. Clearly this is not to suggest that all males, or even the majority of males, are in a structurally dominant position. With the development of class stratification, a group of male wage laborers who do not *own* the means of production develops. But the essential difference here is that, to the extent that they are involved in social production of the resources of the society, their work is social rather than private. The exclusion of women from access to the major means of production, in the context of stratification, means that they are unequal to the men of their class.

Marginalization, however, is not automatically a loss of power or status. It may result in labor segregation, and this may, in turn, mean more control over so-called women's jobs. As Milkman (1976) points out, the rate of unemployment among women during the Great Depression was lower than among men not because women were cheaper labor but because they were concentrated in the least vulnerable sectors of the economy. The major difficulty with the thesis about female displacement and male control over the means of production, however, can best be seen by looking at the advanced countries, where the means of production are controlled either by conglomerates and multinationals or by government monopoly. In this economic context it is neither desirable nor possible for women to regain control over the means of production. In the advanced countries with monopoly capitalism or monopoly socialism or some mixed version, equity depends on participation in decision-making, on mechanisms of accountability, and on access to formal education as well as training in managerial skills. The point cannot be made strongly enough, for women, like generals, are often fighting the last war.

Economic indicators either of poverty or equality measure something more elusive, a psychological shift and a new value system that provide the motivation for a more aggressive approach to economic behavior, a determination to solve problems rather than surrendering to them fatalistically, a more scientific and secular mind. Sociologists have been concerned more than economists with defining and measuring the motivational principle of modernization. Folk, peasant, and feudal mentalities, they have argued, may coexist with urban, industrial society, and they may, in a limited sense, be functional, but they cannot serve as the dominant modes of thinking without threatening the continuity of the system and without limiting wide participation in the postpeasant, postfeudal society. Whether the modern mind is a precondition for development or superstructure matters less here than the recognition that neither large-scale capitalism nor large-scale socialism can function without it.

The simplest indicator of modernization is the extent of literacy, for without literacy there can be change but no serious commitment to industrialization. Illiteracy, like poverty, is a drag on development that must be drastically reduced before development can commence. Empirical studies, however, are less interested in literacy than in industrial and business organization. And it is at this critical point that women disappear from the research and no questions are asked. Singer (1975), for example, who was interested in the fit or lack of fit between the joint family (in India) and modern industry, interviewed nineteen male heads of industries and concluded that the joint family, far from being a hindrance to industrial development, may serve as a positive resource. Another example is a study conducted by Kahl (1974) in Brazil and Mexico. Kahl's subjects were 740 men in Mexico and 627 men in Brazil, stratified by occupational level. He found no statistically significant differences between the two countries, which confirmed his general hypothesis that industrialization is creating a common culture. None of these studies questions the absence of women from entrepreneurial roles or from skilled factory occupations; it is a given, and, having accepted it, the authors conclude, as do Inkeles and Smith (1974: 26), that change moves through the system from husband to wife, not jointly or in the reverse direction:

> Most of the traditional societies and communities of the world are, if not strictly patriarchal, at least vigorously male dominated. . . We predicted that the liberating influence of the forces making for modernization would act on men's attitudes, and incline them to accord to women status and rights more nearly equal to those enjoyed by men. We tested the men's orientation through questions on a woman's right to work and to equal pay, to hold public office, and to freely choose her marriage partner.

Thus women are not studied and are seen as remaining premodern. Their exclusion from industrial life may be explained as either a biological necessity or a cultural phenomenon, like the exclusion of women from sacred totemic sites. But either way, biological or cultural, exclusion (partial and in many instances total) is a reality that soon becomes an attribute, a seemingly built-in incapacity for participation in the public industrial life or politics. This, in turn, justifies excluding women from or limiting their participation in societies that value excellence, or, at any rate, must catch up in a hurry.

Elsewhere I have discussed the sexist bias of this type of thinking in political studies (McCormack, 1975). Here I want to draw attention to the modernization of patriarchy. If men remain in control of economic and political institutions but give women allowances and the vote, the bottles have changed but the wine has not.

To summarize, I have tried to suggest here that the literature on modernization and development has, in different ways, not addressed the women's issue in all of its complexity. Substituting the family for the male gives a greater understanding of how the domestic economy controlled by women contributes to the overall economy. Since occupational census data usually reflect the monetized sector of the economy, corrections need to be made that recognize the economic importance of the nonmonetized sector. Yet, this does not shed any critical light on the family itself.

The second issue was the legacy of a liberal tradition that sought to protect small-scale societies from abuse, that is, from innovations that would disrupt harmony and integration. But in protecting these societies against plastic trinkets, bubble gum, and Coca Cola, the liberal tradition was also protecting patriarchy. Against the background of Auschwitz, patriarchy in the islands of the Pacific could seem almost idyllic, yet it is a fact that just about every other form of inequality was exposed and treated with derision by scholars. Later, when questions about equality of the sexes were raised, some of the research findings supported the view that no change or only very small, incremental change might be preferable, at least for women, than the more dramatic and drastic introduction of capital-intensive agriculture and industrial systems (Boserup, 1970).

The third issue discussed was the poverty or equity debate. Equity, as we noted, does not refer to the status of women, but to the economic status of countries and to groups within countries. Therefore, although the findings of these studies have little relevance to women, they suggest a new model of differential impact of economic growth. Thus, development produces new forms of economic stratification. For feminists who believe that this process should be reversed, that women should regain control over the economy or create an alternative economy, we suggested that in a highly developed economy, ownership of land or simple technology conceal the newer forms of discrimination in education, occupational choices, mobility, and participation in decision making. Finally, we touched on the discussions of modernization which we would now like to develop further.

III

Just as development policies have not eliminated class or status differences, so they have not eliminated patriarchy. But there is one major difference: economic growth may depend upon resources; democratization does not. It is therefore a question of attitudes and ways of organizing social life that determine problems of equality.

The expectation that modernization would eliminate patriarchy was based on the assumption that the nature of authority itself would be radically altered, becoming more situational than diffuse, more rational than conventional, more universal than personalistic, more instrumental than moral. Above all, because authority would cease to be rooted in ascriptive criteria and would cease to be passed down through the male line, the whole system of patriarchal authority in premodern or traditional societies would die out. Not at once, for in any major transformation of social life on the scale implied by traditional-modern there would be adjustments, survivals of archaic patterns, hidden injuries, and pockets of resistance. Yet in the long run the imperatives of modern economic organization would prevail with compelling advantages for women. Indeed, the traditional household would become a woman-centered model of specialized and professionalized activity, a husband-wife partnership.

The shock, then, is that patriarchy was itself modernized. It is differentiated into expressive patriarchy (rape, machismo, symbolic misogyny in the arts) and instrumental patriarchy (job discrimination and differential access to education, health, legal services, and political office). It is legitimated not through references to holy texts or sacred scripts but to scientific studies of the brain, of psychological differences, of personality development. Male preference, male privilege, and male norms constituting standards of excellence are the outcome of a process which, in theory, should have given us a gender-free division of labor, a set of gender-free standards of achievement, and gender-free institutions.

Whether the new patriarchy is in some ways preferable to traditional patriarchy, whether it is a step toward equality or a horizontal movement going nowhere, are questions that can be argued. However, it is not necessary to hold, as some do, that it is a regressive development and that therefore development should be resisted. Modernization, we suggest, is the thin edge of the wedge that makes it possible for women to organize around issues of equality.

Affirmative action, we have suggested, is the common element in all programs for equality; it is to social equality what income transfer payments are to economic equality, a necessary but not a sufficient condition. It can unify women throughout the world without indicating which substantive forms of inequality are more important than others. Above all, it is a political principle that puts women on the offensive rather than the defensive—that requires women to set agendas, to set quotas, and to evaluate existing policies in terms of the speed of implementation. Finally, it introduces a new factor, sexual equality, into classificatory or ranking systems, and a new measure, rate of achievement.

Development with equity, then, is a new concept. We have tried to suggest here that it is more than a metaphor to say that women live in an underdeveloped culture throughout the world. But the term "development" is more cumbersome than not. Accordingly, we have suggested a world systems approach in which the various connections and linkages among women are traced. Like the new feminist historiography, it is an exercise in rediscovery, and is, in itself, a form of affirmative action.

Nevertheless, one must still deal with those processes—social, economic, political, psychological—that constitute a paradigm or series of paradigms that can be called modernizing. In retrospect, we can now appreciate that the promise of modernization based on a social theory of authority has not been met. Morally, the new forms of patriarchy are as odious as the old, and intellectually the modernized forms of patriarchy constitute a challenge to contemporary social and political thought, a challenge that is long overdue. For women who live in the developed sector, there is an undoing process; for women who live in the developing sector the activity can be more creative. But it is appropriate to conclude here that communication between them is reciprocal.

REFERENCES

ADELMAN, I. and C. T. MORRIS (1973) Economic Growth and Social Equity in Developing Countries. Stanford, CA: Stanford University Press.

BENDIX, R. (1967) "Tradition and modernity reconsidered." Comparative Studies in Society and History. 9: 292-346.

BLUMBERG, R. L. (1976) "Kibbutz women: from the fields of revolution to the laundries of discontent," pp. 319-344 in L. B. Iglitzin and R. Ross (eds.) Women in the World: A Comparative Study. Santa Barbara, CA: ABC-Clio.

BOSERUP, E. (1970) Woman's Role in Economic Development. London: Allen & Unwin.

CHANEY, E. M. (1974) "The mobilization of women in Allende's Chile," pp. 267-280 in Jane S. Jaquette (ed.) Women in Politics. New York: John Wiley.

DAVIN, D. (1976) Woman-Work: Women and the Party in Revolutionary China. New York: Oxford University Press.

DEERE, C. D. [ed.] (1979) "Peruvian peasant women's work," pp. 26-46 in Women in Latin America. Riverside, CA: Latin American Perspectives.

EICHLER, M. (1979) "The origin of sex inequality: a comparison and critique of different theories and their implications for social policy." Women's Studies International Quarterly 2, 3: 329-346.

EISENSTADT, S. N. (1966) Modernization: Protest and Change. Englewood Cliffs, NJ: Prentice-Hall.

———(1968) Comparative Perspectives on Social Change. Boston: Little, Brown.

ELLIOTT, C. M. (1977) "Theories of development: an assessment." Signs 3, 1: 1-8.

FRIEDL, E. (1975) Women and Men. New York: Holt, Rinehart & Winston.

HAFKIN, N. J. and E. G. BAY [eds.] (1976) Women in Africa. Stanford, CA: Stanford University Press.

HEILBRONER, R. L. (1963) The Great Ascent. New York: Harper & Row.

IGLITZIN, L B. and R. ROSS [eds.] (1976) Women in the World: A Comparative Study. Santa Barbara, CA: ABC-Clio.

INKELES, A. (1980) "The emerging social structure of the world," pp. 483-515 in H. D. Lasswell et al. (eds.) Propaganda and Communication in World History, III. Honolulu: University of Hawaii.

INKELES, A. and D H. SMITH (1974) Becoming Modern. Cambridge, MA: Harvard University Press.

JANCAR, B. (1974) "Women under communism," pp. 217-242 in J. S. Jaquette (ed.) Women in Politics. New York: John Wiley.

KAHL, J. A. (1974) The Measurement of Modernism. Austin: University of Texas Press.

LAPIDUS, G. W. (1974) "Modernization theory and sex roles in critical perspective," pp. 243-256 in J. S. Jaquette (ed.) Women in Politics. New York: John Wiley.

LEACOCK, E. (1979), "Women, development, and anthropological facts and fictions," pp. 7-16 in C. D. Deere (ed.) Women in Latin America. Riverside, CA: Latin American Perspectives.

McCORMACK, T. (1975) "Toward a nonsexist perspective on social and political change," pp. 1-33 in M. Millman and R. Kanter (eds.) Another Voice. Garden City, NY: Doubleday.

MEAD, M. (1974) "Changing perspectives on modernization," pp. 21-36 in John J. Poggie, Jr., and R. N. Lynch (eds.) Rethinking Modernization. Westport, CT: Greenwood.

MILKMAN, R. (1976) "Women's work and the economic crisis: some lessons from the Great Depression." The Review of Radical Political Economics 8, 1: 73-97.

MITCHELL, J. (1975) Psychoanalysis and Feminism. New York: Vintage.

MULLINGS, L. (1976) "Women and economic change in Africa," pp. 239-264 in N. Hafkin and E. G. Bay (eds.) Women in Africa. Stanford, CA: Stanford University Press.

NISBET, R. (1971) "Ethnocentrism and the comparative method," pp. 95-114 in A. R. Desai (ed.) Essays on Modernization of Underdeveloped Society, 1. Bombay: Thacker.

PAPANEK, H. (1978) "Comment on Gusfield's review essay on *Becoming Modern.*" American Journal of Sociology 83, 6: 1507-1511.

PARSONS, T. (1966) Societies' Evolutionary and Comparative Perspectives. Englewood Cliffs, NJ: Prentice-Hall.

REITER, R. R. [ed.] (1975) Toward an Anthropology of Women. New York: Monthly Review Press.

SCOTT, H. (1974) Does Socialism Liberate Women? Boston: Beacon.

SINGER, M. (1975) "The Indian joint family in modern industry," pp. 167-198 in I. A. Brady and B. L. Isaac (eds.) A Reader in Culture Change, II: Case Histories. New York: John Wiley.

STACEY, J. (1979) "When patriarchy kowtows: the significance of the Chinese family revolution for feminist theory," pp. 293-348 in Z. R. Eisenstein (ed.) Capitalist Patriarchy and the Case for Socialist Feminism. New York: Monthly Review Press.

STIEHM, J. (1976) "Algerian women: honor, survival and Islamic socialism," pp. 229-241 in L. B. Iglitzin and R. Ross (eds.) Women in the World: A Comparative Study. Santa Barbara, CA: ABC-Clio.

TALMON, Y. (1972) Family and Community in the Kibbutz. Cambridge, MA: Harvard University Press.

VAN ALLEN, J. (1976) " 'Aba Riots' or Igbo 'Women's War'? ideology, stratification and the invisibility of women," pp. 59-85 in N. J. Hafkin and E. G. Bay (eds.) Women in Africa. Stanford, CA: Stanford University Press.

WEBSTER, P. (1975) "Matriarchy: a vision of power," pp. 141-156 in R. R. Reiter (ed.) Toward an Anthropology of Women. New York: Monthly Review Press.

WHARTON, C. R., Jr. (1975) "The green revolution: cornucopia or Pandora's Box?" pp. 309-320 in A. Brady and B. L. Isaac (eds.) A Reader in Culture Change, II: Case Histories. New York: John Wiley.

WHITE, L. A. (1975) "Man's control over civilization: an anthropocentric illusion," pp. 23-45 in I. A. Brady and B. L. Isaac (eds.) A Reader in Culture Change, I: Theories. New York: John Wiley.

WOLF, E. (1966) Peasants. Englewood Cliffs, NJ: Prentice-Hall.

PART II
THE IMPACT OF CHANGE ON WOMEN

2

RURAL WOMEN IN DEVELOPMENT

RAE LESSER BLUMBERG

During the decade of the 1970s, two issues have aroused increasing concern in the "mainline" international development community: (a) "development with equity," and (b) food. In this chapter, I suggest that it is *poor rural women* who constitute the hitherto largely invisible but crucial common element—indeed, perhaps the ultimate determinant of success or failure—in guaranteeing both development with equity and food in the Third World.

To make this argument, we shall examine the present conditions and contributions of rural women in comparison with their menfolk. This comparison will include the relative position of women as (1) producers, (2) property controllers, and (3) people. The first involves the sex division of labor in the group's main economic pursuits. The second involves the sex division of resources, i.e., each sex's relative control over the means and fruits of production. The third involves the sex division of noneconomic life opportunities and well-being. In previous work on a cross-societal paradigm of sex stratification (Blumberg 1978, 1979a), I have suggested that *women's relative economic power* is the main determinant of their relative equality as people, regarding a wide variety of life options and aspects of well-being. *Work,* in and of itself, does not seem to enhance women's relative equality in "life options"[1]—although in most societies it does seem to be a prerequisite for women's acquisition of substantial economic power.

It was Ester Boserup who first suggested that the processes of Third World "development" (i.e., the combination of unplanned macroeconomic trends in the world political economy and planned development policies in various Third World countries) frequently have led to the greater economic marginalization of women (1970). In terms of the three factors listed above, such "development" often has had the general consequences of (1) increasing rural women's workload, while (2) decreasing their resource base (both absolutely and relative to their menfolk), and, consequently, (3) decreasing their well-being and opportunities as people. In turn, it will be argued, what happens to poor rural women profoundly affects both their country's agricultural system and its general level of well-being.

DEVELOPMENT WITH EQUITY

The emergence of the development-with-equity issue has signaled the gradual eclipse of the "modernization" approach to development. That focus stressed capital-intensive projects, used GNP growth as the measure and goal of Third World advancement, and assumed that development could be fostered almost without reference to the underlying social structure of the country or its position in the world economy. In contrast, the development-with-equity approach speaks to the question of "Development for whom?" It stresses the distribution of the economic pie, rather than its mere growth. Little more than a decade ago, development-with-equity was an isolated cry from the "periphery" (both the countries on the periphery of the world economy and the iconoclasts or radicals within the development "community"). Today it has been taken up in many quarters—even among the ranking development planners in the core countries themselves. It involves both an internal and an external perspective.

Core country development experts tend to be more sensitive to the *internal* ramifications of the development-with-equity issue, since evidence has been accumulating that the combination of capital-intensive development projects and trends in the world economy have contributed to an increasing gap between the haves and have-nots within Third World countries. For the limited beneficiaries, the world economy-oriented pockets of development have brought high technology and luxury-oriented consumer goods. For the many, it has meant labor displacement in the countryside and an ever-growing shortfall of jobs as urban industrialization fails to generate sufficient employment. One result of the changing relations of production is a swelling tide of temporary and permanent migration, of people searching for subsistence. Another is soaring rates of landlessness and impoverishment, due to conversion to wage labor and the increasing concentration of land holdings.

Current international statistics classify fully 800 million of the rural poor as "destitute" (FAO, 1979: i) and their numbers are expected to increase rapidly (the World Bank [IBRD] estimates that by the year 2000 about 1.1 billion people in the noncommunist developing countries will be suffering from absolute poverty). And many statistics document the widespread erosion of real income (Stokes et al., 1979: 65). Recognition of these facts and the potentially massive instability that they engender has prompted a new concern with development projects aimed at filling "basic needs."

The development-with-equity issue has an *external* component as well. In fact, many advocates of this position claim that the negative internal trends documented above result from the increasingly unfavorable position of the non-oil-exporting Third World countries vis-à-vis the developed nations, particularly the industrial capitalist ones. The external emphasis of the development-with-equity issue is symbolized by the call for a New International Economic Order. By the end of the "second decade of development," the gap between rich and poor countries had widened unrelentingly. Most of the non-oil-exporting developing countries remain suppliers of a limited range of primary export (usually agricultural) commodities under increasingly unfavorable terms of trade. Not only is the gap between prices of the developing world's primary exports and those charged by the core countries for manufactured goods widening (Emmanuel, 1972), but prices received by Third World countries have fallen farther behind those charged for the *cereal grains* that a growing number of these lands must import from the United States and Canada (Omvedt, 1975). This brings us to the world's growing food crisis, which also has an external and an internal aspect.

FOOD AND THE FEAR OF FAMINE

The *external* aspect of the food crisis is represented by the fact that more and more Third World nations (largely agricultural producers themselves) are becoming net importers of food, dependent on the world's number one food exporter, the United States. The United States plus Canada account for an estimated 90 percent of the world's export cereal grains (principally wheat); six multinational corporations account for roughly 90 percent of that 90 percent (Cox, 1974). The United States controls more of the world food economy than OPEC controls of the world petroleum economy.

All indications are that Third World food dependence will continue to increase over the short term: "Current production and demand trends indicate that the cereal deficit of the developing world, which stood at 16 million tons in 1970, will rise to over 90 million tons by 1985" (FAO, 1979: iv). And while there is no dearth of Western experts predicting catastrophic famine, most seem to take little cognizance of how agricultural production is organized in Third World countries.

The most popular scenario for disaster remains runaway population growth outstripping food supply growth. In addition, since 1972, an exceptionally devastating year of widespread bad weather, climatic trends—either cooling or heating—have been increasingly invoked as the cause of future famines. Still other experts fear the potential for ecological/plant genetics destruction as ever more of our food is grown under conditions of monoculture agriculture.[2]

In contrast, recent work on the *internal* aspect of the Third World food deficit focuses on the *social relations* of agricultural production that tend to promote vicious circles of agricultural stagnation and shortfall. On the one hand, faced with growing numbers of rural landless and urban poor who must buy food with extremely limited cash, developing country governments must keep food prices as low and as stable as possible. On the other hand, the combination of low prices for food and increasingly marginalized food producers exacerbates the shortfall in food production (see de Janvry and Garramon, 1977). Nutritional standards fall, and the nation must spend scarce foreign exchange to stave off starvation. Contributing to the problem is the fact that most of these countries devote most of their inputs assistance (research, extension, credit, seeds, fertilizer, pesticides, and so on) to producing export crops—frequently inedible—while food crops are all but ignored. But is it "benign neglect"?

In many instances, governments have not intervened until the crisis point. For example, in recently drought-wracked Upper Volta, it was observed that not until the famine of 1973 did the satisfaction of food requirements figure in the list of governmental priority development objectives (Société africaine d'études et de développement [SAED], 1978: 23).

Between crises, the emphasis on export cash crops typically means food crops are grown on increasingly marginal land by an increasingly hard-pressed labor force, hardly able to grow enough for their own families, let alone to produce a marketable surplus. Moreover, subsistence-oriented food producers, unwilling to take chances with their families' lives, stick with the tried and true varieties characterized by low yields, but also by low *variance* of yield (Scott, 1975). Meanwhile, the contradictions deepen and the food crisis grows.

WOMEN: THE TRUE "INVISIBLE HAND" IN THE WORLD FOOD SYSTEM

The above discussions of development with equity and the food crisis typify the literature on these questions in that *women are nowhere mentioned.* From such discussions, who would suspect that poor rural women are disproportionately driven into *deeper* marginalization than their menfolk, both by the local impact of world economic trends and by most development plans aimed at rural populations? Even more to the point, who would have suspected that the majority of the world's food is produced by women?

Yet both seem to be the case. This chapter attempts to document what happens when women are at the bottom of development priorities. The women themselves tend to lose control of whatever means or fruits of production they previously had at their disposal, and find themselves plunged into circumstances of greater uncertainty and marginality. To the extent that this neglect typically results in lower nutrition, pro-natalist pressures, and greater concentration of resources in the hands of a narrow male elite, even GNP development is slowed. Concomitantly, development with equity may be aborted.

The problem begins with national statistics that rarely record the work poor rural women do (Deere, 1977; Garrett, 1976). However, recent United Nations (1978: 5) estimates indicate that they are doing more than almost anyone suspected:

> "It has been estimated by ESCAP and ECA that women provide 60 to 80 percent of the agricultural labour in Asia and Africa; in Latin America, according to ECLA, the percentage is 40 percent."

Only in sub-Saharan Africa and parts of Southeast Asia have women been perceived as agricultural producers. This recognition (often disapproving) has been most manifest in those areas of *horticultural* production characterized by Boserup (1970) as "female farming" zones. Even here, national statistics concerning women's agricultural participation vary wildly and none approach the 70 percent estimated by the Economic Commission for Africa in Table 2.1. As little appreciated as the extent of women's contribution to food production is the degree to which women's role extends throughout the entire food *system:* 50 percent of storage, 100 percent of processing, 60 percent of marketing—as well as 100 percent of cooking. Often, women's contributions to areas of the food chain other than cooking are even more "invisible" than their participation in production. Women's access to nonformal education (Table 2.1, part C) may be characterized as reflecting "a perception of women's roles which has been translated into development programs and policies" (Zivetz, 1979: 1). Specifically, it is primarily women's "noneconomic" roles that have been translated into training programs. Thus, not only are the women themselves and their families being short-changed; development itself is short-changed by failure to build on women's economic activities.

Table 2.1 raises two important questions: (1) Have women been this productive throughout most of human evolutionary history? If so, it rarely has been recognized outside a narrow circle of specialists.

Table 2.1. African Women's Participation in Production/Supply/Distribution, Household/Community, and Nonformal Educational Access

Responsibility	Unit of Participation
Production/supply/distribution	
Food production	0.70
Domestic food storage	0.50
Food-processing	1.00
Animal husbandry	0.50
Marketing	0.60
Brewing	0.90
Water supply	0.90
Fuel supply	0.80
Household/community	
Bearing, rearing, initial education of children	1.00
Cooking for husband, children, elders	1.00
Cleaning, washing, etc.	1.00
House-building	0.30
House repair	0.50
Community self-help projects	0.70
Areas of Access to Nonformal Education	
Agriculture	0.15
Animal husbandry	0.20
Cooperatives	0.10
Arts and crafts	0.50
Nutrition	0.90
Home economics	1.00

NOTE: Units of participation are calculated on the basis of estimates of women's time as a percentage of all the time expended in a particular task. Units of participation were proposed in Data Base for Discussion on the Interrelations between Women in Development, their Situation, and Population Factors, U.N. Economic Commission for Africa, 1974. Units of participation were determined first for areas within countries, then for countries, then for Africa.

SOURCE: The Changing and Contemporary Role of Women in African Development, U.N. Economic Commission for Africa, 1974; Country Reports on Vocational and Technical Training for Girls and Women, U.N. Economic Commission for Africa, 1974; studies, mission reports, discussions. This table was compiled from versions of these materials in U.N. A/33/238, Effective Mobilization of Women in Development: Report of the Secretary General, 1978: 9; and Zivetz, Laurie, "The Impact of Rural Development on Women and Its Consequences for Fertility in Africa," 1979: 2.

(2) Do similar patterns of female participation in production appear at different levels of development? It appears that sex division of labor in production varies significantly by social class and development pattern and is being greatly affected by contemporary trends in the world economy. Before exploring the specifics of female economic roles around the world and summarizing the evolutionary/historical patterns, let us sketch in some of the changes that are occurring in the lives of both men and women among the rural poor as they attempt to adapt to the contemporary economic trends and development policies that are transforming Third World agriculture.[3]

MANIPULATING FERTILITY, GEOGRAPHIC MOBILITY, FAMILY, AND FEMALE LABOR FOR SURVIVAL

The penetration of the world capitalist economy generally increases uncertainty in the lives of the rural poor, and often displaces them. Also, traditional systems of "social security" and crisis aid, undermined by the cash economy, have not been replaced by new formal institutions in most of the Third World. Thus, poor people's survival may depend on their coping responses.

Two responses may be labeled "demographic": (1) changes in *fertility*, and (2) changes in *migration* patterns. In turn, these intensify "modernization"-induced changes in two other areas: (3) *household/family structure,* and (4) *sex division of labor and resources.* The first three will be discussed briefly in this section as a prologue to the region-by-region examination of the fourth topic, emphasizing women in agriculture.

FERTILITY

One adaptive strategy is adjustment of fertility. Diverse data indicate that a "fertility spurt" has almost invariably accompanied the intrusions and dislocations of the cash economy (American Association for the Advancement of Science [AAAS], 1974). The affected people are not poor because they have too many children, Mamdani (1972) argues; rather, they attempt to use their children to solve the problem of their poverty. Children of poor rural people in many parts of the Third World seem to bring net positive benefits, often from a fairly early age (White, 1975; Schnaiberg and Reed, 1974). In addition, extra children may eventually work as local wage laborers or as migrants. But though this strategy may better some families and individuals, it undercuts the position of the poor *as a class.* It also places the entire country at a disadvantage, for those nations where, as in India, some calculations indicate that each new mouth represents a net drain on the nation's resources (Enke, 1960).

Women, too, may favor increasing fertility if it is not incompatible with their economic activities. Even very young children may help women with their burdens of fetching wood and water and endlessly processing food (Youssef, 1979). Where children can help with *production* tasks, this motivation should be reinforced.

MIGRATION

Development trends tend to take away jobs of the rural poor and to leave them without alternative employment in the urban cash economy. Where peasant populations are ejected en masse, the immediate results for the individuals involved are surely disastrous. However, such wholesale displacement is rare. More often, *some* family members migrate to seek work and provide occasional cash and other assistance to close kin left behind. Selective migration thus offers a possible survival strategy.

Most migration is sex-selective, usually with profound consequences for both family structure and the sex division of labor and resources. In most of the world, males dominate migration streams. Even in Latin America, where rural-urban migration streams are largely female, *seasonal* migration tends to be more heavily male.

HOUSEHOLD/FAMILY PATTERNS

A major consequence of male-majority migration streams has been a great increase of de facto as well as de jure *female heads of household.* Recent United Nations estimates indicate that women "serve as head of *over one-third* of the rural households in the developing world" (Leeper, 1978: 129; see also Buvinic et al., 1978; Blumberg with Garcia, 1977). Since female-headed units are almost invariably poorer than their male-headed counterparts (reflecting both women's lower remuneration and fewer income producers in the average woman-headed household), problems of family well-being in these households tend to be magnified. Migration can affect household composition and thus family well-being in various ways. Retention of additional income earners or additional dependents can lift or depress family economic welfare. Among the poorest rural Third World families, children's small, and often occasional, cash remittances may make a big difference.[4] And the poorest families are precisely those who seem likely to form flexible *sharing networks* among kinfolk, as a kind of mutual insurance (Stack, 1974). In short, although household and family patterns appear to be strongly influenced by economic factors, people also appear to make survival-enhancing adjustments wherever they can.

SEX DIVISION OF LABOR AND RESOURCES

As suggested, women's well-being and relative equality are more affected by the extent of their relative control over the means of production than by the extent of their labor. In these terms, recent agricultural development has been negative for women: capital-intensive technologically oriented strategies tend to increase women's work while decreasing their control over resources.

This may hurt family welfare as well, for men and women apparently spend new income differently. For example, Stavrakis and Marshall (1978) found that introducing sugarcane production in Belize resulted in (1) the decline of food production, (2) the loss of women's resource base, and (3) no improvement in the generally poor prevailing level of child nutrition. Greater sugarcane production, controlled by men, generated quite a bit of income locally, which accrued to the men. However,

> money flowed out of the system as fast as it came in, spent on drink, trucks, travel and purchased female companionship. By and large it did not benefit the women at home tending the children and animals [Stavrakis and Marshall, 1978: 158].

In contrast, there is some indication that women use the income that they control for family welfare. This seemed to be the case in a rural mango puree canning operation established by a women's cooperative in Honduras (author's observation, 1978). Research is needed to generalize this finding.

To reiterate, over and above the sex division of labor within a class is the sex division of resources. Changes in the sex resource base appear to affect what is *done* with increasing or decreasing resources in the class. Thus, we hypothesize:

> Increasing the proportion of a class's resources in the hands of its females will have more rapid and more immediate consequences for the level of individual well-being than comparable increases in the hands of its males.

If this is so, then we have added still another "contradiction of development" to those causing marginalization and malnutrition among more and more of the Third World's rural poor. If women's relative position declines then, because of their unique relationship to food and family welfare, the life- and equity-enhancing aspects of development may suffer disproportionately. This implies that even successful programs intended to make more equitable the distribution of resources between have and have-not classes (within developing countries, and between have and have-not nations within the world system) may not be enough to benefit the world's rural poor. It follows that a concerted effort to recognize, preserve, and enhance the role and resource base of women vis-à-vis the entire agricultural system—including food production, processing, storage, marketing, preparation, and consumption spheres—is required.

We turn now to women's place in each of these spheres of the agricultural system in the developing world's major regions. How are both the unplanned economic trends and the planned intervention programs affecting women? We will consider in turn the three areas: (1) production, (2) control of property, and (3) life options.

WOMEN, FARM WORK, AND FARM WEALTH AROUND THE WORLD

AFRICA

Africa offers the best documentation of what women do in agriculture and specific examples of how economic change and development programs hurt women. Quantitative studies of African women's agricultural system involvement (e.g., Cleave, 1974; Clark, 1975; Weil, 1973) show very high female involvement, often far surpassing male involvement. Since most of these societies have a horticultural base, this is to be expected: According to the data in the 1170-society computer version of Murdock's Ethnographic Atlas (1967), males are the main labor force in only about one-fifth of known horticultural (hoe-cultivation) societies.

Even though colonial administrators may have found it unseemly that women raised so much of the food, their colonial policies capitalized on this fact—and "used women's labor in subsistence agriculture to subsidize the export economies" (United Nations, 1978: 21).[5]

Colonial policy not only pushed men to migrate to plantation, mine, and other wage labor jobs; it also pushed them to grow export cash crops in their home villages. Over time, men predominated in the growing village money economy, controlling most of the earnings from local export crops even though women provided most of the labor. Women added this burden to their responsibilities for growing, processing, storing, and distributing the local food crops. Thus a pattern emerged whereby woman's workload tended to *increase* while her control over the means of production tended to *decrease*. This pattern has persisted to the present day. Let us examine the causes and consequences of both the increased labor and the diminished economic power.

More Work. Other factors above and beyond women's added work on a new series of cash crops increased their labors: (1) Those most likely to migrate for wage labor are the young males who had provided the labor for clearing and tree-felling. (2) An increasing proportion of the children attend school rather than helping with household tasks. (3) The land on which women grow food crops has become increasingly marginal, since the better acreage is almost invariably devoted to cash crops. Thus, women have had to raise the food on land that is either farther from their homes (the closer fertile lands having been switched to male-controlled cash crop use), or worn out from overcropping with insufficient fallow time (Chaney et al., 1979). The amount of land for food crops has also decreased.

Less Economic Power. But even more serious for women is the widespread erosion of their relative control over the means of production. When colonial policy and the concomitant commercialization of agriculture replaced corporate kinship control of land with individualized land rights, women lost out in various ways. Even in matrilineal areas, the new individual legal titles to land overwhelmingly went to men. In areas of heavy male migration, men who had become absentee owners could and sometimes did sell the land out from under their rural wives and children. In the most common situation, patri-kin-controlled land passed to individual men and women lost their traditional *use rights* to land, but not their obligation to cultivate it. All in all, women increasingly could be considered *tenant* farmers on land now controlled by males (Chaney et al., 1979).

Again, it should be stressed that women's farming *competence* does not lag behind. For example, Fortmann (1978) found that in Tanzanian Ujamaa villages there was no significant sex difference in scores indicating "good maize practices" within groups of purchasers and of nonpurchasers of improved inputs (seeds, fertilizers, insecticides, and herbicides).

Men, however, seem able to outspend women on inputs such as seeds, fertilizers, herbicides etc., since, in addition to their own higher cash incomes, they typically have much, much greater access to credit. Concerning loan information, for example, Staudt (1978) found that households with a male present were *fourteen times* more likely than those headed by a female to have received detailed data. And men are likely to receive more information about new, improved farming practices of all kinds, because they receive the overwhelming share of agricultural extension and training services (see Table 2.1).

Moreover, men's privileged access dates from colonial days, when the original extension and training services were set up along Western models. Thus, although colonial administrators were presumably aware of women's central role in most African farming, they offered agricultural assistance to men; women were given home economics training (in embroidery and table decoration, for example) instead. Today, now that the tide is turning and women are being considered for more agricultural services, the result is often that the female extension agents, primarily home economists, have to add agricultural duties to schedules already filled with responsibilities for nutrition, family planning, and so on.

Nutrition has frequently been a casualty of women's increasing marginalization. Eide et al. (1977: 41-42) discuss this issue and provide examples:

> In Ghana, the introduction of cocoa increased women's workloads because men left the yam crop to cultivate the new crop in order to raise cash. As yams require a high labour input and as women's time for growing food was limited due to their many other responsibilities, they replaced the yam with cassava, which can be planted at almost any time during the year and needs little weeding. But cassava has less nutritional value than yam and cannot be intercropped with vegetables and legumes because it depletes soil nutrients more rapidly than yams.

Other studies, while less detailed, also cite the decreasing variety, quality, and/or quantity of the foodstuffs available to African women (SAED, 1978; Simmons, 1975). Yet many programs assume that "traditionalism, or passivity or ignorance" keeps women from enhancing the nutritional content of their diet, rather than the income, time, and other resource constraints usually to blame.

The "ignorance" argument implies that the latest fashion in Western nutritional gospel should replace the allegedly "backward" and low-nutrition crop currently in disfavor. Yet further study may indicate that the women's food practices make good nutritional sense when viewed as part of a total *system.* For example,

> in some countries, efforts are still going on to make women stop planting manioc and replace it with more "protein-rich" crops even though the most recent studies indicate that manioc is the best crop for many poor soils, that the replacement crops often serve nutritional needs poorly, and that traditional cooking practices make manioc more protein-rich than urban nutritionists realized [April et al., 1974, cited in Boulding, 1978: 32].

In fact, the total *system* approach to agriculture may be the missing key to providing meaningful food crop assistance to African women. Currently, it appears, most programs promoting new food crops to women tend to "blame the victim" if they fail. However, these programs themselves usually fail to take into account the many subtleties behind women farmers' decisions to adopt food crop innovations. Some questions women might raise regarding potential new food crops include: Does it mean the possibility of more money (from sale of surplus under their control) as well as food? Does its timing for planting, cultivation, weeding, and harvesting conflict with other demands on women's labor and time? Does it have high variance of yield (cultivators living near the subsistence level cannot risk planting high-variance crops)? Is it easy to harvest (high-yield varieties, HYVs, are often dwarfs with difficult-to-harvest, short, thick stems)? Is it easy to process and to store (since women typically are responsible for both processing and storage)? As a food, is it easy to cook, does it taste good, and does it combine well with traditional foods? Is it easy to market (i.e., is it easy to transport, and is there local demand)?

These questions emphasize that efforts to introduce new higher-protein food crops will require not only adequate extension/inputs aid, but also examination of how the proposed new crop fits into the entire agricultural/food system.

Female marketing activities also deserve close attention. Female own-account, local-level foodstuff traders' positions often have been eroded by the intrusion of male-dominated, larger-scale patterns of wholesaling, distribution, and retail trade (Boserup 1970; Human Resources Development Division, UNECA, 1972). Given the 1974 Economic Commission for Africa estimate that 60 percent of marketing still is done by women (see Table 2.1), further erosion of their position will have widespread consequences. Declining participation in trade will generally mean fewer income sources and less cash for women, and will accentuate the outflow of agriculturally generated surplus to urban centers. This presumably will further limit the local market, and advance the process of rural impoverishment vis-à-vis the city. Worse still, if women cannot expect to market surplus food for extra income, they may not produce that surplus in the first place, thus making their country's food shortfall worse.

If the food crisis intensifies, it is likely that more attention and aid *will* be directed at African female farmers; new evidence of their importance in cultivation is mounting too rapidly for development experts to ignore.[6] But will aid be confined to their role as producers? Unless their control over *property* and the quality of their lives as *people* are actively promoted (and they rarely are), it is unrealistic to expect women to increase agricultural production.[7]

ASIA

Most of Asia is agrarian, and it is more stratified and commercialized than Africa:

> In contrast with Africa, where women are primarily engaged in subsistence agriculture as self-employed farmers and family workers, a large number of women engaged in agriculture in Asia work as wage earners in commercial farms and on plantations.[8]

But while large proportions of the female agricultural labor force are hired workers throughout Asia, there are subregional differences in sex division of labor patterns by both social class and type of cultivation.

Where irrigated intensive agriculture is *not* prevalent (e.g., Northern India), usually only the poorest, landless rural women work as hired labor. For peasant class women, confinement in or near the house (except perhaps during peak periods) symbolizes class differentiation. In contrast, under the more labor-intensive conditions of irrigated cultivation, women at all levels tend to do considerable agricultural work. In general, in areas of extensive irrigation systems and paddy rice, women weed, transplant, harvest, and probably sow. Men dig irrigation ditches, construct and repair terraces, and lift water from canals. With paddy rice, each person can usually produce a bit more than his or her subsistence costs. And the prevalent patterns of unequal land tenure, landlordism, and parcelization typically require that the entire family pitch in for mutual survival. This has had a profound effect on the large-scale export crop sector, since

> male labour cannot, therefore, be recruited without providing for the women and the children, in contrast with Africa, where subsistence agriculture is predominately women's work. . . . The most expedient means of keeping the effective wage rate low, then, is to employ the entire family [United Nations, 1978: 25].

As the United Nations report points out, the plantation can thus avoid paying *male* workers a "family wage" in both Africa and Asia because of the agricultural work of the *females*. In Africa, women's subsistence food production permits the maintenance and reproduction of the labor force. In Asia, rural female wage earners are available as a dividend of the family hiring system. In Latin America, yet a third pattern (discussed below) precludes the necessity of paying male workers enough to maintain their families.

The employment situation in Asia's plantation sector (as in much of the developing world) is affected by a worsening "price/cost squeeze." Because revenues tend to be declining and/or unstable while production costs continue to rise, there have been widespread attempts to minimize the resident, permanent labor force. This has tended to hurt women along with men. However, the widespread sex differential in wages *may* increase employer preference for female labor. An International Labor Office (1970) study of plantations notes:

> In Sri Lanka, for example, the average minimum wage of females on both the rubber and tea plantations was about 80 percent of the male wage for the period 1960-66, in spite of the fact that women tend to work longer and produce more than men in certain tasks. . . . During the same period, the price of rubber and tea exports declined steadily. The participation of women on the rubber and tea plantations then increased from 46 to 49 percent and from 40 to 43 percent, respectively [United Nations, 1978: 26].

Labor displacement in export crop plantation agriculture often has been paralleled by labor displacement in *food* crops, when these are grown by larger owners using the new Green Revolution high-yield varieties.

The amount of labor displacement accompanying mechanization and/or introduction of Green Revolution "packages" appears to vary greatly by crop and specific techniques introduced, and, moreover, to vary in ways that may differentially affect one sex or the other. The result has been more marginalization of female than male labor (United Nations, 1978: 13; Billings and Singh, 1970). Other studies rarely spell out the implicit differential impact of mechanization on males and females. In Thailand, the traditional combination of broadcast rice with buffalo farming involved 8.8 "man days" per rai (Inukai, 1970, cited in Stokes et al., 1979). If tractors were introduced and broadcasting continued, labor use dropped to 5.5 "man days." If, however, the tractors were combined with the more labor-intensive technique of transplanted rice, labor use *rose* to 10.5. As transplanting is usually a female task, this would probably disproportionately involve women. Also suggestive is Abercrombie's (1972) study detailing labor reductions of 6 to 19 percent from increasing mechanization in potatoes (a horticultural crop), as against 50 to 90 percent labor reductions for wheat (an agrarian field crop).

The grim impact of agricultural mechanization and other Green Revolution innovations on those who are both landless (or near-landless) and female, in the *absence* of major ameliorating structural change, may be seen in Java today (Stoler, 1977; Milone, 1978), where women have long been crucial to wet-rice cultivation and enjoy considerable economic autonomy. During the last century, both land scarcity and concentration in Java rose steadily because of (1) the leasing of peasant land for estate crops such as sugar, and (2) the (probably resultant) increase in population pressure (Milone, 1978: 84; Geertz, 1963). By the 1970s, "over 75 percent of the villagers were without enough rice land to sustain themselves and had to seek off-farm sources of income" (Milone, 1978: 86). Women, particularly poor ones, usually harvested rice for such income.

Then the Green Revolution varieties of rice and the mechanical rice huller came to Java. The HYV rice, with a heavier stalk, is difficult to harvest with the traditional bamboo knife; thus steel scythes, too heavy for many women, are used. Much of the harvesting is now by crews of scythe-wielding males brought in by the middlemen who buy the crop. This devastating blow to the landless and near-landless women has been followed by the introduction of the mechanical rice huller. Previously, the in-kind shares earned through rice-pounding supplied an important source of subsistence to poor women, as did transporting small amounts of rice to local markets. But the mechanical rice huller, a much less labor-intensive operation using *male* workers, is rapidly displacing women. Poor women are losing a direct food source: "By 1973 less than 50 percent [of rice] was hand-pounded, and some observers suggest as little as 10 percent" (Milone, 1978: 153). Also, rice began to be bulked, right in the field, into large sacks, too heavy for many women to carry.

I have hypothesized (Blumberg, 1979a, 1979b) that women's position and autonomy rest on the proportion of the means of production they control, and have proposed that, in class societies, this hypothesis be tested by comparing resource control by sex within classes. The preceding discussion of Asian women supports this hypothesis, to the detriment of women. The expected relationship also appears in certain parts of Indonesia, where women, controlling the bulk of the means of production, have been beneficiaries, not victims, of mechanization:

> In West Sumatra, the women's clans still own the land, and the effect of the introduction of the HYVs was entirely different than in Java. In fact, *women* buy the costly inputs, own the rice hullers, and employ *men* with knives and scythes to help in the harvest. Before these developments, Minangkabau women kept control of earlier technological innovations, such as mechanized spice grinders and the water driven mills which they still own and use to grind flour. In Aceh, as well, where women can own the rice fields, they have kept control of earlier labor-saving devices, such as mortar and pestle for rice pounding, and now use hullers to reduce losses and produce a better quality of rice [Milone, 1978: 156-157; emphasis added].

But this case, clearly an exception, offers little grounds for optimism. In today's world, those instances in which women maintain control over a substantial or majority share of the group's means of production appear to be both sharply limited and shrinking.

LATIN AMERICA: A BRIEF OVERVIEW

This region offers another variation on the basic patterns observed elsewhere. For Latin America as a whole, the importance of agriculture has been declining in recent decades and the rate of labor absorption in agriculture also has been decreasing steadily (United Nations, 1978: 28). But statistical examinations of the region are plagued by gross but idiosyncratic underenumeration of female involvement in agriculture (Deere, 1977; Garrett, 1976; United Nations, 1978). Thus, it is hard to assess what has happened to women, especially in the less industrialized areas. In Bolivia, Ecuador, Mexico, Peru, and north and northeast Brazil, actual rates of female participation in agriculture—as distinct from government census statistics—are estimated to be about 50 percent to 60 percent (United Nations, 1978: 28).

As its agriculture has moved relentlessly toward commercialization in recent decades, landholding in rural Latin America remains "dominated by an extraordinary degree of concentration through the latifundia-minifundia [large estate-smallholding] pattern" (Stokes et al., 1979: 40). Although this has resulted in an overall pattern of proletarianization of the labor force, three trends are involved, all of them greatly affecting women's work and well-being. First, the *resident, permanent workforce* on the large holdings has been declining in both relative and absolute terms, with women suffering the bulk of the displacement (Garrett, 1976, documents nearly 100 percent elimination of females in such jobs in Chile's Central Valley by 1965). Second, *temporary, seasonal wage workers* have increased dramatically, often displacing the permanent workers; since these are mainly male, female-headed households frequently result when the men fail to return. Third, both unpaid family workers and proprietors on the minifundia also have increased; many of the unpaid family workers, especially, are women. The net result for females often has been deeper poverty or total displacement from the rural economy—i.e., migration to the city for domestic work or marginal informal-sector activities (see Youssef, 1979; Chaney, 1978).

The coming of capitalist agriculture to Colombia's Cauca Valley provides an example of still another way women's control over agricultural means of production is eroded. As the plantation monoculture of annual cash crops (especially sugar) replaces year-round subsistence crops often farmed by female-headed smallholder families, many women have been forced off their holdings (Rubbo, 1974). Not all have been displaced by the voraciously expanding plantations. Others have cut down their trees and cleared their gardens at the urging of sons, who, encouraged by male extension agents, have introduced annual commercial crops. Families are then deprived of a steady food supply and exposed to the vicissitudes of the world market, with the result that many smallholders go under. The women become increasingly dependent on male access to wage labor and/or are recruited into labor gangs of temporary female farm workers who reside in the towns and work at the lowest wages. In general, women are again losing both absolutely and relative to men as they lose control over their means of production.

What, then, of agrarian reform? How have women—especially female family heads—fared under the redistribution and resettlement schemes aimed at reversing rural pauperization? First, it appears that land reforms to date have been largely ineffective in changing unequal patterns of access to the means of production. Second, it also appears that land reform has been neutral or actually detrimental for women's position. A woman is extremely unlikely to be named as the legal beneficiary of agrarian reform or the officially recognized "member" of any resulting cooperative control structure. (Even a female head of household with no male present, although theoretically equal to men, is rarely so named in practice; such women are disproportionately underrepresented in the reformed sector.) Without such recognition, she is unable to receive credit and many other forms of assistance.

Resettlement schemes tend to emphasize cash crops for men and thus have been particularly hard on women. If women are included, they typically get a minute "kitchen garden." Sometimes (as in Honduras) it is legally impossible, under the terms of the agrarian reform/resettlement law, for women to be allocated land for women's cooperative production. This leaves the women completely dependent on their men in a strange and difficult environment.

Neither poor men nor poor women have increased their access to land or employment under Latin America's old and still-dominant latifundia-minifundia pattern. But the evidence indicates that women have suffered more than men from commercialization. These increasingly marginalized rural females seem to suffer from a combination of the negative consequences of both the African pattern (where women work harder with less help to grow more of the food crops in the subsistence sector) and the Asian pattern (where women work for wages in the cash crop sector, but at the lowest-paid and least stable jobs). And their plight is distinctive in its extreme invisibility: More than elsewhere, their labor contribution is in categories that "fall between the cracks" of national statistics.

THE MIDDLE EAST: AN EVEN BRIEFER OVERVIEW

Similar "invisibility" exists in relation to the role of women in the Middle East. The stereotype of rural Middle Eastern women is that they play at best a very marginal role in agriculture, have low skills, and participate little (aside, perhaps, from the peak seasons of the yearly cycle). This view is consonant with national statistics, which show generally the lowest rates of female economic activity in the developing world.

Yet here, too, detailed village studies are providing evidence that women are much more active than previously thought, both in crop production and (particularly in North Africa) in animal husbandry (see Badran, 1972). Van Dusen (1977: 23), citing Nassif (1976), reports:

> For instance, against the Tunisian estimate that 13.2 percent of rural Tunisian women were economically active in 1972, Nassif found that approximately 40 percent of the adult women in a small Tunisian village she was studying had economic roles, from which they derived some income.

Van Dusen points out that this statistical discrepancy exists in part, because traditionally, the entire informal market system is excluded in specifying "economic activities." However, in addition, "the pressure of cultural norms would [also] explain, in part, the underenumeration of working women in agriculture, since farmers are generally reluctant to report that their wives and daughters have a gainful occupation" (United Nations, 1978: 27, citing Youssef, 1977).

Moreover, trends in the region seem to indicate that women's participation in agriculture and other economic activity is increasing and likely to rise in the future. A major cause is international migration, which (except in Turkey) is heavily male. For example, in Yemen, approximately half the male labor force is out of the country at any given time, employed in the Persian Gulf oil-producing countries. Rising rural male outmigration may prove linked to the rising proportion of female-headed households and rising divorce rate observed in Morocco. Even where male migration is not outside the country, it can have a profound effect. Oil-producing Algeria "reported that female participation in agriculture more than doubled between 1966 and 1973, primarily owing to male migration, which resulted in an increased importance of female labour in self-managed farms" (United Nations, 1978: 22).

In sum, under the impact of internationally generated economic trends, Middle Eastern customs are changing and traditions are accommodating to new and urgent survival necessities. There is no evidence of any group anywhere choosing economic ruin rather than permit a change in the traditional economic role of its womenfolk—if no alternative labor force (e.g., expatriate males) can prudently be recruited. Rather, as history shows, if survival necessities are urgent enough, and alternate workers unfeasible or politically problematic, women may move almost overnight into tasks considered both "inappropriate" and "incompatible." But, as in the other regions surveyed, increases in women's agricultural activities may not positively affect their autonomy or well-being. Once again, it is proposed, the less women control the means of production (and in the Middle East their relative economic power seems generally the lowest of the major regions reviewed), the less they can control the conditions of their participation in production—or "progress." Recent and conflicting tendencies in Khomeini-influenced Iran, on the one hand, and Marxist-influenced South Yemen, on the other, may be subsumed under this proposition.

SUMMARY OF HYPOTHESES AND IMPLICATIONS

Throughout this chapter the central hypothesis of the author's paradigm of sex stratification—that women's level of economic power (especially their relative control of the means of production) relative to the men of their class or group is the most important predictor of their relative equality in other areas of life—has provided an important "handle" for interpreting the diverse but often negative ways in which development trends and policies have affected Third World women in the regions surveyed. This hypothesis and some of its corollaries and related propositions (e.g., that although women's participation in production apparently is a necessary precondition for economic power, of itself, it does not predict their relative equality in the sorts of "life options" described in note 1) have received strong empirical support in the author's pilot study of a sample of 61 preindustrial societies. The three major types of such societies, in evolutionary order, are foraging societies (hunters and gatherers), horticultural societies (hoe and digging stick cultivators), and agrarian societies (plow cultivators). These and other ethnographic data reveal that human historical evolution has witnessed a variety of productive arrangements, in many of which women dominate production and enjoy considerable control over both the means and the fruits of production (see Blumberg, 1978, for details and references).

To summarize this historical material, in hunting-gathering societies, women have high participation in production and control over the means (and fruits) of production that is relatively equal to men's. In horticultural societies, women continue to have high participation in production, but, in general (with some spectacular exceptions, such as the Iroquois), less control than their menfolk over the means of production. In agrarian societies (especially among non-irrigated cultivation), women tend to be low in both contribution to production and control of resources, and are found to be almost universally subjugated. In short, the subservient and relatively less productive roles of women found in many agrarian societies (including the antecedents of all of today's industrialized nations, both capitalist and socialist) are not representative of most of human history, let alone all Third World nations today. Yet, exaggerated by the flawed picture of low female productivity drawn by most national statistics (which rarely measure the non-wage-labor rural activities in which most Third World women engage), it is this image of women that is the implicit model common among most development policy makers and practitioners around the globe. This model provides them with the blinders so often apparent in the regional material presented in this article. But one must not presume that it represents the limits of human female experience. The more valid assumption is that rural "women's fate" owes little to biology, much to socialization, and even more to the social relations of production.

Elsewhere (see especially Blumberg, 1979b), I have presented additional hypotheses relevant for the construction of a preliminary theoretical framework for interpreting and predicting how different groups and classes of women are affected by specific development trends. Many of these hypotheses relate to predicting women's *production* activities in terms of (a) the degree of compatibility of the activity with women's special child-care responsibilities (e.g., lactation), (b) the demand for labor relative to the available male supply, (c) the nature and extent of the larger stratification system, and (d) the position of the woman's country within the world economy. One can conceive of these four factors as a sort of intensity scale, in that the last one, relating to international political economy, impacts on the two preceding factors, which generally prove more important than the biologically linked "compatibility" factor.

As an overall hypothesis linking women's economic position and development, we can suggest that the greater the control over the means of production, the greater the control over the impact of development. This proposition should apply to both male large landholders and female smallholders as well as anyone between. If women's resource control is reduced, it is thus assumed to have negative consequences for their own lives and the well-being of their children. But if the women in question play large and unheralded roles in the world's food system, as argued here, then the consequences of ignoring or injuring their economic base and roles are of much greater magnitude.

Almost every day, headlines underscore the deepening of some aspect of the world crisis of hunger and the growing gap between have and have-not. Already some voices (such as those of Lappe and Collins in *Food First*) are arguing the connection between the two problems. But even they have all but overlooked the "female factor" in their analysis of the approaching agricultural apocalypse.

In sum, no policy prescription for achieving either "development with equity" or an equitable supply of food for the people of the Third World can be written until female contributions to farming and food systems are *recognized, preserved* where threatened, and *enhanced* in an equity-promoting manner. The present synthesis of extant data and hypotheses focuses more on the problem than the solution. Will the next act feature policy proposals from above or popular protest from below? Stay tuned for the 1980s.

NOTES

1. Originally conceived in my sex stratification paradigm as opportunities/issues existing in all known societies, the "life options" include women's relative freedom to decide marriage and divorce, control sexuality pre- and extramaritally, regulate fertility patterns, enjoy freedom of movement, have access to available educational/training opportunities, and exercise household power and decision-making.

2. A National Academy of Science study notes that of roughly 100,000 edible cultigens, only some 30 are emphasized as commercially viable (Irene Tinker, personal communication, 1979).

3. The overall impact of the penetration of the world capitalist economy on the Third World countryside frequently has been a "cultivation crunch" that has increased uncertainty in the lives of the rural poor while displacing many of them. Many Third World governments, attempting to boost foreign exchange earnings via export crops, have encouraged their "modernization" via strong incentives to import the latest technology. Under conditions of unequal concentration of the means of production, the technological innovations introduced tend to be capital-intensive and labor-displacing.

Larger landowners reap most of the benefits from the usually resultant increase in yields and land values. Meanwhile, although the exact scenario varies according to the local situation, often smallholders are undercut, tenant farmers are evicted, and/or employees on the large holdings are dismissed. The net results typically include further concentration of landholdings, and some combination of outmigration and/or conversion to seasonal wage labor (Stokes et al., 1979, summarize an extensive literature; see also their Figure 1, p. 67, and related discussion).

4. For example, Michaelson (1975) discusses the case of a young teenager who had migrated to Bombay and found work as a houseboy. The remittances he sent home a couple of times a year were quite small, yet were an important part of yearly family cash needs.

5. Men were recruited to work in the mines, plantations, and other "modern sector" large-scale export enterprises, at wages manifestly insufficient to provide for the family, since women were able to do almost all operations of the agricultural cycle unaided by men. Thus, the women supported the children and the old people, absorbing the costs of sustaining and reproducing the labor force from one generation to the next.

6. A grim recent example, however, indicates that development experts' vision retains many blind spots. In the 1970s international outpouring of disaster aid to the drought-stricken Sahel, it was the cattle of the men, rather than the smaller ruminants (e.g., goats) typically controlled by the women, that were replaced (Cloud, 1978). Not only did women lose their economic independence, but the group's ability to weather future drought was placed in doubt, since the different animals fill diverse ecological niches and thereby provide survival insurance (e.g., the quick-breeding goats better resist and recover from drought since they can exist on browse if necessary, still providing palatable milk and meat). This example typifies the development "horror stories" first chronicled by Boserup (1970) and Tinker (1976), in which developers' blindness to women's property, productivity, position, and problems ultimately harms not only the women themselves but also the developers' larger projects.

7. Concern for women's relative resources with regard to *property* is even rarer than attention to their production activities, and statistics are almost nonexistent. In particular, special concern for women's rights to land is needed—not only in existing villages, but also in new cooperative or agrarian reform/settlement schemes where women are almost never given title to land. Two of the most pressing "women as *people*" issues are: (1) Attention to reducing females' largely ignored drudgework in processing grain and supplying water and fuel for the household. Appropriate technology could: (a) simultaneously reduce women's burdens, (b) save energy (since these activities inefficiently use up to half of all rural energy consumed), and (c) ease pro-natalist pressure (since children are so useful at these tasks). (2) Attention to female-headed families, since these are increasing rapidly, are estimated to involve even now one-third or more of Third World rural households, and constitute the very poorest and most vulnerable.

8. "Thus, in Sri Lanka 72 percent of the female workforce in agriculture are salaried workers, comprising almost 40 percent of the total number of wage earners. . . . In the tea plantation industry of India, where around two-thirds of the total plantation labour force is engaged, women constitute approximately 50 percent of this labour force. . . . In Malaysia, about 45 percent of the hired labourers for all types of crops were women" (United Nations, 1978: 25).

REFERENCES

ABERCROMBIE, K. C. (1972) "Agricultural mechanization and employment in Latin America," International Labor Review, 105-106: 11-45.

American Association for the Advancement of Science [AAAS] (1974) Culture and Population. Washington, DC: Author.

APRIL, J. E. et al. (1974) "Cassava's role as a food staple." Preliminary Report for the Office of Nutrition, Bureau for Technical Assistance. Agency for International Development, University of Colorado.

BADRAN, H. (1974) "The 'cost' of a child." CERES 7, 4: 25-30.

BILLINGS, M. H. and A. SINGH (1970) "Mechanization and the wheat revolution: effects on female labour in Punjab." Economic and Political Weekly 5, 52: A-169-A-172.

BLUMBERG, R. L. (1978) Stratification: Socioeconomic and Sexual Stratification. Dubuque, IA: Wm. C. Brown.

———(1979a) "A paradigm predicting the position of women: policy implications and problems," pp. 113-142 in J. Lipman-Blumen and J. Bernard (eds.) Sex Roles and Social Policy. London: Sage Publications, Ltd.

———(1979b) "Rural women in development: veil of invisibility, world of work." International Journal of Intercultural Relations 3: 447-472.

BLUMBERG, R. L. with M. P. Garcia (1977) "The political economy of the mother-child family: a cross-societal view," pp. 99-163 in L. Leñero-Otero (ed.) Beyond the Nuclear Family. London: Sage Publications, Ltd.

BOSERUP, E. (1970) Woman's Role in Economic Development. New York: St. Martin's.

BOULDING, E. (1978) "Women, peripheries and food production," in Proceedings and Papers of the International Conference on Women and Food. Tucson: University of Arizona.

BUVINIC, M., N. H. YOUSSEF, and B. VON ELM (1978) "Women headed households: the ignored factor in development planning." Report submitted to the Women in Development Office, Agency for International Development.

CHANEY, E. (1978) Testimony before the House International Relations Committee, March, Washington, D.C.

——— E. B. SIMMONS, and K. A. STAUDT (1979) "Women in development." Office of Women in Development, Agency for International Development, Washington, D.C.

CLARK, B. A. (1975) "The work done by rural women in Malawi." Eastern African Journal of Rural Development 8, 1/2.

CLEAVE, J. H. (1974) African Farmers: Labor Use in the Development of Smallholder Agriculture. New York: Praeger.

CLOUD, K. (1978) "Sex roles in food production and distribution systems in the Sahel." Presented at the International Conference on Women and Food, University of Arizona, Tucson.

COX, P. (1974) "Who controls the world food system?" University of Wisconsin, Food/Climate Research Institute.

DEERE, C. D. (1977) "The agricultural division of labor by sex: myths, facts and contradictions in the Northern Peruvian Sierra." Presented at the Joint National Meeting of the Latin American Studies Association and the African Studies Association, Houston.

de JANVRY, A. and C. GARRAMON (1977) "The dynamics of rural poverty in Latin America." Journal of Peasant Studies: 206-216.

EIDE, W. B., E. SKJONSBERG, A. PALA, and A. BATHILY (1977) "Women in food production, food handling and nutrition with special emphasis on Africa." PAG Bulletin 17, 3-4. (published by the Protein-Calorie Advisory Group, United Nations, New York)

EMMANUEL, A. (1972) Unequal Exchange: A Study of the Imperialism of Trade. New York: Modern Reader.

ENKE, S. (1960) "The gains to India from population control: some money measures and incentive schemes." Review of Economics and Statistics 42 (May): 175-180.

Food and Agricultural Organization [FAO] (1979) "Review and analysis of agrarian reform and rural development in the developing countries since the mid-sixties." Reference Document for the World Conference on Agrarian Reform and Rural Development, Rome, July 12-20. (WCARRD/INF.3)

FORTMANN, L. (1978) "Women and Tanzanian agricultural development." Economic Research Bureau Paper 77.4, University of Dar es Salaam. (mimeo)

GARRETT, P. M. (1976) "Some structural constraints on the agricultural activities of women: the Chilean hacienda." Land Tenure Center, University of Wisconsin.

GEERTZ, C. (1963) Agricultural Involution: The Processes of Ecological Change in Indonesia. Berkeley: University of California Press.

GOTSCH, C. H. (1973) "Tractor mechanization and rural development in Pakistan." International Labour Review 107, 2: 133-166.

Human Resources Development Division, UNECA (1972) "Women: the neglected human resource for African development." Canadian Journal of African Studies 6, 2: 359-370.

International Labor Office [ILO] (1970) "Conditions of work of women and young workers on plantations." Report III of the Sixth Session of the Committee on Work on Plantations, Geneva. (mimeo)

INUKAI, I. (1970) "Farm mechanization, output and labour input: a case study in Thailand." International Labour Review 101, 5: 453-473.

LAPPE, F. M. and J. COLLINS (1978) Food First. New York: Ballantine.

LEEPER, D. S. (1978) "Assistance, hunger and malnutrition: the commodity systems approach." Presented at the International Conference on Women and Food, University of Arizona, Tucson.

MAMDANI, M. (1972) The Myth of Population Control: Family, Caste, and Class in an Indian Village. New York: Monthly Review Press.

MICHAELSON, K. L. (1975) "Family size: the reproduction of the labor force: the case of Bombay." Presented at the annual meeting of the American Anthropological Association, San Francisco.

MILONE, P. (1978) A Preliminary Study in Three Countries: Indonesia Report. Prepared for the Office of Women in Development, Agency for International Development, Washington, D.C.

MOOCK, P. (1976) "The efficiency of women as farm managers: Kenya." American Journal of Agricultural Economics 58, 5.

MURDOCK, G. P. (1967) World Ethnographic Atlas. Pittsburgh: University of Pittsburgh Press.

NASSIF, H. (1976) "Women's economic roles in developing Tunisia." Presented at the meetings of the Association of Arab-American University Grads/Middle East Studies Association.

OMVEDT, G. (1975) "The political economy of starvation: imperialism and the world food crisis." Scientific Socialist Education Trust Publication No. 2, Bombay.

RUBBO, A. (1974) "The spread of capitalism in rural Colombia: effects on poor women." in R. Reiter (ed.) Toward an Anthropology of Women. New York: Monthly Review Press.

SCHNAIBERG, A. and D. REED (1974) "Risk, uncertainty and family formation: the social context of poverty groups." Population Studies 29.

SCOTT, J. (1975) "Exploitation in rural class relations." Comparative Politics (July).

SIMMONS, E. B. (1975) "The small-scale rural food processing industry in northern Nigeria." Food Research Institute Studies 14, 2: 147-161.

Société africaine d'études et de développement [S.A.E.D.] (1978) "Social and economic development in Upper Volta: woman's perspective." U.S. Agency for International Development, Regional Economic Development Services Office, West Africa.

STACK, C. B. (1974) All Our Kin: Strategies for Survival in a Black Community. New York: Harper & Row.

STAUDT, K. A. (1975-1976) "Women farmers and inequities in agricultural services." Rural Africana 29 (Winter).

———(1978) "Agricultural productivity gaps: a case study of male preference in government policy implementation." Development and Change 9: 439-457.

STAVRAKIS, O. and M. L. MARSHALL (1978) "Women, agriculture, and development in the Maya lowlands: profit or progress?" Presented at the International Conference on Women and Food, University of Arizona, Tucson.

STOKES, C. S., W. A. SCHUTJER, T. McCOY, and C. H. WOOD (1979) "Rural development, land and human fertility." Prepared for the South-East Consortium on International Development.

STOLER, A. (1977) "Class structure and female autonomy in rural Java," in Wellesley Editorial Committee (ed.) Women and National Development: The Complexities of Change. Chicago: University of Chicago Press.

TINKER, I. (1976) "The adverse impact of development on women." in I. Tinker et al. (eds.) Women and World Development. New York: Praeger.

United Nations, Economic Commission for Africa (1974a) "Country reports on vocational and technical training for girls and women."

———(1974b) "The data base for discussion on the interrelations between women in development, their situation, and population factors in Africa." Presented to the Regional Seminar on the Integration of Women in Development with Special Reference to Population Factors, Addis Ababa.

———(1977) "The changing and contemporary role of women in African development." Economic Bulletin For Africa.

United Nations, Report of the Secretary General (1978) "Effective mobilization of women in development." (UN/A/33/238)

VAN DUSEN, R. A. (1977) "Integrating women into national economies: programming considerations with special reference to the Near East." Submitted to the Agency for International Development, Office of Technical Support, Near East Bureau.

WEIL, P. (1973) "Wet rice, women and adaptation in the Gambia." Rural Africana 19 (Winter).

WHITE, B. (1975) "The economic importance of children in a Javanese village," in M. Nag (ed.) Population and Social Organization. The Hague: Mouton.

YOUSSEF, N. (1979) "Rural development activities, fertility and the cost and value of children: review of the paper's consideration of women." Submitted to the Research Triangle Institute and the South-East Consortium for International Development.

——— (1977) "Women and agricultural production in Muslim societies." Studies in Comparative International Development 12, 1.

ZIVETZ, L. (1979) "The impact of rural development on the status of women and its consequences for fertility in Africa." Submitted to the Research Triangle Institute and the South-East Consortium for International Development.

3

SINGAPORE WOMEN

Work and the Family

JANET SALAFF

From 1974 to 1976 after the first decade of Singapore's economic and social development program we conducted extensive interviews with 100 young Singapore Chinese women and their families, a sample including both employed and homemaker wives. The critical importance of women's work to their families is demonstrated by the labor force experiences of the 52 young women of my sample who continued full-time jobs through marriage and childbearing. These women are the main concern of this paper.[1]

Our study finds that women work in response to the economic needs of their families and that they direct their earnings to enhance the prospects of family and children. They do not work primarily for their own satisfaction or self-expression, although many find pleasure in their work. The dependence of these employed women on family

AUTHOR'S NOTE: The data for this chapter were collected as part of a larger study jointly conducted with Professor Aline Wong, Department of Sociology, University of Singapore, under a grant from the International Development Research Centre. I wish to express my appreciation to the IDRC for its support. The present chapter expresses the views of the author and does not necessarily reflect those of the IDRC. The study is currently being updated with reinterviews of a sample of the 1974-1976 respondents.

support to aid them—in particular, assistance from other women—is striking and not sufficiently documented by other studies of working-class women.

BACKGROUND

Singapore obtained independence from Great Britain in 1959. The party-state is animated by a social democratic ideology that affirms that the capitalist market system can be improved by state economic regulation to avoid the usual mass impoverishment attendant upon early industrialization in the more laissez-faire nations of the South and North Asian region. As part of this policy, Singapore promotes the labor force participation of women.

In view of Singapore's small size, the ruling party concluded early that the city-state could not by itself provide internal markets, sufficient capital, or managerial expertise to build the industrial foundation needed for an import substitution policy. Active state promotion of industrial investment by transnational corporations and a launching of a substantial social services program is directed at ameliorating the liabilities of colonialism (Goh, 1976; Yoshihara, 1976). These liabilities included widespread poverty, massive unemployment, congested and rundown housing, and an economy dominated by a labor-intensive service sector built on Singapore's position as entrepôt for the primary products of the hinterland and principal British military base east of Suez. The party-state development scheme links Singapore closely to the capitalist world market. In 1959 industry accounted for only 13 percent of Singapore's gross national product (GNP). However, from the mid-1960s to the mid-1970s, the government-directed investment program encouraged labor-intensive manufacturing industries that would absorb unemployed workers and all school leavers. By 1972 industries with some foreign capital constituted 64 percent of the Singapore workforce (Yoshihara, 1976: 180). By 1975 industry formed 35 percent of Singapore's GNP, and manufacturing contributed over one-quarter of the labor force employment, the unemployment rate had fallen sharply, the price of labor had risen, and a labor force shortage was anticipated (Singapore Bulletin, 1979).

The development strategies that center on the state promotion of labor-intensive manufacturing industries with foreign capital and markets have had a paramount impact on the position of women in the economy. By 1975 Singapore had become one of Asia's leading centers for electronics assembly, and Singapore's workers were becoming stitchers of inexpensive garments for the world market. The workforce in the Singapore fashion and garments industry more than doubled, growing from 12,690 workers in 1970 to 32,792 in 1978. In addition, the majority of workers in electronics industries are semi-skilled women (Lim, 1978). The percentage of economically active females rose as a proportion of women aged 15 and over, from 22 percent in 1957 to 42 percent in 1979 (Singapore Economic Bulletin, 1980; Ministry of Labour, 1979).

Singapore industrialists pay women low wages on the grounds that their products must be competitive in the international marketplace. A 1975 compilation found the median working wage for Singapore Chinese males was $319 and was under $200 for females.[2] Another study that spanned all of Singapore's principal ethnic groups (Chinese, Malay, Indian) found that women production workers earned 60 percent of the wages of their male counterparts (Deyo and Chen, 1976; Ministry of Labour, 1975). However, by the mid-1970s the city-state was losing its attractiveness to investors seeking large pools of cheap labor (Goh, 1979). Housewives formed a potential labor source, but many are illiterate and without work experience, and lack inexpensive child-care assistance. For these and other reasons, the chief source of low-wage labor since 1970 has been guestworkers from Malaysia.

In the late 1970s the government launched the restructuring of the economy in favor of high value-added industries, and Singapore is pioneering the introduction of capital-intensive manufacturing industry in the ASEAN region (Singapore Bulletin, 1979). The wages of most workers are to be raised to encourage management to replace labor-intensive methods of production with machinery. Light industries no longer receive state subventions, and many textile and electronics assembly firms that spearheaded the Singapore industrial revolution are transferring their operations to other nations in the region.

In order successfully to carry out the transition to advanced manufacturing in the 1980s, Singapore will need to implement fully a new program for enhancing labor force skills and to introduce universalistic criteria for job search and advancement by merit. However, few of the many women who work in the light manufacturing sector that is now being downgraded have the broad, flexible education or the manual training necessary to take advantage of the technical upgrading courses being offered to retrenched workers. Personal connections and introductions have formerly been required and are still useful for Singapore workers to obtain their jobs. Women who do not have extensive job-finding networks or female role models have been relatively disadvantaged in the labor market, resulting in extensive labor force segregation by sex and class, as will be seen in this chapter.

In addition to job creation, the Singapore state finances ASEAN's most extensive social service infrastructure to improve the quality of the new industrial labor force. These programs include a contributory pension plan that covers most employees and hourly workers, large blocks of working-class housing in which nearly two-thirds of the populace resides (HDB flats), and a means to finance the purchase of these apartments through the pension plan. The state has made available secondary-level education and technical training for youths (including some women) and virtually free hospital care for families. Employment of women has been further facilitated by government-sponsored family planning measures and an improvement in working conditions for pregnant women. However, day-care facilities are minimal. To bolster the positive measures, stringent socioeconomic penalties are deployed in the cause of economic growth and political stabilization. For example, in 1973 a population limitation program raised accouchement costs after the first birth and reduced school enrollment choices for the fourth- and higher-parity children (Wong and Salaff, 1979).

These and other social services elevate the popular living standard, but the government does not promote income equalization or even a comprehensive welfare system for fear of restricting the inflow of transnational capital, alarming indigenous capitalists, and burdening the public sector. Mass educational efforts stress family advancement by means of hard work and saving for the future. Singapore citizens are encouraged to assume personal responsibility to avail themselves of the opportunities for work and education opened by the state's industrial and social service programs (Nair, 1976).

Under these conditions, the labor force participation of women has risen in general in post-independence Singapore, but marital status, age, and the number of children continue to be important determinants of the decision to work. Of all 20- to 24-year-old women, married and single, 73 percent were working in 1978, but only 53 percent of the 25-29-year-olds were working, and the proportion continues to decrease with age (Nair, 1980). The 1973 Singapore Family Planning and Population Board Survey (1974: 30) found that 37 percent of the childless married women aged 15 to 24 worked, while 16 percent of the mothers in the same age range worked.

The socioeconomic policies of the Singapore government require that the populace develop farsighted family plans if it wishes to optimize its chances for long-term family upgrading. The labor force participation of women is one of the cardinal means employed by families to improve their living standards and quality of life. The present chapter assesses the impact of women's workforce participation on their family economies.

WOMEN'S WAGES, WORK EXPERIENCES, AND SOCIAL CLASS

WAGES

This study is based on a sample that divides naturally into two groups of families. Group I consists of 58 lower and median working-class families classified on the basis of four components: socio-economic status of the couple's parents, and the educational level, occupation, and combined monthly income of the couple. Group II, which comprises the remaining 42 families of my sample, consists of the affluent working class (Group IIa) and the middle class (Group IIb).[3]

Fifty-two of the women in this study are employed full-time in non-agricultural labor: 47 factory workers, a domestic servant, a waitress, a teacher, a newspaper writer, and a government civil servant. In addition, 3 women work part-time outside the home: an accountant, a domestic servant, and a saleswoman for Tupperware. There are 5 others who take in piecework sewing for nearby factories. The remaining 5 women work part-time without pay for their relatives on farms or in small family businesses. Thus the group of 52 full-time workers, the primary focus of this study, is augmented by a further set of 13 part-time working wives.

All the employed women of this panel, except those of the higher-ranking Group IIb families, perform tedious repetitive work. Table 3.1 displays the differences in salary among the 52 workers. Service women earn the lowest wages, followed by operatives in small- and medium-sized locally capitalized enterprises. These firms trim their wage bills to maximize their share of intensely competitive markets. Thus, 6 of the 11 poorest-paid women (who receive under $200 monthly) are textile and garment workers, whereas only 2 of the respondents who receive relatively good women's wages ($300 or above) toil in these two key industries. One of these women is a section leader on a production line and the other operates a small dress-making school in her apartment. The better-capitalized transnational electronics firms in Singapore are able to pass their higher wage bills to the consumer and generally pay their workers somewhat more than the small garment factories and shops. Of the 27 electronics workers in this panel, only one earns under $200, while 9 of the 14 highest-paid women are employed in electronics firms. However, many of the electronics assemblists interviewed in 1974-1975 were forced to work a 4-day week because of the recession in the industry, and feared that their companies would terminate local operations entirely.

The type of assistance that women's wages provide to the economic and social goals of their families differs between the two groups. Group I women seem to be forced into labor by sheer economic necessity, whereas Group II women toil primarily to brighten the reasonably assured futures of their families. The motivations of our female respondents to work for a wage are affected by their earnings as well as the economic goals of the family. After the costs of child care, transportation to and from work, and canteen meals are subtracted, Group I wives may net very little. It seemed clear to our interviewing team that $200 was the amount below which it was uneconomic for most women in Group II and many in Group I to work. Nevertheless, as Table 3.1 shows, 10 Group I wives earn under $200 and only 2 gross more than $300.[4] The 10 Group I women who earn under $200 told us that dire poverty forces them to work, and that their family finances remain afloat only by the addition of their very small net wage.

The average basic monthly wage of our men is as follows: Group I, $437; Group II, $906. In fact, 64 percent of our Group I men earn less than $300. This sum is under the median for all Singapore Chinese men and insufficient to support a wife and children (Ministry of Labour, 1975). Most of these men work overtime, and a few hold a second job to supplement their earnings. The household incomes of these low-earning men are in 70 percent of the cases augmented by the earnings of their wives.

An example is Wu Kim Luk, a Group Ib husband (formerly a waiter and now a driver for an import-export firm) who earns $250 monthly, and his wife, Wu Mui Huay, who earns $7.50 daily as a seamstress in a medium-sized garment factory. Kim Luk commented that he would have been able to manage comfortably on his present salary five or more years ago, but with the high cost of living these days his earnings are barely enough to support his family.

> That is why, although I would have liked to see my wife staying home as a housewife giving all her attention to our son, this is not possible. I'm thankful to have a wife who is willing to help me out financially, although I don't feel too happy at the idea of her working. If I make more money she won't be working in a factory the way she's doing now.

Forty-one percent of the wives whose husbands earn over $300 monthly are employed full time, and indeed these wives do not work

Table 3.1. Women's Wages by Social Class Position, Fill-Time Wage Earners (number of women)

Women's Wages	Group I	Group II	Total
–$199	10	1	11
$200 – $299	13	15	28
$300+	2	11	13
	25	27	52

NOTE: Women's wages are gross wages in Singapore dollars. $1 U.S. = $2.45 S in 1975.

for low wages. Wives of the more affluent men themselves possess better education, connections and longer job tenure, and can earn reasonably good wages (for a woman) at factory assembly positions. Table 3.1 shows that 11 of the 27 employed Group II wives earn $300 or more. The sole low earner (under $200) had earned around $300 until a production slowdown in her electronics factory reduced the work week and her wages. It should be emphasized that only 5 of the entire sample of 52 working wives command over $400 a month: 3 hold administrative or semiprofessional posts, the fourth is a factory instructor who regularly works overtime, and the fifth holds two jobs. Far more men in our sample at all class levels are able to remit $400 or more to their families each month.

The wages of working women are important for families of all social stations, however. Table 3.2 shows that Group IIa women are the most likely of all to work. This finding probably reflects in part the great urge of the better-off proletarian families to anchor and upgrade their position in society by drawing on all the available resources at their command. My analysis of these relatively affluent working-class men has shown that most are able to upgrade their positions in the labor force, and the present study finds that their wives also make a substantial contribution to the families' economic futures (see Salaff, forthcoming). At the time of these interviews, Group II families pursued the major chances for family betterment provided by the social service and educational sectors of Singapore. These opportunities include purchase of an apartment in the public sector, secondary education for their children, and limitation of family size to a 2- or 3-child family. In addition, wives in Group II couples have higher education than Group I wives, which renders them eligible for better-paying assemblist positions.

Table 3.2. Wives at Full-Time Labor, by Social Class

Socioeconomic Class	Percentage (number) Working Wives	Number of Families in Each Class Group
Group Ia	47% (8)	17
Group Ib	41% (17)	41
Group IIa	79% (15)	19
Group IIb	52% (12)	23

NOTE: Group Ia = lower working class;
Group Ib = average working class;
Group IIa = affluent working class;
Group IIb = middle class.

Group IIb women have the highest expectations from their employment, and will only work for a good woman's wage (over $300 a month at interview time). These middle-class women estimate the direct costs incurred in their paid employment higher than the others, and they perceive considerable nonmonetary costs when they labor outside the home. In particular, employed wives regret their limited time to supervise their children's studies, help in their husbands' work, and entertain in the home. Many IIb women consequently withdraw from the labor force.

An example is Low Wah Poh, a homemaker married to Tze Shen, a Group IIb aircraft refueling supervisor. The couple has two children, aged 4 and 6 years. After she graduated from commercial secondary school Wah Poh worked for five years in a clerical capacity for various firms at the Singapore airport. Wah Poh quit her job in order to go on a honeymoon with Tze Shen, and has never returned to the workforce. When our interviewer asked Wah Poh whether she planned to go back to work, she explained her decision to remain at home.

> There is nothing new or interesting about being a full-time housewife, but I have gotten used to it. Unless I could get a job that pays me over $300 a month, it would not be worthwhile for me to work. I would have to pay at least $150 for a servant, besides providing her with food. I would also need to spend at least a hundred dollars for my own transportation and lunch. So how much money will there be left? Besides, my husband doesn't believe in having other people look after our children.

Wah Poh has found considerable work at home to occupy her. She is proud of her household interior decoration in the Lows' new HDB flat, and she devotes considerable time to its upkeep. Her account also emphasizes care of her children:

> Some modern women think more about their own career and happiness than having children. If they don't want children, they'd better not get married. When a woman is still young she is alright without children, but she will feel very lonely when she gets old.

Low Tze Shen concurred:

> A mother should not go to work because no one else could possibly give the care, love, and discipline that a child needs. A man's world is outside of the home, while a woman's world is the home.

He added, "Besides, it is not worthwhile economically for a mother to work."

WORK EXPERIENCES

Group I women receive a lower economic remuneration than Group II women, their apparent motivation to work is different (they work from short-run necessity, whereas Group II women are able to think of the future), and their work experiences also differ. Group I women experience less job continuity and fewer possibilities for promotion; their work commitment is lower than that of Group II women.

Group I women change their employers frequently in search of better pay, but usually without much success. Only 2 of the 25 Group I women who work full-time have remained at the same job since they entered the labor force. They considered that a search for a better job would be futile. Out of a total of 25 currently employed Group I women, the number who have been employed by three or more firms is 15, and of these, 5 worked for at least five different companies. These 15 women are markedly more typical of Group I employment experience than their two peers, who held only a single workforce position. Like their husbands, most of the 15 were either forced to switch by layoffs or else chose other employment in an effort to increase their earning prospects. Still others in this group left work temporarily in response to their families' needs.

The case of seamstress Wu Mui Huay illustrates the great difficulties that Group I women face in balancing home and workforce demands. She reported:

> As a working woman I'm in a difficult position in many ways. We must put in several hours of overtime at least. My supervisor is not happy if I escape overtime work too often, but Kim Luk, my husband, is cross

> when I come home late from work. He has overtime sometimes, too, but he complains at *my overtime* because he says the spirit of a home is lacking when the wife is at work and the husband is forced to cook dinner at home. Since I can't please my supervisor and my husband at the same time, I often decide to suit one at the expense of the other. This last month I did no overtime work for several weeks for the sake of Kim Luk. Now I must begin overtime, however, which means that on some days I won't leave work until 8 at night, and so I won't be able to pick up our son from his babysitter until late, and Kim Luk will have to collect him instead. He won't like that at all.

Few Group I women aim for promotion on their jobs. Singapore factory managers do not instill the ethic of vertical advancement for women shop-floor workers. In addition, most of these ordinary working-class women lack the educational qualifications, role models, or self-assertiveness to compete for the limited number of section leader positions, which are in the main occupied by women from more affluent working-class backgrounds.

I estimated earlier that $200 monthly is the minimum economic wage for my working women. However, many of the lower-ranking Group I mothers with little education or training are unable to command salaries at or above the $200 level. These women desire, nevertheless, to supplement their families' incomes, and they seek informal working arrangements that enable them to care for their children on the job. As an alternative to the formal labor market, some Group I women take in sewing or wash clothing for neighbors while caring for their own children in their residences. But even these tasks cannot always be pursued continuously.

Government workforce tabulations reveal few formal part-time positions for married women to supplement their family income. Moreover, at the present stage of developing industrialization in Singapore, family social services are rudimentary, and day-care or crêche facilities for working mothers are limited. Only recently has union attention been directed toward meeting this need (Nair, 1980). This forces all of the working mothers in our sample to rely on extended family and other personal networks for the maintenance of the household while they toil in factories. However, our study suggests that undocumented part-time positions—as washerwomen, unlicensed hawkers, neighborhood day-care mothers, and home seamstresses—that enable women to watch their youngsters while they work, may be underreported in the Singapore workforce statistics.

Siah Loo Chan is a Group Ib homemaker, married to Wen Yen, a bookstore clerk who earns $250 monthly. The case of Siah Loo Chan shows how the multifaceted roles of young mothers force them to leave the labor force and even to abandon part-time work at home. Loo Chan was able to sew clothes at home only until her second child was born. Loo Chan said,

> When you are sewing uniforms for the factory, you must put together each batch of goods on schedule, so it was impossible for me to continue piecework sewing when my second child came along. He was active and needed my full attention all the time.

She added,

> I don't think I'll ever go back to the factory. Even when the kids reach school age, they still need a mother to take them to school, to fix meals for them, and to be around when they get home from school in the afternoon.

Loo Chan is considering laundering clothes for neighbors or caring in her home for children of neighbors who are at work. Other respondents nurture the hope of reentering the labor market in the more flexible role of a hawker, but it is nevertheless true that most jobs in contemporary Singapore are in large-scale organizations, and opportunities for independent, self-employed entrepreneurs are decreasing. For these reasons, Group I women with two or more children who would like to earn some money and are encumbered by their daily homemaking routine cannot find the opportunity to work.

Group II women are more likely than Group I women to remain with the same firm throughout their careers. Of the 27 Group II working women, 10 remain in the firm where they first began employment, and these firms pay more than those of Group I workers. (As I have already noted, only two Group I women remain in their first place of employment.) Fewer Group II women have held numerous jobs: Only 10 changed jobs three or more times, and a sole woman held five or more positions.

Group II women also are more likely than those of Group I to attain promotion. Four Group II women hold supervisory positions, and others are in line for such posts. Group II women are equipped with superior education, English language proficiency, connections, and the interpersonal skills needed to gain promotion in higher numbers than Group I women, and they are more confident that their efforts to improve their position in the workforce will bear fruit. As noted, Group II women who lack help with child care may decide not to work in factories, and some do wage labor at home. Group II women, however, tend to pass up the least remunerative positions, such as laundering, babysitting, or the poorly paid garment-seaming at home, that their Group I counterparts are forced to accept.

MOTIVES FOR WOMEN'S WORK: USES FOR WOMEN'S WAGES

Some sociologists of the family argue that women enter the labor force to fulfill personal needs. In this view, married women do not "need" to work, and thus working-class women are said to toil for pin money and middle-class professionals to work mainly for interest. These sociologists claim, further, that married women are able to enlarge their circle of social contacts, to improve themselves, or to test new social roles at work (Fortney, 1972; Hoffman, 1975; Salaff and Wong, 1977). In contrast to these assertions, my research shows that the earnings of Singapore women are essential to their household budgets. Moreover, few married Singapore Chinese women use their labor force participation for self-improvement, for enlarging their circle of social contacts, or for testing new social roles.

It is indeed the case that before their marriages Singapore women looked to their jobs to enlarge their circle of contacts, gain information, and develop important social skills, although these were not the prime motivations for seeking employment. They bantered and socialized with their co-workers on the job, and in the evenings and on weekends they organized group outings with their fellow workers and former classmates. These unmarried women learned to dress and date and to deport themselves outside the family circle in the peer group culture of the workplace. Even for such women, however, the main reason for their employment was to make economic contributions to their families. Beyond this, the objective of these women who were primarily in their late teens or early twenties was to conclude a good marriage (Arrigo, 1980; Kung, forthcoming; Lim, 1978; Salaff, 1981).

In contrast to their experiences as unmarried working daughters, in the eyes of these married women and their families the social aspects of their jobs cannot compete with homemaking tasks and roles. In Deyo's (1976: 9) sample of Singapore factory women, 48 percent of the single working women engaged in one or more social activities with their co-workers during the week prior to the interview. In contrast, over the same period only 18 percent of the married women workers met their workmates socially. My findings support Deyo's conclusion that married women do not toil in order to develop and enjoy social relations with co-workers or enrich opportunities.

In general, we see that the level of and need for women's wages are the crucial determinants of women's entry into the labor force. Increasingly, Singapore families need more money. Enmeshed in the money economy, all of our sample of wives are motivated to work from present-day necessity and for a brighter future for their families. The size of the combined husband-wife income then determines the use the families make of the wives' earnings. Economic exigencies predominate in the lower ranks of the ordinary working-class families (Group Ia), while hope for the future becomes increasingly important as family income rises in Group Ib and Group II.

Group Ia women need money for essentials, and half the Group I women are willing to work for even the low wages they command, because their husbands' earning power in every case under consideration is greatly limited, and wives' contributions are needed. In Group I homes women spend their wages first to buy clothes and toys for their children and next to maintain the families' enveloping networks of kinship connections, such as allowances to the members of the older generation and gifts on the occasion of visits, marriages, birthdays, and other ceremonial occasions. Remaining funds are used for personal clothing and other household essentials, and to enable these women to share a modest social life with workmates, other peers, and relatives in their limited leisure times. Women openly express the filial desire to help their aging parents with occasional funds. For these purposes, it is important for Group I women to possess private funds amounting to between $20 and $40 a month.

Group I women cannot obtain extra money for these purposes from the household money, which in most cases is limited. Women also must sometimes struggle with their husbands to gain spending money. Thirteen women of the panel of 100 (Groups I and II, working and nonworking women alike) receive little or no cash from their husbands for their personal use; 57 women receive some form of personal allowance from their spouses; and only 30 have complete control over household finances. Women who have no control over the household budget may desire to go out to work simply to obtain funds over which they have complete say, but it is not "need" as defined in this way that distinguishes the employed from homemaker women. Whether or not women are able to enter the labor force depends, rather, on their family support and uses of funds. Moreover, those women who do receive regular funds from their husbands still need to work. Even Group Ib women who receive money from their husbands must often supplement these funds, since the husbands of many Group Ib women have little to give them.

By entering employment, women are able to support their relatives at a higher level than they could if they paid these relatives an allowance out of their household budget. As Siah Loo Chan (a Group Ib homemaker) put it,

> It's not that my husband is stingy. Wen Yen is a good-natured man. When we have the money we spend it. There just isn't enough these days for me to donate to my parents. . . . When I was sewing uniforms at home I had money to buy things and could give my parents $10 and $20 occasionally. Now that I'm not working at all, I have no extra money to contribute anymore. Only on festivals can I bring some small gifts to my family. Two of my sisters who are working full-time give Mother and Father some money every month, and I wish I could do the same.

It is common for working women to reimburse close relatives for the child-care services they provide. Others pay their neighbors to care for their infants on a daily or weekly basis. Women of the older generation, the mothers of these respondents, have borne large families, and many are still raising their youngest child when their eldest children are married and have offspring of their own. The older generation of women are unable to leave the home to work; moreover, they rarely have experience in the modern industrial sector and cannot locate a well-paying job. Many of the mothers of the working women of this sample worked as domestic servants, took in laundry, or operated hawker stalls for a living until their children were able to support them, and some still do. Since none of these grandmothers receive pensions, and many are widowed or separated from their husbands, they accept a nominal payment for their child-care help in order to survive. In this way working women's wages, even though small, distinctly benefit their relatives. In the socioeconomic circumstances of Group I families, if the wives did not work it would be impossible for the couples to budget $100 monthly for support contributions to a mother or an aunt. Our sample of employed mothers pay between $50 and $120 for child-care services, and their relatives are the prime beneficiaries. Siah Loo Chan explained,

> It's very difficult for a married woman with children to work full-time unless she has a mother-in-law to look after the kids for her. For one thing, you don't have to pay Mother-in-Law too much money for babysitting, and for another, you can be sure that your mother-in-law will take good care of your children. Unfortunately, Wen Yen's mother is already watching the children of her daughter, while my own mother is watching my sister's kids. Sister works in her husband's own business and can pay Mother $170 for caring for her child all week long.

Like Group I women, the Group II sample toils to improve their household budget. However, since this second group is situated well above the economic poverty line, members who work can save with the long-term betterment of their family unit in mind. With a higher level of schooling, Group II women earn considerably more and dispose of much-improved prospects for job advancement.

The highest proportion of working women occurs in Group IIa, the affluent working-class families. Although all IIa men draw serviceable working-class wages, they nevertheless aspire to exploit the opportunities for economic advancement proffered by Singapore government programs. In order to realize their family betterment plans, Group IIa families need two income earners, and in four-fifths of this group the wives' workforce participation is actively promoted by the husband and the extended family. Group IIa working women devote their earnings to longer-term family development: purchase of an apartment in the public housing sector, secondary education and professional training for their children, and appliances for their new flats.

Goh Min Ti, a Group II seamstress, shows us how their somewhat higher wages reinforce Group IIa women's labor force commitment and help their family toward economic achievement. Min Ti also benefits from the availablity of the help of her in-laws, with whom her family of four (husband, wife, six-month-old baby, three-year-old son) live. In 1974 she earned $200 per month sewing woolen jackets and other outer garments in a medium-sized factory capitalized by Hong Kong Chinese. Min Ti is married to Goh Chee Boon, a civil servant who reads electricity meters for the Public Utilities Board and earns $500 monthly. When we first interviewed Min Ti in July 1974 she believed she would never be able to earn more than $200 and planned to terminate her employment. Min Ti looked forward to the opportunity to spend full days with her son, imparting to him the knowledge and values that would encourage his superior performance in school. By 1976, however, Min Ti had advanced to the position of recorder of the output of each worker's finished garments on her work floor and her wages had risen to $300. The couple then decided that Min Ti would continue to work and contribute to the payments for the apartment they planned to purchase. In mid-1976 the Gohs moved into their new flat, and their two offspring remained in the care of Chee Boon's mother during the day.

Many of the middle-class families at the upper reaches of Group IIb can afford actual luxuries, such as a family car, an annual vacation, and dancing and music lessons for their children. However, the contribution of working wives is in some cases essential to fund this higher level of expense.

In sum, although in all cases of working mothers under study these women's earnings contribute to the family budget, the uses of these earnings differ clearly between groups. The wives of Group I couples elevate the family economy above the poverty line, but their wages are insufficient to enable them to obtain postsecondary schooling for their children or to purchase an apartment in the public sector. However, women's earnings in Group II families make it possible for their families to utilize government programs, to purchase public housing, to obtain higher education for their children, and to pursue adult education courses.

WOMEN'S CONTRIBUTION TO THE HOUSEHOLD

In this sample all the women strive to raise their children to become prosperous members of their families and Singapore society, all care for their husbands, and some assist the husbands directly in their work. Married women cement kinship obligations and establish the crucial links to the wider family group that are necessary for survival in times of illness or unemployment. In addition, women negotiate on behalf of their families with the bureaucracies that operate the schools, the health care and housing systems. All of these activities take considerable time.

Most families under study lack domestic appliances generally considered necessary to alleviate homemaking burdens: washing machines, vacuum cleaners, refrigerator-freezers. The absence of washing machines creates a particular burden, because laundromats are not yet popular in Singapore, and working women can only hire laundresses to do their washing for them. Furthermore, as the industrial revolution takes firm hold, domestic servants are becoming scarce. Balancing the general lack of services for working women, however, is Singapore's wide assortment of markets for food produce, including hawker stalls that serve cooked take-out food. Moreover, in the tropical environment light clothing serves adequately all year round and is not time-consuming to purchase and wash.

All homemakers spend considerable time in labor-intensive household tasks, and many devote their daylight hours to the creation and continuation of bonds of friendship, assistance, and mutual obligation with relatives and neighbors. Such interaction is especially essential for the low-income households, which must turn to unpaid assistance at times of emergency or even in their routine homemaking chores (Stack, 1974). All of the study women spend much of their time raising their children to acquire the status long sought by their families. Although the women of this study socialize their children in various ways, most are responsible for the education and moral cultivation of their offspring. Group II women use their education and skills to upgrade the quality of their children's schooling and health to make them more competitive in the Singapore school system. These women, especially those of Group IIb (middle-class families) may decide in conjunction with their husbands to leave the labor force while their children are growing up in order to spend more time improving the quality of family life (for instance, consider Low Wah Poh or Tok Sor Ngee, discussed below). Middle-class families, unlike most Group I respondents, expressed to us their hesitation about entrusting the complete moral and practical education of their children to grandparents and discussed their willingness to forgo short-term income for the benefit of their children.

Approximately 30 percent of our panel are charting an upwardly mobile path. These eight Group I and 22 Group II families budget savings to advance their children's education and to purchase a public housing (HDB) flat, and many seek to improve their jobs. These are termed "planning families." The wives in these planning families spend considerable time in the training of the children and maintenance of the home. Some may decide to forgo remunerative employment, although others, in particular Group IIa wives, insist on working to expand the pool of resources available for family upgrading.

Tok Kim San, a Group IIb husband, operates his own driving instruction car, and Tok Sor Ngee helps Kim San keep his books and answers the business phone. Additionally, Sor Ngee manages the family budget of food, shelter, and savings. Sor Ngee told the interviewer,

> I am a hard-working woman, and I am good at economizing. I handle all of our household finances, I make sure that food and clothing for the children come first, and that we save a little each month. As a result of the planning I've done, we were able to pay cash for this flat and the driver training car as well!

(Other planning families discussed in this chapter include Goh Min Ti, Loh Wah Poh, and Chan Soo Lee; see below.)

Like Tok Sor Ngee, who helps her husband manage his business appointments, a number of Group I and II women assist their husbands with work in a family store or farm. Such family businesses are particularly demanding. Even if women do not themselves serve in the store, their mothers-in-law may do so, which reduces the number of hands able to carry out the housework. Moreover, the housework is heavier in homes that operate family firms. In shopkeeping families, where all available capital must be channeled into the family business, the pressure on the family budget is particularly intense and the women frequently make and repair their own clothing at home and economize in other ways. Thus, paid employment is not the only way of contributing to the family economy, and several wives in small business households who do not earn a wage aid the business nonetheless. Participation in family ritual, such as meals, promotes cohesion in the common endeavor, while separate meals for each family reflect the weakening of the family structure. In the case of the close family relationships witnessed in several business families, women spend considerable time organizing family gatherings and are unable to plan to enter the labor force to earn money. These homemaking women contribute to their family economy substantially, but generally do so indirectly and from the home.

FAMILY STRUCTURE AND SUPPORT OF WIVES AT WORK

Young mothers can work only with the assistance of a supporting network for their household chores and parenting tasks. This assistance is facilitated by residence in an extended family. Married women who reside with parents and other female adults can benefit from the larger number of hands and obtain increased opportunities for wage labor.

The key feature of the patrilocal household favored in Singapore is the family economy, to which all sons contribute their productive labor or an agreed-upon, large proportion of their monthly pay packet (Cohen, 1970, 1976; Freedman, 1957). The household head redistributes the family income in the form of food, clothing, and other essentials and cash for the members' expenses, including education and medical fees for the children. The members of the household practice equality of consumption, and when there are several nuclear families living under one roof, families with more dependent members and greater expenses receive a larger allowance than the others.

The patriarch or matriarch of this extended family determines the family division of labor with the authority of the religious patriliny. When several married women reside under one roof, production and consumption benefit from economies of scale, and the division of labor frees some of the women from homemaking tasks. It is therefore somewhat easier for these married women to remain in the labor force. Under such circumstances, it is understandable that the decision for a young married woman to work for a wage is made only by common counsel. In most Group I and II working-class families in this panel, the willingness of others to relieve young mothers of their homemaking chores is the precondition of their labor force participation. Some families make use of the services of neighbors, but most respondents either depend entirely upon the help of their kin or combine the two forms of assistance.

Women who remain in the labor force tend therefore to reside in households that contain close relatives. Half of all our families reside in stem or extended households. Women who work full-time outside the home for pay are more likely to reside with relatives than are women who are outside the labor force: Two-thirds of the full-time workers live in such enlarged households, whereas only one-third of the homemakers do so.

Enlarged households help women to work, but other options nevertheless are sought. Women who do not live with relatives and who desire to work take measures to expand their circle of helpers. They attempt to achieve this assistance by a flexible combination of paid and unpaid neighbors and relatives. Some couples choose to reside apart from but near one or both sets of parents to facilitate grandparental relations and services. These couples dine daily at the home of the grandparents and thereby reduce homemaking time. Husbands and wives living apart from their elders nevertheless pay visits to them, two or three times each week, and the old folks can babysit for or foster their grandchildren during the week. Some grandparents who cannot watch their grandchildren are able to visit the neighboring family that does care for their grandchildren, to ensure that the children are content.

In this analysis, couples are classified into two groups: "interacting" and "isolated" families. The former group either lives with one or the other set of parents, lives apart but visits at least twice a week, or has its children cared for by grandparents. The latter group visits parents once a week or less.

There are few isolated working wives in our sample: 90 percent of the full-time earners are interactors, compared with 65 percent of the homemakers. All but two of the full-time working women in Group I and all but three in Group II are interactors, which makes clear the importance of family support to women.

Apart from the informal child-care and housekeeping arrangements these female respondents contract, they have access to no collective services to facilitate their full-time employment. Indeed, several of the family policy and housing programs designed by the Singapore government to elevate the quality of family life have as their unintended outcome the partial separation of young couples from their community of kin.

At the time of the interviews, 73 families resided in HDB apartments, and 27 in private homes, rooms, or farms. Public housing encourages resettlement from private, low-density housing to high-rise flats, and with that a trend toward smaller families and neolocalism. Only 41 percent of my public housing residents live with their elders, compared to 70 percent of those who live in private housing. Private farms and village housing can hold multiple three-generation family units of parents, married brothers, and their families. Two-room HDB flats, however, can house at most a stem family of parents, a married son and his family, and the parents' yet-to-be married children. But many of the Group I respondents can afford only to rent a one-room HDB flat. This constraint of housing size does not in itself isolate parents from their married children who live apart, because young married couples attempt to select apartments in close proximity to their parents. They are not always successful, however, and, moreover, multiple three-generation extended families, with their wider assortment of kin, free wives for work outside the home far more readily than can stem families.

When in the future regular part- or full-time employment for middle-aged women becomes available, fewer older women will be willing to supply child care for the low wages that Group I and IIa working women can afford. These findings show the desirability of government initiatives to establish low-cost child-care services within or near public housing blocks.

ROLE MODELS

A woman of our sample who has in the past worked continuously and who expects to extend her workforce participation in the future is termed a "work-committed woman." Work-committed women generally enjoy their colleagues' friendships at the workplace, conscientiously apply themselves to their job and frequently seek promotion. The interviewing disclosed that a work-committed woman is much more likely than is her nonwork-committed peer to have a mother or mother-in-law who at one period worked regularly for pay. Such a female relative who has worked is willing to provide tangible assistance and make sacrifices for her work-committed daughters and daughters-in-law. Moreover, the mother-in-law who has worked often has raised her sons (the husbands in our sample) to help her in the home, and so the work-committed respondent finds her husband is willing to accept his wife's wage labor and may encourage it.

Since working-class women depend on extended circles of family and in-laws in order to work, these work-committed women rely on those of their more experienced elders who worked for a wage both for concrete assistance with their children and to learn how to combine work with motherhood. Middle-class women of this sample absorb child-care information from a wider range of sources, but even Group IIb women are inspired to work by mothers and mothers-in-law who had careers. In sum, a work-committed woman is likely to be one who obtains considerable support for her work from her family, as well as one who is interested in her work and its environment and who maintains a continuous work history.[5]

When the 52 respondents who are engaged in full-time paid labor are assessed along these dimensions, their levels of commitment are as follows: high work commitment, 9 women; medium work commitment, 23 women; low work commitment, 20 respondents. Most of the high-work-committed women are Group II wives.

The case of Chan Soo Lee, a Group Ib high-work-committed woman, dramatically illustrates these several dimensions of work commitment. Chan Soo Lee is married to a construction worker, Chan Tuan Kwok, and the couple has two children. Tuan Kwok is an irregular worker by choice. Soo Lee's father is a low-paid *jaga* (warehouseman) who gambles part of his monthly wage. The two families live in a single household and are essentially supported by Soo Lee and Soo Lee's mother, who operates a food vending stall in a Sembawang army camp. Upon her marriage at age 18 Soo Lee took employment as an ironer in a laundry and followed this three years later with an assemblist position in the large National Semiconductor electronics factory, where she still works at the time of the interviews. During this period Soo Lee and Twan Kwok moved with their two children into a new, spacious, three-room rented flat with Soo Lee's parents. Soo Lee's younger sister helped her care for her children.

Soo Lee is a conscientious worker who acquires skills rapidly and now earns $10 per day in the transformer section of the electronics factory. She frequently helps newcomers with their tasks and performs some of the lead-girl activities on her own initiative. Soo Lee told us proudly that she was under consideration for promotion to section head.

During a 1974 production slump at the National Semiconductor electronics factory, rumors circulated of an imminent factory shutdown. At that time Soo Lee formulated plans against her possible dismissal, withdrawing $1000 from a chit fund in which she participated. She used Mother's hawker permit and with her starting capital purchased the equipment to sell *laksa*, a popular, pungently spiced regional vegetable and shrimp soup with a coconut milk base, in a six-table stall in the new market in her housing estate. Mother taught Soo Lee to prepare and serve *laksa*, and recruited two of her sons, aged 12 and 16, as work assistants. Clearly her household backs Soo Lee's ambitious scheme.

National Semiconductor did not close its doors after all, and Soo Lee, while maintaining her position there, moonlights at the stall. She awakens at 5 in the morning to prepare the *laksa* ingredients in her kitchen. Her younger brothers leave first and by daybreak have set up the tables. Soo Lee cooks at the stall until after lunch, and then returns home for a rest before her 3 p.m. shift. Her brothers remain behind to shut down the stall and wash up. When Soo Lee is at the factory, Younger Sister cares for her two children.

Soo Lee's success pleases and inspires Mother, who plans to transfer her own hawker trade to a pitch nearer home. Tuan Kwok hopes to leave construction labor to assist Soo Lee expand her food stall. Soo Lee remits part of her approximately $800 in earnings each month to Mother, and gives Father $30 monthly for pocket money. Soo Lee's substantial earnings guarantee not only family survival but also education for her children and her younger siblings, and the rent for the three-room HDB flat for the two families.

Soo Lee recounted an incident that illustrates the central household role that she has acquired by virtue of her earnings.

> Several months ago when I was at work my brother pushed my little boy, who is smaller than he, down on the floor. When I came home that night and learned about this, I scolded Younger Brother and told Mother that we would return to our own flat if such a thing happens again. This frightened Mother and she pleaded with me on her hands and knees not to go away. This scared me too, and we both went to bed trembling.

Despite the fact that Soo Lee held two jobs and earned in excess of $800, unique in Group I family histories, her case illustrates my three main conclusions about extended family support for women at work. First, the young mother who is keen to improve her family's finances and living standard will often integrate herself into an extended family household to free herself from household duties in order to punch a factory clock or work in another occupation each day. Second, work-committed women have the best chances of locating such supporting networks when their extended families contain older women who encourage their employment. Third, women who earn well over $200 monthly command more respect and tangible support for their continued employment than those women whose earnings are too meager to augment the family purse in any significant manner.

CONCLUSION

Singapore Chinese women accept outside employment on behalf of their families. As unmarried daughters they dutifully contribute their unpaid family labor, and in contemporary industrializing Asian cities they enter the labor force and faithfully remit their wages to their families (Arrigo, 1980; Kung, forthcoming; Salaff, 1981). Upon marriage Chinese women toil long hours as homemakers, and when they enter the labor force they also devote their wages to further the health, welfare, and prosperity of the families they have formed. The ways in which women's earnings are used for family survival and advancement and for the education of the young generation, by no means unique to the Chinese culture area, is determined in Singapore by the family class position. A substantial proportion of Singapore women hold positions with low wages and few prospects for upward mobility, which reduces these women's desire to work. It also hinders their contribution to the generation of family plans beyond maintenance at the present level. The more substantial earnings and enhanced opportunities for advancement of higher-ranking women, on the other hand, make feasible the formulation of their higher family aspirations and anchors their families' superior status.

In this early phase of first-generation industrial participation of Singapore women, the family plays a vital role. These women depend closely on family support services to free themselves from some household chores; however, the expansion of semiskilled factory labor has already decreased the availability of women to perform the support services working women need. Group I women previously served as domestic servants for Group IIb women, but no longer do so in large numbers, preferring instead to enter factories. If part-time industrial jobs for women come into existence, more of the parents of my young mothers will seek regular work outside the home, instead of taking in laundry or caring for grandchildren or for the children of neighbors. The cost of labor-intensive support services needed for women to work will increase and become prohibitive to Group I women. Thus, it is important that attention be devoted above all to the living and work conditions of Group I women.

On the basis of my Singapore experience, I recommend that developmental planners incorporate the following objectives in their industrial and nation-building programs: extension to women of advancement by merit programs and sufficient jobs at a living wage for women; adequate home- and neighborhood-based support systems for working mothers; and job training and upgrading for unskilled women. The city-state of Singapore has indeed taken certain measures to fulfill these job objectives as part of its socioeconomic and social service programs. Considerable effort is yet required to narrow the wide gap between wages and conditions of women and men at each level of income, and between the poorer working women and those from better-off homes.

NOTES

1. This study is based on a quota sample stratified in terms of socioeconomic and demographic characteristics to reflect as nearly as possible the social class and occupations of young married Singapore Chinese. One-half of the women in the sample were homemakers whose names were obtained from the registers of four geographically distributed Maternal and Child Health Clinics, and one-half were women factory workers. Working wives were oversampled in our study to ensure adequate cases for analysis. We interviewed the wives four times and husbands once, in five 90-minute sessions. All cases discussed in the paper concern real people whose names have been changed; factories have also been given pseudonyms.

2. Henceforth all wages are expressed in the Singapore monetary equivalent. In 1975 $1 U.S. = $2.45 Singapore.

3. The socioeconomic measuring stick that analyzes the data generated by the interviews, and is the basis for the partition of the families into Group I and Group II, is the product of computations internal to our process of data-gathering and analysis. The ranking resembles that employed in other sociological studies of Singapore. For further information on the scoring procedure, see Salaff (forthcoming).

4. The two Group I women who earn over $300 monthly are skilled electronics assemblists with a record of continuous labor force participation. One of the two, Chan Soo Lee, holds two jobs. The women's husbands are poorly remunerated, uncommitted workers, and their family economic background is deprived. Hence, our socioeconomic scoring procedure places these women in Group I.

5. See Salaff and Wong (1977) for further discussion of the index of work commitment that includes a measure of:

(1) *work continuity:* continuous work record after marriage; intention to continue employment in the future
(2) *technical-environment considerations:* enjoyment of colleagues' friendships, work as escape from home tensions; conscientious work habits; interest in promotion
(3) *social structural support:* division of household labor which helps women to work; husband's support of wife's work; wife's mother or mother-in-law worked continuously for pay

REFERENCES

ARRIGO, L. G. (1980) "The industrial work force of young women in Taiwan." Bulletin of Concerned Asian Scholars 12, 2: 30-37.

COHEN, M. (1970) "Development process in the Chinese domestic group," pp. 21-36 in M. Freedman (ed.) Family and Kinship in Chinese Society. Stanford, CA: Stanford University Press.

——— (1976) House United, House Divided: The Chinese Family in Rural Taiwan. New York: Columbia University Press.

DEYO, F. C. (1976) "Marital status, job orientation and work commitment among semi-skilled factory workers in Singapore." Sociology Working Paper 54, Department of Sociology, University of Singapore.

DEYO, F. C. and P. CHEN (1976) Female Labour Force Participation and Earnings in Singapore. Bangkok: FES/ILO.

FORTNEY, J. (1972) "Achievement as an alternative source of emotional gratification to childbearing." Presented at the annual meeting of the Population Association of America, Toronto.

FREEDMAN, M. (1957) Chinese Family and Marriage in Singapore. London: Colonial Research Studies 20, Her Majesty's Stationary Office.

GOH, C. T. (1979) "Restructuring the economy through higher wages." Presented at the 47th Annual Dinner of the Singapore Manufacturers' Association, Neptune Theatre Restaurant, June 29.

GOH, K. S. (1976) "A socialist economy that works," pp. 77-85 in C. V. D. Nair (ed.) Socialism That Works. Singapore: Federal Publications.

HOFFMAN, L. W. (1975) "The employment of women, education and fertility," pp. 104-122 in M. T. S. Mednick et al. (eds.) Women and Achievement: Social and Motivational Analyses. New York: John Wiley.

KUNG, L. (forthcoming) "Lives: Taiwan women," in M. Sheridan and J. W. Salaff (eds.) Lives: Chinese Working Women. Bloomington: Indiana University Press.

LIM, G. P. (1974) "Factory workers in Jurong." Academic Exercise, Department of Sociology, University of Singapore. (unpublished)

LIM, L. Y. C. (1978) "Women workers in multinational corporations: the case of the electronics industry in Malaysia and Singapore." Michigan Occasional Paper No. IX, University of Michigan.

Ministry of Labour and National Statistical Commission (1975, 1979) Reports on the Labour force survey of Singapore, 1975, 1979. Singapore: Author.

NAIR, C. V. D. [ed.] (1979) Socialism That Works: The Singapore Way. Singapore: Federal Publications.

——— (1980) Opening address to the seminar, "The role of young women in social progress and development." Singapore, May 11.

SALAFF, J. W. (forthcoming) "Structuring an industrial society in Singapore: social class, state policy and family plan." Toronto.

——— (1981) Working Daughters of Hong Kong: Filial Piety or Power in the Family? Cambridge, England: Cambridge University Press.

SALAFF, J. W. and A. K. WONG (1977) "Chinese women at work: work commitment and fertility in the Asian setting," pp. 81-145 in S. Kupinsky (ed.) The Fertility of Working Women: A Synthesis of International Research. New York: Praeger.

Singapore Bulletin (1979) "The new economic directions." December: 4-5.

——— (1980) "Economic woes fail to dampen ASEAN'S growth." February: 11.

Singapore Economic Bulletin (1979a) "Dr. Mattar on retraining." 6 (New Series), October: 39.

——— (1979b) "30,000 Singapore workers may be redundant." 6 (New Series), November: 52.

——— (1980) "Excerpts from a speech by Dr. Ahmad Mattar, Acting Minister for Social Affairs and Chairman, Vocational and Industrial Training Board on 21 December, 1979." 7 (New Series), January: 44.

Singapore Family Planning and Population Board, and National Statistical Commission (1974) "Report of the first national survey on family planning in Singapore, 1973." Singapore: Author.

STACK, C. (1974) All Our Kin. New York: Harper & Row.

WONG, A. K. and J. W. SALAFF (1979) "Planning births for a better life: working-class response to population disincentives," pp. 109-132 in P. S. J. Chen and J. T. Fawcett (eds.) Public Policy and Population Change in Singapore. New York: The Population Council.

YOSHIHARA, K. (1976) Foreign Investment and Domestic Response: A Study of Singapore's Industrialization. Singapore Eastern Universities Press.

4

HOUSEHOLD ECONOMIC STRATEGIES IN KINGSTON, JAMAICA

A. LYNN BOLLES

The purpose of this chapter is to examine some of the strategies of survival[1] utilized by working-class women and their households in Kingston, Jamaica. Since over a third of the households in Jamaica are headed by women, it is useful to analyze the activities of the domestic unit via the participation of its female members in addition to and in relation to that of its other residents (Jamaican Government, Department of Statistics, 1979a: 10). Urban, working-class household systems of production, distribution, and consumption make use of the participation of household members in various activities, incorporate social networks, and engage in both formal and informal sectors of the urban Jamaican economy. Moreover, the fashion in which these economic systems manipulate members' participation in the two sectors can be best understood in terms of the dependency that exists between informal and formal economic activities. The relationship between the

AUTHOR'S NOTE: The research for this chapter was conducted in Jamaica in 1978-79. Fieldwork was funded by National Research Service Award IF31MH07997-01 (SS) of the National Institute of Mental Health, and a predoctoral fellowship of the Inter-American Foundation. Parts of the chapter are further developed in a dissertation, "The Impact of Working Class Women's Employment on Household Organization in two economic sectors is a direct outcome of the structure of the Jamaican economy as it has appeared over the years, based on Jamaica's peripheral position in the world economy.

This chapter suggests that urban Jamaican working-class households can survive because of the nature of the relation between the formal and informal economic sectors. That is, in an economy with high rates of unemployment, various informal jobs become just as important as formal employment for generating an adequate income for household subsistence. In addition, the organization of working-class households often connotes the best usage of that relationship between the formal and informal sectors for short-term and long-term economic planning.

To illustrate this position, data gathered from interviews and visits with 127 working-class women, who are employed in factories in Kingston, Jamaica, are utilized. During the fieldwork the International Monetary Fund's anti-inflation program was instituted in Jamaica. The impact of the effects of the IMF's program on these household economic systems at that time is also noted.

The discussion is divided into three sections. The first describes the theoretical argument of the relation between formal and informal economic sectors in an urban setting. In the second, the organization of these 127 working-class women and their respective households is described, with emphasis on the "economic" activities of individual household members. The final section portrays the usage of social networks by households and their members.

ECONOMIC DEVELOPMENT AND THE FORMAL AND INFORMAL SECTORS

FORMAL SECTOR

The formal economic sector is represented by those production processes that are operated by the state or are state-regulated private enterprises. What differentiates formal from informal economic activities lies in the production process—large-scale, capital-intensive, or imported techniques and, most often, foreign financing characterize the formal sector (see Weeks, 1975: 89).

Kingston, Jamaica." The women(n=127) who participated in this study represent those factory workers and some of their family who agreed to be involved in the project. During the research period, the social, economic, and political situation was tense, and the author is indebted to these working women for their time, patience, and kindness. The author is also grateful to Nora Groce and Rhonda Levine for their comments, Helen I. Safa and Alejandro Portes for their inspiration, and Noma Petroff for her editorial assistance.

In the case of Jamaica, the formal sector has contributed to the economic expansion of the country in the past thirty years. Between 1950 and 1970, Jamaica's increase in gross domestic product (an annual growth rate of 8 percent) was based on the expansion and/or creation of the mining, construction, tourist, and manufacturing sectors (Jefferson, 1972: 2). The type of development process that prompted this expansion in Jamaica was called "industrialization by invitation."

One of the best examples of the economic problems exacerbated by the industrialization-by-invitation plan can be seen in an analysis of the manufacturing sector, specifically, in its employment of working-class women. Manufacturing in Jamaica, in accord with this development plan, was financed primarily by North American capital. It was often based on the utilization of cheap female labor (in comparison to U.S. labor costs), imported raw materials and components, income tax concessions, and import duty relief—with little internal control on the outflow of investment income. The type of industry established was referred to as "screwdriver" industry, which implied its production process: assembly, processing, or repackaging of goods, with little investment in the physical plant in Jamaica. Another term applied to this kind of industry was "footloose," which indicated its minimal integration and commitment to the generation of growth in the Jamaican economy, as well as to the lack of investment in the physical plant. Over the years, this type of production process has served as the prototype for the establishment of multinational corporation subsidiaries and "offshore production" in many other Third World countries (Lim, 1978; Fernández, 1980).

In terms of employment for working-class Jamaican women, footloose, screwdriver production posed a number of problems for both workers and the national economy. Manufacturing, specifically during the "boom" years, provided employment to some degree for the population. For example, between 1943 and 1960, the numbers of women employed in the sector grew from 35,300 to 43,865 (Roberts, 1957: 87; West Indies Population of Census of Jamaica, Vol. 1, Part D, Table 6). However, between 1960 and 1978, the number of women employed dropped by more than half—from 43,865 to 19,400. During the same period, male employment increased from 45,658 to 58,000 (Jamaican Government, Department of Statistics, 1979a: 49). Although the numbers of men employed fluctuated over those years, there was something distinctive about the rapid decline of female employment in the sector.

One of the basic criteria for many investors in the Jamaica development plan was the availability of cheap labor.[2] Albeit cheap labor was, and still is, an essential factor in the labor-intensive production of garments, tobacco, and (to a lesser extent) food-processing, it was the small investment in physical plants made by the footloose concerns that allowed them great ease for abandoning production, particularly when their locale was no longer suitable for their needs. In Jamaica, as is the case in many parts of the Third World, these footloose, screwdriver industries were the principle employer of female industrial workers. The decline of women employed in the manufacturing sector has been attributed primarily to the exodus of garment firms from Jamaica in the early 1970s, resulting in a loss of approximately 8000 jobs (personal communication, Jamaica Industrial Development Corporation officer).

The reason behind the departure of garment firms from Jamaica appears to have been twofold: political and economic. In 1972, when the Manley government came to power, its goal was to give the majority of the population greater access to the resources of the society. These plans were implemented through a variety of social and economic programs, e.g., land reform, a minimum wage, health clinics, and an adult literacy program. Another charge of that government was to redefine Jamaica's terms of international trade on a basis more equitable with the industrialized world.

Such policies undermined the "cheapness" and open receptivity of Jamaican labor for many footloose industries. Local labor was no longer cheap compared with that in other nations of the Third World. Protective labor legislation and organized labor were promoted by both labor and the Jamaican government; a minimum wage was instituted; and the government took greater control over the import and export of goods and the outflow of investment income. In addition, Jamaica's renewal of friendship with Cuba was viewed by many U.S. investors as a move toward bringing communism to the island. Plants were abandoned, and many Jamaicans were left unemployed, particularly working-class women.

On another economic level, the Jamaican government had depended on foreign investors not only for the development of industry but also to finance its own public expenditure, as it lacked a sufficient tax base. Eventually, by the 1970s, with its dependence on foreign investment and financing and the lack of ability to generate its own internal finances, Jamaica's growth came to a halt.

The economic situation was further aggravated by the world financial "oil" crisis in 1973. At that time, the world demand for bauxite—Jamaica's highest earner of foreign exchange—dropped, and the price of sugar, the other major export, also declined. In addition, the tourist trade experienced a drastic reduction of visitors.

The changes in the demands of the world market, the burden of the deficiencies on the Jamaican economy as a whole, and the high price of government programs resulted in a balance-of-payments problem for Jamaica. In 1976 the country was forced to seek financial assistance from a number of international lending agencies to ease the pressure on the economy. At the same time, the U.S. government (a major economic support) decreased its aid to Jamaica.

In July 1977 Jamaica received a standby agreement from the International Monetary Fund in order to pay some of its debts and creditors. Ten months later, the Jamaican government accepted the stringent fiscal controls of the IMF in order to receive an additional U.S. $240 million loan. The terms negotiated for the three-year loan included a 15 percent devaluation of currency; reduction of commercial bank credit lines; foreign exchange controls; liberalization of import controls; control of wage increases; weakening of consumer price controls; and greater hospitality to foreign investment.

The harsh impact of the IMF program was keenly felt by the majority of the population in four ways: (1) Within eight months of the agreement (May-December 1978), the cost of living increased by 30 percent (Jamaican Government, Department of Statistics, 1979b: 169). (2) Consumer price controls were weakened. (3) Many workers were laid off because of the lack of foreign exchange available to manufacturers for purchasing the imported raw materials needed in production.[3] (4) Those workers still employed could not receive a salary raise without lengthy bargaining sessions, and even then, salary increases never approached cost-of-living increases.

In short, over a period of approximately thirty years, the Jamaican economy has become deeply dependent on foreign capital for its sustenance. Economic dependency has ranged from industrialization-by-invitation investiture to the intrusion of IMF policies into the social order. Jamaica's increased dependency has made the country quite vulnerable to the effects of shifts in foreign capital investment and to the movements of the world economy in general. It is clear that employment in the formal economic sector is considered most desirable on one hand, yet on the other hand, given its dependency on the world economy, it is often very unstable. The case of women factory workers exemplifies how unreliable that kind of employment can be. Because of the instability of formal-sector employment, particularly for working-class women, their households must rely on informal systems to overcome dependency on the formal sector. These systems incorporate a number of economic survival strategies that are carried out in the informal economic sector.

INFORMAL SECTOR

In the past, the informal sector of the economy, particularly in the Third World, has been defined as a formation of small-scale activities conducted outside the state and state-regulated private sectors (Portes, 1980: 23). Despite the traditional conception of the nature of these activities (e.g., food-peddling, shoe-shining), informal jobs constantly change to meet the requirements and new circumstances of the "modern" formal economy. As Portes (1980: 30) states, "Informal sector activities are neither traditional nor transitional but very 'modern' features of the system of capitalist accumulation, and, as such, continuously reproduced by the operations of the system."

The following are examples of informal-sector activities:

• A higgler (market woman)—a traditional female Jamaican occupation—sells primarily plastic kitchenware as well as an assortment of other goods, such as flour, cornmeal, and local spices. The primary product this woman vends is nontraditional. She is dependent on a local plastics manufacturer for her goods, and when supplies of tubs and pans are low, she concentrates on other, less profitable, items (e.g., spices). The higgler has stopped buying her wares from a retailer, the traditional buy-and-sell practice of nontraditional goods marketing. She now procures her plastic goods directly from the wholesaler to improve her own markup percentage.

• In Kingston, "robots" are illegal minibuses that travel regular bus routes, picking up passengers. Although robot fares are a bit more expensive than those of state-sanctioned buses, they are quicker, many times more convenient, often flexible in destination, and reliable for commuting workers and passengers.

• In downtown Kingston, a third kind of informal-sector activity also expands on the conventional notion of buy-and-sell operations. A man sells plastic shower slippers, which are made in Korea. He has just returned from a "buying"trip to Panama, where he bought these slippers for about J$4 a pair. The entrepreneur passed customs with the goods, declaring that the slippers were not for resale, but intended for his large, extended family—hence the many sizes. Since shower slippers are desirable, hard-to-get items in Jamaica, this man is doing a bristling business on the streets of Kingston, selling the zoris for J$20 a pair.

The activities discussed above represent three types of informal-sector jobs. One is an offshoot of a traditional, "nonmodern" informal-sector function—higgling. The second is an informal-sector activity only because it operates outside state regulation. The third demonstrates the utilization of formal-sector activities in the informal sector by "traditional" vendors in their business ventures. In all three cases, the operations of the informal activity are linked to and dependent on the formal sector. The higgler follows more institutional marketing procedures, linking her to the formal sector by her purchases from a wholesaler; in addition, she continues to sell more traditional items, such as pimento and ground black pepper. Robot drivers are successful because the formal-sector state-regulated city bus service suffers from numerous problems (including poor scheduling), and consumers gladly choose an alternative despite its illegalities. Moreover, the vendor utilizes the formal sector on an international scale, benefiting from trade agreements between Korea and Panama. Hence, the functions of the world economy are quite discernible on the local-level entrepreneurial scale. Because of the nature of dependency and uneven development—all based on Jamaica's peripheral postition in the world market—informal-sector activities become necessary and thrive.

HOUSEHOLD ORGANIZATION

There are a number of anthropological and sociological studies concerning household organization in Jamaica (Henriques, 1953; Cohen, 1955; Clarke, 1966; Smith, 1962; Davenport, 1961). All these studies approach the investigation of the household organization via marital status of the head of household.[4] Utilizing a similar methodology, the organization of households in the present discussion has been divided into three types, according to the marital patterns of the group of 127 women workers: (1) married (n = 19) and common-law (n = 33), which are combined to stress *stable union* (total n = 52);(2) women who head households, but have steady boyfriends—*visiting union* (n = 52); and (3) women as sole supporters and heads of their households by the dissolution of marriage—i.e., widows (n = 2), separated married (n = 1), separated common-law (n = 9), or no current relationship (n = 11)—the *single woman* group (total n = 23).

The largest households were those in the stable union category, with an average of 6.8 persons. Following second were those in the single woman grouping, averaging 6.4 persons. Third, the visiting union households showed an average of 5.6 persons per unit. What differentiates household membership within these three types is the number of extended kin in residence, the presence of men in the father/partner role, and the presence of children. Visiting unions have, by far, more sisters, brothers, mothers, and other kin living with them than the other two marital types have. However, stable unions have, by definition, spouses/partner men as household residents. Stable unions also have more children per unit than do the other two categories.

The composition of these household units becomes most relevant when the residence is analyzed as an economic unit. In this manner, who is employed and in what economic sector, and who is responsible for domestic chores such as child care and housework denotes the level of cooperation among members and offers further insight into the lifestyles of the 127 women and households discussed here.

For example, Marcia, a teenage high school student, has the primary household responsibility of doing well in school. Her mother has worked hard to earn Marcia's school fees and knows that when Marcia finishes school, she can get a well-paid job. Marcia still has housework to perform, such as washing dishes and helping around the kitchen, but these tasks are scheduled around her school day and homework. In contrast to Marcia's situation, cousin Avis, also a teenager, has housework as her primary function in the same residential unit. Avis has a primary school education, and migrated to Kingston from the country to find employment. However, because jobs are so scarce Avis does most of the housework, and job hunts when the opportunity arises.

In order for their household to sustain itself, Avis currently has assumed a greater role in domestic activities, while Marcia's household responsibility, a good job, is planned for the future.

Analysis of Table 4.1 shows that the situation of Cousin Avis is not an isolated case. In visiting unions, over a quarter of the nieces (n = 7) are involved in housework. Of the nieces in the single woman category residences, 50 percent perform those tasks necessary to the survival of the household. Children are also important houseworkers, depending on their age and whether or not they are enrolled in school. One mother of three boys, aged 8 to 15 years, encourages her sons to "look after themselves." The boys help her prepare meals, run errands daily, and clean the house on Saturdays. One woman, over 40, was quite pleased that since her eldest daughter had finished school she was able to assume the upkeep of the house while her mother was on the job. Another group of participants in housework were the sisters of these 127 women workers. On a full-time basis, visiting union and single woman households had more sisters responsible for domestic chores than did stable union households.

It is clear that many of these domestic-chore workers were female members of these households. The important point, however, is that domestic labor, though performed by women and unpaid, is not depreciated in the view of other household members. Those who perform domestic chores are appreciated for carrying out activities that are valuable and necessary to the unit's viability (see Larguía and Dumoulin, 1975: 3). Reproductive functions, which encompass restorative, nurturing, mending, feeding and similar activities, are crucial and are recognized as such especially by members of visiting union and single woman households.

On the other hand, stable union households, particularly legally married units, are organized under the patriarchal tradition, and that system of social organization tends to devalue female labor, paid or unpaid. In this study of working-class Jamaicans, the functioning of the patriarchal tradition among stable unions is not so consistently strict as has apparently been the case in other studies (Larguía and Dumoulin, 1975). For example, although 70 percent of the women in stable union households referred to their spouses/partners as heads of household, 56 percent of these women indentified themselves as important decision makers in the home.

Another aspect of the household as economic unit concerns how and where income is generated for the benefit of the household. It should be noted from Table 4.1 that stable union households have more formal-sector wage earners (n= 161) than do visiting union (n = 96) or single woman households (n = 55). What distinguishes the three groups is the percentage of formal-sector wage earners per unit. Thus, 45 percent of stable union household members are engaged in the formal sector, while about 32 percent of both visiting union and single woman household residents are active in that sector. These percentages include the women workers—the respondents in this research.

According to Table 4.1, 45 persons state that they are active in the informal economic sector. The eight spouses/partners listed as participants in the informal sector are all unemployed formal-sector workers. For example, Mr. Brown worked as an unskilled construction worker for fifteen years. However, since the construction business is slow, he has been out of work for five years. Therefore, Mr. Brown has taken up doing odd jobs in the "build your own" housing scheme where he lives. Not only does he have the expertise to construct extra rooms for these tract houses, but also he knows where to get supplies, and at a good price.

Another example of work in the informal sector is provided by the brother of a woman in a visiting union. Ricky arrived from the "country" in the past year.[5] He recently left school and is seeking a job. However, steady jobs in the formal sector are scarce, so he takes jobs in that sector whenever there is a need for extra workers (see Portes, 1980: 18). For instance, in the past nine months Ricky has

Table 4.1.

	Stable Union Numbers engaged in:					Visiting Union Numbers engaged in:					Single Woman Numbers engaged in:				
	Totals	formal job	school	house-work	informal job	Totals	formal job	school	house-work	informal job	Totals	formal job	school	house-work	informal job
Respondent	52	52	–	–	–	52	52	–	–	–	23	23	–	–	–
Spouse/Partner	52	42	–	2	8	–	–	–	–	–	–	–	–	–	–
Children	220	63	138	15	4	138	11	95	24	8	86	15	42	26	3
Sister	1	1	–	–	–	26	14	4	7	1	7	5	–	2	–
Brother	1	1	–	–	–	19	11	–	2	6	2	2	–		–
Momo	3	–	–	3	–	8	1	–	1	6	2	–	–	2	–
Niece	7	–	5	2	–	26	1	15	7	3	8	1	4	2	1
Nephew	2	1	1	–	–	9	1	5	1	2	6	1	4	–	1
Other	4	–	–	4	–	12	4	–	8	–	5	2	–	3	–
Da Baby Fa	1	1	–	–	1	1	1	–	–	–	2	1	–	–	1
Grandchild	10	–	–	–	–	–	–	–	–	–	7	–	–	–	–
Totals	353	161	144	26	13	291	96	119	50	26	148	50	50	35	6

worked for a week in a canning factory and for six weeks in a furniture factory, and has packed groceries in a supermarket during the Christmas holiday season.

Another example of informal jobs is illustrated by the sister of a woman in the single woman category. The sibling wants to start a small buy-and-sell business in downtown Kingston. Goods to be sold include soap, detergent, rice, and other often hard-to-find items. In order to start the business, the two siblings combine their efforts. The woman who is employed in factory work finances the operation, while her sister supplies the labor and business expertise.

In the following section, another kind of household management of scarce resources will be examined.

SOCIAL NETWORKS FOR SCARCE RESOURCES

None of the three categories of urban, working-class households limited its economic participants to the in-residence members of the household. Economic networks encompassed other family members, close friends who lived nearby, and some who lived farther away (see Stack, 1974, for a U.S. example). Relatives and friends made regular visits to these households—the frequency depending on the distance they had to travel—and visits were reciprocated. With those relatives and friends living within short distances, such as next door or in the same area of town, there was a constant flow between households. Goods, services, gossip, and (when needed and available) cash traveled back and forth. Often the goods exchanged were items from these relatives' and friends' respective jobs. For example, one sister working in a canning factory had access to her company's commisary, and bought canned foodstuffs, to be exchanged for dressed chicken from her cousin's place of work. The woman from the chicken-processing plant, in turn, bought clothing from a garment worker who "liberated" (pilfered) goods on occasion.

Often relatives from the country visited these urban households. Visits depended on the time of year or on whether the relatives had business to conduct in town, either on an occasional or a regular basis. For example, two women in the study had sisters who lived in the country and were professional higglers in the Coronation Market in downtown Kingston. On every weekend that these market women came to sell in Kingston, they stayed at the homes of their sisters. The higglers gave their sisters some of their produce, and in exchange the urban kin would often collect for the higglers items that were hard to find in the country, such as cooking oil.

During the holidays, urban women and their children, laden with food and gifts, traveled to the country parishes to visit their kin. During Christmas 1978, one woman took as much cooking oil, detergent, and bar soap as she could carry to her country relatives for their Christmas gift. Only 27 women in the sample were born in Kingston. Most of the women had left the country when their schooling was finished, at about age 15.

The following account of the "ackee connection"[6] describes how a scarce item, in this case a vegetable, is distributed through an informal network of exchange.

Miss Ivey and her sister, Miss Ruth, help each other in a number of ways on a daily basis. The two sisters are close in age and have been giving each other a helping hand for as long as either of them can remember. Their houses are two streets apart. Miss Ivey is employed at a factory that frequently lays off its workers; Miss Ruth has been a helper (maid) for an upper-class family for the past fifteen years. Both jobs provide continuing employment for the sisters. However, while Ivey's factory job holds the higher status, Ruth's job offers other benefits—access to food.

The family for whom Miss Ruth works owns a farm in the countryside. Every week, Mr. S (her boss) travels to the farm to check on operations and returns to Kingston with fresh fruits and vegetables from his land. It has been Mr. S's habit to give Miss Ruth a portion of this produce. Miss Ruth, in turn, shares her vegetables and fruits with Miss Ivey.

One day, Mr. S gave Miss Ruth two very full bags of ackees. The ackee trees on the farm had produced abundantly, and Mr. S had filled a couple of boxes with the vegetable. He planned to have Miss Ruth boil and freeze the ackee for future use. When Mr. S arrived home, there had been a substation power outage. The generator for the deep freeze had shorted out when the current returned. Mr. S had to dispose of his ripened vegetables quickly. Hence, he gave Miss Ruth more than her normal share, as he searched for alternative means to store his portion.

Miss Ruth was quite burdened with the two large bags, but managed to return home without incident. Immediately, she sent her daughter with word to her sister that there was "plenty ackee today." When Miss Ivey saw the amount of the vegetable, she was surprised. Ackee could be quite expensive at times. Both sisters decided to divide the vegetable between themselves, and to share some with a good woman friend with whom they attended church and visited regularly.

There are two important aspects of these subsistence networks. First, special attention should be paid to the cultural component. Who is incorporated into these networks, and what is the basis of their membership? Initially, these networks of exchange comprise the family and close friends. One of the crucial aspects of Afro-Caribbean and Afro-American household structures and networks is the sharing of resources. This system is based on reciprocity (see Stack, 1974: 90-125), and members are incorporated and dropped according to that principle. The second aspect of these networks is that they manipulate the formal sector (e.g., by swapping goods) for household benefit. The fact that goods are taken from the worksite refers to the wage level usually offered in the firms and to the nature of worker-management relations on the job.

CONCLUSION

It is evident that urban Jamaican working-class households attempt to utilize as many economic opportunities as are available to them. These activities originate from traditional forms of subsistence, "modern" formal-sector employment, and both traditional and "modern" types of informal-sector opportunities.

Jamaica's economic situation provides a classic example of the shortcomings of economic development programs based on foreign investment and imported technology—all under the umbrella of government receptivity (i.e., "stable politics") to such activities. In addition, the case of Jamaica also demonstrates what can befall a country when it attempts to take an alternative path.

The household activities described here are significant because they maximize the efficiency of urban subsistence activities, and they maximize the numbers of people who can benefit from them (Portes, 1980: 37). However, most important to understand is the relative position of these particular domestic units in the society. Each household has at least one full-time wage earner in the formal economic sector, in a labor-organized factory. That in itself separates this group from members of the working class employed in seasonal labor (tourism and agricultural sectors), and the lumpenproletariat who form the majority of the Jamaican population.

How these households manipulate their opportunities is admirable. However, the reasons workers must employ such mechanisms, and the reasons that Jamaica itself must try different tactics for its own survival, indicate that something is needed beyond a mere questioning of the capitalist system that perpetuates such activity.

NOTES

1. The term "survival strategies" is used to imply the maneuvering, management, and mediation of resources and situations for personal or group (e.g., household)

benefit. All of these actions are the result of a particular social, historical, economic, and political context.

2. Cheap labor (low wage scale) is the reason for the operations of multinational corporations and foreign investment in the Third World (see Safa, 1978). Labor is cheaper in the Third World than in the United States, and this guarentees higher profits, especially when guarded by tariff laws. Since greater profits are the target of local capitalists, low wages are also part of local enterprise operations.

3. In 1978, the national unemployment rate was 26 percent, 15.7 percent for men, and 37.7 percent for women (Jamaican Government, Department of Statistics, 1979: 26).

4. Most of the investigators were seeking answers for the high rate of illegitimacy and the low rate of legal marriage in Jamaica.

5. The term "country" refers to parishes outside the Kingston metropolitan area.

6. Ackee is a vegetable that grows as the fruit of the ackee tree, originally of West Africa, but since the late eighteenth century widely cultivated in the West Indies, particularly in Jamaica. Ackee and salt fish, a former diet of the enslaved population of Jamaica, is now the country's national dish.

REFERENCES

CLARKE, E. (1966) My Mother Who Fathered Me (2nd ed.). London: Allen & Unwin.

COHEN, Y. (1955) "Four categories of interpersonal relationships in the family and community in a Jamaican village." Anthropological Quarterly 3 (October): 121-147.

DAVENPORT, W. (1961) "The family system in Jamaica." Social and Economic Studies 10, 4: 420-454.

FERNANDEZ, M. P. (1980) "Maquiladoras and women in Ciudad Juarez: the paradoxes of industrialization under global capitalism." Graduate Program in Anthropology, Rutgers University. (unpublished)

HENRIQUES, F. (1953) Family and Colour in Jamaica. London: MacGibbon & Kee.

Jamaican Government, Department of Statistics (1979a) Labour Force.

——— (1979b) Statistical Abstract, 1978.

JEFFERSON, O. (1967). "Jamaica's post-war economic development." New World Quarterly 3, 3: 1-12.

——— (1972) The Post-War Economic Development of Jamaica. Kingston: Institute of Social and Economic Research, University of the West Indies, Mona.

LARGUIA, I. and J. DUMOULIN (1975) "Aspects of the condition of women's labor." NACLA's Latin America Empire Report 9, 6: 1-13.

LIM, L. Y. (1978) "Women workers in multinational corporations: the case of electronics industry in Malaysia and Singapore." Michigan Occasional Paper No. IX.

PORTES, A. (1980) "Unequal exchange and the urban informal sector," Chapter 3 in A. Portes and J. Walton (eds.) World Exchange and Domination: Essays in the Political Economy of Development. New York: Academic Press.

ROBERTS, G. W. (1957) The Population of Jamaica. Cambridge, England: Cambridge University Press.

SAFA, H. I. (1978) "Multinationals and the employment of women in developing areas: the case of the Caribbean." (Available from author, Center for Latin American Studies, University of Florida, Gainesville.)

SMITH, M. G. (1962) West Indian Family Structure. Seattle: University of Washington Press.

STACK, C. B. (1974) All Our Kin. New York: Harper & Row.

WEEKS, J. (1975) "Imbalance between the centre and periphery and the 'employment crisis,'" pp. 86-105 in I. Oxaal et al. (eds.) Beyond the Sociology of Development. London: Routledge & Kegan Paul.

5

WOMEN'S WORK AND WORTH IN AN ACADIAN MARITIME VILLAGE

NANCIELLEN DAVIS

> Why is there inequality among men? Where do its causes lie? Can it be reduced, or even abolished altogether? Or do we have to accept it as a necessary element in the structure of human society [Dahrendorf, 1969: 17]?

If we alter the first sentence in the above quote to ask, "Why is there inequality between men and women?" the passage then poses the central questions in the study of the status of women. Women in some preindustrial societies held considerable power and influence in political, religious, and economic spheres (Brown, 1970; Smack, 1977), and cultural evaluations did not universally entail the derogation or subordination of female to male (Leacock and Nash, 1977). However, other preindustrial and all industrial societies have been characterized by an asymmetry in the prestige and power differentially accorded men and women over basic resources and decision-making. Why this asymmetric relation favoring males originated, why it persists, and

AUTHOR'S NOTE: This chapter is a revision of a paper presented at the Conference on Women, Mount Saint Vincent University, Halifax, Nova Scotia, November 1976. Some points made in this chapter are also found in Sealy (1979).

under what sociocultural conditions it is altered are questions that have recently been explored in a variety of theoretical frameworks and empirical contexts.

This chapter focuses on the status of women in Saint-Simon,[1] an Acadian village in northeastern New Brunswick. The region has experienced considerable socioeconomic change in the last three decades, especially planned development during the last ten years. Development and modernization do not always improve the life situations of the people involved, and whether the change engulfing Saint-Simon has improved or eroded women's status is problematic.

Status is defined in several ways in anthropological literature. It can refer to the positions individuals fill in economic, political, religious, and familial networks (Matthiason, 1974: xix); examples are "fisherman," "mayor," "witch," and "aunt." I refer to these as social positions and reserve the term "status" for the ranked position of individuals in society. Women's status is the "ranking, in terms of prestige, power, or esteem, accorded to the position of 'women' in comparison with, or relative to, the ranking—also in terms of prestige, power, or esteem—given to the position of 'men' " (Buvinić, 1976: 225). The relative power of the sexes can be viewed in terms of

> (1) the control of the production and, even more importantly, of the domestic and extradomestic distribution of strategic economic resources;
> (2) rights to participation in political, ritual, and religious activities and to leadership in them; and
> (3) the degree of autonomy enjoyed in decisions concerning sex relations, marriage, residence, divorce, and the lives of children [Friedl, 1975: 6-7].

Friedl proposes these indicators as useful in assessing women's status in preindustrial societies (specifically, in hunting-and-gathering societies and horticultural societies), and, with modification, the indicators are useful in the study of women in industrial societies as well. This chapter focuses on women's work in an industrial society. I use socially valued employment as a strategic economic resource and wish to analyze the effects of development on Saint-Simon women largely from this perspective.[2]

THE STUDY OF WOMEN AND DEVELOPMENT

Until recently, development and modernization were assumed to improve women's status in both the home and work worlds.[3] However, recent studies suggest that the contrary often occurs: Women's status is eroded rather than improved. The point is well illustrated in the literature on women and development in the Third World (Boserup, 1970).

More generally, both the actors in and the observers of indigenous settings often view development strategies and their results as incongruous and destructive of traditional life ways. That such changes are nevertheless allowed or encouraged is linked to the advantages that some local people perceive to be forthcoming; or, more likely, the changes are part of a development "package" imported without the choice or consent of the local community. Because the disruption in cultural tradition may be negatively valued, in other than feminist terms, support may come from several directions to rechannel development along lines that are traditional. According to the context, the return to tradition may be advantageous to women. For example, teaching West African women who were traditionally farmers modern farming techniques could be considered, rather than a radical program for modernization, a return to the status quo ante.

The study of development and its effects on women's status in Western contexts reveals a different set of circumstances. Modernization here does not entail a break from recent tradition, but instead an intensifying and extending of it, and may not be perceived by local people as disadvantageous to anyone, much less women. Furthermore, as the changes in the status of women are in some ways slight rather than dramatic, they may be difficult for the observer to assess. Some aggregate comparisons of women and men may be made, but the variation in individual experience makes the devising of a single scale to assess relative status difficult, if not impossible. The effects of development are differentially experienced by women and men according to various features, including ethnicity, class, and age. In addition, even if a case against certain development strategies (as contributing to the erosion of women's status) can be supported, how does one go about redirecting development in areas like northeastern New Brunswick? Considering the traditional base on which development is planned, the needed alterations *may* be radical and unacceptable to policy makers and their constituents.

The following discussion of development in one of Canada's poorest regions touches on some of these problems. A brief description of that region is in order.

VILLAGE, REGION, AND DEVELOPMENT

The region known as northeastern New Brunswick in federal-provincial development programs comprises Gloucester and

Restigouche counties, and Alnick Parish in Northumberland County. The region is bounded on the north by the Bay of Chaleur, and on the east by the Gulf of St. Lawrence. Early settlement was along the coasts, and most of the population is found there today. The area is predominantly rural; few settlements have more than 1000 people. Francophones, largely of Acadian descent, constitute the majority of the population; in Gloucester County, wherein Saint-Simon is located, 83 percent of the population is French-speaking.

At the northeasternmost tip of this region is Lameque Island, whereon Saint-Simon is located. The island is but a mile from the mainland, to which it has been connected by a bridge since the mid-1950s. Saint-Simon is part of Shippegan (civil) Parish; about 60 percent of this parish's rural labor force are employed in fishing and fish-processing. Women make up 90 percent of the labor force in fish processing plants (*usines*), which are almost the only source of employment available to women. Fishing and fish-processing are limited to the warm summer months; during the rest of the year unemployment is high. Incomes are low. In 1961 the average family income in Shippegan Parish was about 37 percent of that in Canada as a whole ($1807: $3906).[4] In the region there is a high birthrate, a high outmigration, and a relatively low percentage of economically productive adults (Even, 1970: 76-109 passim). Educational and health problems also reflect features of a depressed region.

Regional development to alleviate the socioeconomic problems of northeastern New Brunswick began in the mid-1960s. Immediate goals were realized in improving highways and schools. Long-range goals included relocating rural residents to approved centers and rationalizing the fishery. Government monies were employed to improve the fishery: *usines* were built and enlarged; loans for the purchasing of modern offshore fishing vessels were provided through the Fisherman's Loan Board; and a Fisheries School was built for the training of offshore fishermen.[5]

Generally, government strategies have been aimed at economic growth, understood as "a change in the volume of goods and services produced, [and] of purchasing power" of area residents (Belshaw, 1974: 521). Development, understood as the increasing specialization and interdependence of roles and institutions, also resulted. Rationalization of the inshore fishery, for example, entailed decreasing the number of fishermen in order both to prevent over-fishing and to improve the incomes of the fishermen. Some men who might have preferred to enter or remain in the inshore fishery have found positions in the expanded offshore fishery. Others, however, have become dependent on land-based wage labor; in the Shippegan area, this is most apt to be in the *usines*. These former fishermen, because of actual or felt loss of control of economic livelihood, experienced alienation and dissatisfaction with their work. But women, who form the majority of the labor force in *usines,* also describe their labor as boring and tiresome. It is not men alone who experience the "benefits" of development.

With this description in mind, let us consider the socioeconomic changes in Saint-Simon and their effects on women's status.

VILLAGE SOCIOECONOMIC ACTIVITIES

TRADITIONAL ACTIVITIES TO ABOUT 1940

The traditional economic activities of Saint-Simon villagers were subsistence farming and fishing. The household was the unit of production and consumption, and often, but not always, consisted of an extended family. Household men fished and farmed together; the women cared for vegetable gardens, raised domestic fowl, processed and preserved foodstuffs, and reared large numbers of children. Prior to 1940, fish catches were salted and dried before sale, and much of the processing labor was performed by women. Women daily set out and turned the fish on the stages, and, on the return of the boats each day, aided the men in cleaning and preparing the fish for preserving. Lobster was usually sold fresh to local canneries, where some women and youngsters were employed.

Fishing provided little cash income. Men received household supplies, fishing gear, and other equipment from company stores, to which they provided fish in return. Frequently the debts of the past winter were barely cleared when the household was yet again plunged into debt. Villagers had little control over the distribution of their most important product, the fish catch, since most of it was owed to the local company before the season opened.

The household financial affairs were conducted by men. Ownership of land, buildings, and fishing gear was usually passed from father to son. Occasionally property was given to or inherited by daughters. In short, women's overt control of property and socially valued goods was limited.

Villagers' extradomestic activities were centered in the church and were overseen by the resident priest, whose influence extended beyond ritual and religion to matters of education, work, and politics. Although school teachers were usually women, men assumed most other secondary roles in the parish; they were the founders of the local cooperative, the advisers of the priest on parish affairs, and those who held special participatory roles at Mass.

The priest and the Church also influenced matters of sex, marriage, and the family. Villagers were forbidden to marry non-Catholics, practice birth control, or be divorced. Large families were common; women currently living in the village and who had been married prior to 1940 had an average of ten live births. If villagers chose to marry non-Catholics or to obtain a divorce, they did not reside in the village and would have encountered stiff opposition had they attempted to do so. Men held the position of authority in families. This position was undoubtedly strengthened by the importance of male kinship bonds in matters of work, postmarital residence, and inheritance, and by the teachings of the Church. The latter conferred authority to men and prestige to women who accepted the traditional subordinate role of the wife and mother. In sum, men held greater authority in the household and community than did women. However, women's important contribution to household work probably supplied them with a basis for wielding influence within the home.

CONTEMPORARY ACTIVITIES CIRCA 1971

During the last 30 years the Shippegan fishery has been industrialized and mechanized, and farming has all but disappeared. Around 1940 the first modern seafood-processing plant opened locally, and, to provide a reliable volume of fish for processing, the offshore fishery was greatly expanded. Inshore fishermen also began to sell their fish fresh to the plants. In 1971 about three-fourths of the employed villagers of Saint-Simon worked in the fishery; approximately half of these villagers worked in the *usines,* and half worked on the sea (see Table 5.1).

Although the fishing technology is vastly more sophisticated than that of 30 years ago, the organization of work and the relationships among crew members are like those of the past. Work settings are small and involve close interaction. Most boats on which Saint-Simon men fish are privately owned, and crew members commonly are kin, fellow villagers, or parishioners. In 1971, half of the inshore fishing crews comprised brothers, brothers-in-law, or double first cousins. In contrast, although *usines* vary in size, most locally would employ more than 100 persons. Though workmates in *usines* are frequently kin or neighbors, they are more likely to be so on fishing vessels.

Today men who fish together do not necessarily live together. The increased availability of cash allows the establishment of independent

Table 5.1.
Occupations of Villagers

Seasonal Jobs	Men	Women
Inshore fisherman	22	
Offshore fisherman	16	
Laborer in usine	13	20
	51	20
Seasonal Job Totals		71
Nonseasonal Jobs		
School principal	1	
Teacher	2	2
Office or store manager	2	
Owner of business	4	5[a]
Orderly	1	
Office worker	2	1
Salesclerk, waitress	1	3
Bus or truck driver	3	
Woodsman	2	
Construction worker	8	
	26	11
Nonseasonal Job Totals		37
TOTALS		108[b]

NOTE: Listed here is each individual's primary job, the job that supplies the largest part of his/her income.

a. These businesses are village-based and comprise three food stores, one small catering operation, and a pool hall. All but the catering operation are run jointly by a husband and wife.

b. The village population at that time was 387.

households at an earlier stage than 30 years ago, and extended family households are less common. About 60 percent of the 75 village households are made up of nuclear families.

Most villagers no longer carry out income-producing activities in the household context. Unremunerated work there is performed by both men and women. Men exchange labor and perform chores, such as house repairs. However, regular household work has become almost exclusively women's work, and it is less productive than that of earlier village women. Wives are largely the caretakers of house and children and no longer the producers of nearly all household food and clothing, or the coprocessors of a market product.[6] Many women maintain vegetable gardens, preserve large quantities of food, and bake their own bread. However, even these activities are most characteristic of older women.

The development of the fishery has provided women with opportunities to engage in wage labor.[7] Women seek employment either before they marry and have children or after their children have reached school age. Of the 31 working women, 7 are unmarried, and only 6 of the 24 working wives have preschool-aged children (see Table 5.2). About one-third of the villagers' jobs are held by women, and the majority of these jobs are in *usines* (20:31). Many men and women hold jobs that are seasonal, low-paying, and uninteresting. However, whereas some men can assume positions of responsibility and financial reward, such as those of school principals and captains of offshore fishing vessels, women are almost exclusively restricted to lesser positions.

WOMEN'S WORK AND WORTH

Today Saint-Simon villagers do much the same work as was done 30 years ago, but the rules, contexts, and rewards associated with that work have changed. The activities are no longer for subsistence, but for cash wages, often small and uncertain. Women's work was essential for the survival of the family and for the successful completion of the husband's work. Today women's wages frequently represent the difference between a household's only getting by and being able to afford "luxuries" that most Canadians take for granted. The villagers' labor was previously legitimized by religious beliefs; now it is guided, stimulated, and rationalized by government policies. Men's and women's labor was household-based; now it is the housewife only whose work is based in the home. What do these changes suggest about women's status today?

Before attempting to answer that question, it must be remembered that Saint-Simon is composed of individuals, and not two groups distinguished by the consequences of gender. Gender influences social interaction and status, but it may be overshadowed by kin and marriage ties, age, education, occupation, income, and residence. For

Table 5.2.
Employed and Unemployed Married Women and the School Standing of their Children

Married Women	No Children	Pre-schoolers	Children in School	Children No Longer in School	Totals
Employed	6	6	9	3	24
Unemployed	2	16	15	4	37

NOTE: Included here are some women without children. Women over 65 years of age are excluded from the unemployed.

example, the college-educated woman, rather than a neighboring fisherman, may be elected to a parish committee; the female elementary school teacher may receive more prestige and enjoy a higher income than the male school-bus driver.

I have suggested employment as a key indicator of status; however, just as gender does not automatically determine status in individual contexts, employment is not the only source and measure of power and prestige. This is particularly important for Saint-Simon women, for, as indicated earlier, nearly two-thirds of the married women are not employed. With these qualifications in mind, let us look at the sources of power and prestige for village women.

EMPLOYMENT

Some might argue that the employment of Saint-Simon women represents an improved status over that previously held by village women. Such an argument assumes that earlier women were not employed and consequently had little status. This assumption is false. Earlier women were not paid for their work, and, thus, they were not officially counted as part of the labor force; their labor and contribution to the household and regional economy were obscured by the criterion defining employment.[8] Yet village women had an economic role complementary to that of men, and that important role was recognized locally. Older women and their labor are now described in near-heroic terms; indeed some of the stories told of them are heroic. At least within the household context women's prestige, as based in familial and economic roles, seems to have been as high as that of men.

Women's participation in the labor force does not necessarily indicate that their work is socially valued (Bossen, 1975: 591). Saint-

Simon women are excluded from the most valued and financially rewarding jobs in the important local industry, the fishery. Also, village women become the teachers and not the principals in local schools. Modernization has contributed to the expansion of *usines,* but this is a context in which women continue to perform in an essentially domestic role—as the preparers of food items, in the company of other women, and under the watchful eye of a male authority figure. The difference lies in the women's receipt of wages, which, however, does not necessarily supply them with financial power. More women were earning wages in 1971 than in 1961, but their earnings continued to compare unfavorably with those of men. The number of women reporting incomes in Gloucester County more than tripled (3,314: 11,225) between 1961 and 1971.[9] However, in that decade the average income of women (in rural nonfarm Gloucester County) decreased from 58 percent to 50 percent of that of men (see Table 5.3). Women's wages and jobs compare unfavorably with those of men, and development strategies contribute to this disparity. In the Shippegan area development programs largely improve opportunities for men. For example, they provide capital and expertise to fishermen. Women participate in the fishery only at the lowest levels, and they constitute a pool of unskilled labor, on which development strategies may be predicated.

As a result of development programs, some fishermen have prospered in the last fifteen years; for example, one Saint-Simon villager recently purchased a quarter-million-dollar offshore fishing vessel. Nevertheless, men's incomes as a whole continue to compare unfavorably with those of Canadians elsewhere (see Table 5.3), and this assures the continued participation of local women in the labor force. The combined incomes of husband and wife provide households with an improved style of living and create the visible signs of regional economic growth. However, this obscures the fact that individual incomes remain unacceptably low.

Certain development strategies negatively influence women's status in many Third World areas, but I do not wish to suggest that such also must be the case in northeastern New Brunswick. Indeed, Saint-Simon women who work, especially those who work full-time, derive prestige and power from their jobs. These women help make decisions regarding household purchases, and they enjoy the physical comforts and heightened prestige that certain purchases supply. The few women who work year-round also tend to be physically mobile; they know how to drive and have access to cars. Even women working seasonally in *usines* have a measure of power, as based in their pay checks and later in their

Table 5.3.
Average Income by Sex

	1961		1971	
	M	**F**	**M**	**F**
Rural (nonfarm) Gloucester County	$1584	$ 908	$3509	$1769
New Brunswick	$2807	$1569	$5042	$2282
Canada	$3679	$1995	$6538	$2883

SOURCE: Statistics Canada.

unemployment insurance payments. Women's salaries are a measure of improving status, but women have not fared as well as a result of development strategies as have men. This is reflected in regional salaries and in the kinds of jobs that women assume.

HOUSEHOLD WORK

All village women are expected to marry and most do, but domestic roles appear to be insufficient as a source of status equivalent to that enjoyed by women in the past. Women have only half as many children today as did their mothers,[10] and in some ways perform less productive work at home. Many contemporary village housewives do not play the "ideal" role that their mothers seem to have approached. Either the ideal role will alter or the younger women may have to choose, on the one hand, to elaborate their actual housewife-mother role so that they are as busy and valued as earlier village women, or, on the other hand, to receive less prestige than their predecessors. In order to secure positions of prestige and power comparable to those of their mothers, housewives may have to engage in wage labor, at least at certain points in the life cycle. The long-run effects on women of this assumption of dual roles is not clear. A short-term effect is ambiguity and uncertainty among women as to what their role should be.[11]

COMMUNITY AND FAMILIAL ROLES

Women play a more active community role now than they did several decades ago. The parish church and associated activities are today administered by laypeople rather than by the priest; the change is a function of the current policy of the Church and of the personality of the present priest. Both men and women have been elected to parish committees, but women hold the lesser offices. Parishioners increasingly participate in religious ritual, but certain roles (for example, at Mass) are restricted to men. In short, women have increased opportunities to participate in and to lead parish activities, but their roles are still subordinate to those of men.

The Church's influence regarding marriage and the family is less pervasive today than several decades ago. Village women are having smaller families for a number of reasons, including the changed "cost" of children, the increased availability of contraceptives, and the diminished role of the Church in promoting large families. However, one of the important holy days celebrated in the parish is that for mothers; there is no comparable celebration for fathers. Villagers continue to marry francophone Roman Catholics, and divorce is still rare in the area. Women have increased freedom in important decisions regarding marital life; however, they are still expected to assume traditional, and thus subordinate, roles.

This section has focused on villagers' work in relation to women's status. As noted earlier, there are many difficulties involved in the attempt to assess the effects of development on people's status. The assessment may vary according to whether a single variable or a cluster of variables is examined; whether the experience of individuals or those of a cohort are studied; and whether the perspective presented is that of the participants in, or the observer of, the society.

I suspect that most Saint-Simon villagers, if given the choice, would prefer present living and working conditions to those of 30 years ago. Villagers enjoy considerable improvement in health and educational facilities, transportation, communication, housing, and social services. The advantages of modern conveniences, whether in the home or elsewhere, are welcomed, and these advantages are in large part a result of government intervention and development programs. The older villagers, however, do regard the changes as a mixed blessing. Perhaps they remember the years of their young adulthood more positively than warranted, but these villagers suggest a social price has been paid for their improved material conditions. For example, the increased availability of cash has diminished the importance of labor exchanges in the village, transactions that involved social as well as work dimensions.

I have tried to indicate that, from the viewpoint of the observer, the material benefits resulting from specific development strategies have a special social cost to women, and to uneducated or unskilled women in particular. Traditionally the work roles people assumed were differentiated according to sex and age. There were some specialized roles (e.g., priest, teacher, storekeeper), and people performed their roles with different degrees of success. In general, however, most people had access to much the same work roles, and their success in filling those roles did not vary greatly. Women's and men's roles in the domestic economy were complementary, and their differential control over scarce resources was limited.

With development has come greater specialization in tasks and work roles and greater variation in the performance of at least some of those roles, such as that of captain of an offshore fishing vessel. I have tried to indicate that development strategies have favored men: The work roles open to men are more varied than those open to women, and some of those roles entail the possiblity for considerable success, as measured in income or prestige. Most women have only these choices in their work roles: To be caretakers of home and children, to work in *usines,* or to do both. Work in the public domain does not guarantee a source of status in any society, and in this region it is particularly the case; women have access to jobs that earn them less prestige and income than do those held by many men. Other status indicators (e.g., women's participation and leadership in community activities and their decision-making in familial affairs) have been only briefly examined here; this examination suggests, however, that although women have an increased role, particularly in the running of parish affairs, they continue to fill roles subordinate to those of men.

VILLAGERS' DOMESTIC AND PUBLIC DOMAINS

The concepts of domestic and public domains have figured importantly in discussions of the status of women:

> The domestic domain includes activities performed within the realm of the localized family unit. The public domain includes political and economic activities that take place or have impact beyond the localized family unit and that relate to control of persons or control of things [Sanday, 1974: 190].

In technologically simple societies, the activities associated with the two domains are intertwined; kinship articulates not only domestic affairs, but political, economic, and religious affairs as well. Extra-domestic positions are not so much different from, as extensions of, domestic ones. In complex societies, these spheres of activity have been described as segregated according to sex, spatially separate, and hierarchically arranged. The more favored public domain is the realm of men, and the domestic domain that of women.

The use of these concepts has recently been questioned (Rogers, 1975; Rapp, 1979; Rosaldo, 1980). Specifically, the analytic separation of the domains and the designation of their political and economic importance may reflect and reinforce the folk belief of what *should* be the case in particular societies; they may obscure, rather than elucidate, the linkages between domains and the real exercise of power and influence in those societies.[12]

I refer to the two domains in this discussion of the spatial separation of men's and women's work. However, in Saint-Simon the sexual segregation and the spatial separation of the two domains are not complete; the presence of women in the public domain does not automatically entail their possession of high status; and the absence of men from the house does not entail their lack of power in the family.

Modernization supports a traditional spatial separation of men's and women's activities in Saint-Simon, the most striking example of which is women's exclusion from fishing. Women are said to bring bad luck or to be too much trouble on fishing trips, and some village women have never been on a fishing boat. Development of the fishery has extended this traditional exclusivity. The modern offshore fishery, for example, provides work opportunities that now make it necessary for men to be absent from the village for much of each week of the fishing season. Only indirectly is the presence of offshore fishermen felt in their homes and in the village during this time. Although offshore fishermen may periodically contact their wives by way of ship-to-shore radios, wives assume additional household responsibility and thereby may increase their influence in family affairs. How much this actually occurs, however, varies according to the personalities of the spouses involved.

The government also inadvertently created a new public area for men when it built a wharf for local inshore fishermen. The men then fished from the wharf, rather than from the shores of their household properties as they had previously done. Several times a day during the fishing season inshore fishermen visit the wharf, ostensibly to check on their boats; other local men also frequent the wharf to check on the day's catch and to exchange information. Women visit nearby neighbors and occasionally meet others at the small village stores, but they rarely visit the wharf and have no daily meeting place comparable to it.

The increased availability of cash has allowed some households to purchase cars or trucks. But men are usually the ones who drive them and who have public places to visit. Most women lack mobility: Few know how to drive, and they do not use bicycles for transportation as their menfolk do. Women gather information by means of their telephones and their highly mobile children, but they lack public settings like the wharf where they may use information and interactional skills to validate or improve their social standing. This does not obviate women's influence on members of the family and neighborhood. However, this influence is not unlike that described of women in Mediterranean rural villages, where "if women have any power to affect the conditions of their lives it is through men and on an individual basis" (Harding, 1975: 308; see also Reiter, 1975).

At the extravillage level, development has included building *usines* in which women are regularly employed. The increasing participation of women in these public work contexts may ultimately be more important in improving women's status than their being employed and earning wages. In *usines,* for example, wider-based networks of association and friendship are forged, which are important for women's potential involvement in trade unions, cooperatives, and political parties.[13]

In spite of women's increased involvement in work outside the home, this work is not an overt source of self-identification; even women who work full-time tend to identify themselves as *ménagères,* or housewives. Until women take their public employment as at least a partial frame of reference for their self-definition, they may continue to demand little from their work in terms of benefits or rights. In an economically depressed area like northeastern New Brunswick, it may be advantageous to define oneself in relation to something other than extradomestic work. Nonetheless, men identify themselves in terms of public work roles. Older men who no longer fish call themselves "retired fishermen"; they have completed their roles in the public work world, but they continue to define themselves in terms of those roles. Women, of course, retain their domestic roles throughout their lives. There are no "retired housewives."

Men who are unemployed during the off-season, and who rely on unemployment insurance payments and social assistance, do not seem to define themselves as "unemployed." They are fishermen (or *usine* workers) who, like their fathers before them, are unable to work during the long winter months. Men's work identity is not affected by unemployment and reliance on government assistance, and their authority in the home as breadwinners is not undermined.

On the basis of a study of rural Newfoundland outports, where many men are chronically or seasonably unemployed, Wadel (1973: x) notes that the wives of unemployed men do not become the breadwinners in their families, and that "this seems to be one basic difference between rural and urban situations of unemployment." This may characterize some urban and rural contexts of unemployment in North America. However, in poor rural areas of the Caribbean, Circum-Caribbean, and Mexico, women's economic resources are often more dependable than those of their men, and matrifocal domestic groups occur in which men have less power or influence than do the senior women (Friedlander, 1975; Smith, 1956). The economic strategies followed by these women do not exist in Newfoundland or New Brunswick, or they exist as specializations which require considerable training and/or capital to carry out. Thus the level of economic development, as well as the local cultural definitions of work and unemployment, affect the domestic status of the underemployed or unemployed male in rural areas.

In discussing development and the role of women in Latin America, Schmidt (1976-1977: 256) suggests that

> opportunities for women, say in the labor force, undergo cycles of expansion and contraction. It is hypothesized that in traditional subcultures women's opportunities for meaningful productive roles are rather large. Economic modernization sets into motion a series of events which may adversely affect women's opportunities, while the accelerated expansion, especially of educational opportunities, eventually produces a new threshold of demand and/or possibilities for women.

In northeastern New Brunswick, development is at that midpoint in which the opportunities for women are limited. The "natural" expansion of opportunities for women seems doubtful, however, and planning toward that expansion is needed.

IMPLICATIONS OF DEVELOPMENT FOR WOMEN'S STATUS

Coming over several generations, socioeconomic changes have been less apparent in Saint-Simon than have been similar changes in the Third World. Where change is rapid, individual lives may be severely disrupted, but the implications for social structure and role systems are nonetheless important where change is slow and cumulative. The removal of Saint-Simon women from the coproducer role was gradual, unobstrusive, and combined with certain obvious "advantages": women were freed from considerable labor associated with fish-processing and farming. Women in Saint-Simon did not object to their decreasing involvement in traditional economic activities as women did in some other areas of the world; for example, the Kon women of

Eastern Nigeria caused "major upheavals" because of "the deterioration of their position as farmers coupled to their fear of losing their land to male farmers" (Boserup, 1970: 63-64). On the contrary, Saint-Simon women expressed satisfaction that their arduous labor of thirty years ago was a thing of the past. However, other dissatisfactions do exist.

Women in Saint-Simon express their alienation in modest terms. Working women are concerned about caring properly for their children, and these women are often those who, in addition to or as a result of their employment, are most occupied with vegetable gardens.[14] Their frustration is based in the difficulty of holding two jobs at once, homemaker and wage earner. On the other hand, non-working women are frustrated at being unable or unwilling to obtain employment and, simultaneously, at seeing the monetary advantages accruing to those who work; as a defense, they criticize women who work or elaborate and upgrade their domestic role to fill time and to create a worthy social position. The frustrations of working and non-working women in Saint-Simon are, of course, those reported for women elsewhere in North America.

The dissatisfaction experienced by women stems partially from confusion about what their contribution to income should be. Denied the traditional role of coproducer, women may become financially dependent on husbands or they may themselves attempt to gain income. If the former occurs, women within households are essentially powerless in an economic sense; by claiming responsibilities (e.g., for shopping decisions) in the absence of power, they may be designated too demanding, domineering and the like. Perhaps descriptions of female domination in North American households reflect the case that women make claims for which they no longer have a power base; in this sense such claims *are* too demanding. However, if women are seen to attempt to dominate illegitimately because they have no power base through contribution to the family income, they have few opportunities to change this beyond employment in the *usines.*

I have suggested that development has contributed to the erosion in the status of area women, but must development programs have this effect? Might programs be planned that also upgrade women's positions, and, if so, what form might such programs take?

The decrease in the Shippegan area fish stocks suggests that the regional economy should be diversified, and diversification could well include industries that create opportunities for women. The creation and stimulation of industries in which women would be given favored access to jobs would not endanger already existing positions held by men in the fishery or increase unemployment among men. Several such industries seem feasible. Recent experiments in growing hot-house vegetables for market could stress the hiring of women rather than men; this is appropriate, as the care of vegetable gardens was traditionally women's work. Some local women have already demonstrated entrepreneurial skills in tourist-related activities, and these women could be given loans, grants, and professional training to encourage the expansion of their activities.

Nevertheless, two problems present themselves. First, work in primary industries and tourism is seasonal only, in this area of long, harsh winters. Seasonal work may have advantages for some, especially women with young children, but it provides little income and few benefits, and does not constitute a means toward job advancement. Second, creating situations in which women engage in work associated with their traditional roles may reinforce notions about the types of jobs women can hold. It may also reproduce in the public work world the structure of female subordination to males associated with the domestic domain. The seasonal basis of certain industries may be overcome (for example, by creating a winter tourist trade), but the second set of related problems calls for more fundamental sociocultural change.

Year-round employment with some semblance of fair or even affirmative action in hiring and training of women might be aided by the establishment of government offices in the area, in which women could secure jobs. Decentralization of federal government departments and their relocation from Ottawa to economically depressed areas of the Maritime Provinces have already occurred, but, one must note, there are many poor areas like Shippegan and only so many government offices to relocate.

By increasing the number and quality of jobs for women, young educated women and their husbands might be encouraged to remain in the area. Many of these people have tended to take up residence in anglophone-dominated urban areas, where acculturation frequently results. Their remaining in the Shippegan area would facilitate the retention of their language and ethnic identity and also provide a pool of future community leaders. The creation of more jobs for women results in other advantages for the community. Economic growth, for example, need not result in a rapid expansion of population and households. Wives and husbands sharing the local jobs can be housed in fewer dwellings than if most jobs are held by men. Consequently, growth problems are minimized: there is less urban sprawl,[15] and governments are not burdened with providing additional schools, sewerage, streets, and other services. Government revenues can be used to increase the quality of existing services, rather than simply to expand them.[16]

Compared to women elsewhere in the world and at different times in Western history, Saint-Simon women are reasonably well off, and development has contributed to this by upgrading health care, expanding educational facilities, and improving transportation and communication systems. However, development has also contributed to the erosion of women's status, as reflected in women's near exclusion from socially valued work. Still, development need not negatively affect the status of women; alternative strategies can be formulated that are good for women, and, not surprisingly, good for the developing region.

NOTES

1. Fieldwork took place during the course of seven months in 1971 and 1972. "Saint-Simon" is a pseudonym.

2. My discussion of women's status in Saint-Simon is based on an analysis of data collected with reference to other topics, and certain limitations in the present analysis result. Specifically, indicators of women's power and prestige should be delineated and *then* investigated in the field. The general indicators presented by Friedl (1975) could be developed into more specific indicators of the relative status of men and women. Dixon (1976) also provides some indicators of status that could be incorporated in future research. Individual women's experiences differ, and these differences need to be explored in the field as well.

3. Obviously, many of women's activities at home constitute "work"; the description of women's unpaid housework as something other than work lends support to a societal arrangement that accords less importance to women on the basis of their nonproductivity, and that then defines them as not entitled to remuneration.

4. See Community Improvement Corporation Planning Department (1968). In 1971 the average family income in Shippegan Parish had risen to 51 percent of the average for Canada as a whole ($4913:$9600).

5. The inshore fishery of Saint-Simon is a small-scale, labor-intensive, daily enterprise. Crews seldom include more than three men. Boats fish lobster and groundfish (e.g., cod, plaice, hake) and usually travel no more than twenty miles round-trip each day. The offshore fishery is a large-scale, capital-intensive enterprise. Crews of at least three and not usually more than a dozen men undertake trips from several days to several weeks in duration, in pursuit of groundfish, crab, or herring. Trips cover hundreds of miles, with return to port determined by weather conditions or the completion of catches. For a fuller discussion, see Sealy (1974).

6. That most women in 1971 were not involved in processing fish while most were thirty years earlier is due to several factors. However, a smaller volume of fish to process is not one of those factors. Due to the expanded offshore fishery, there is in fact a larger volume. Of course the processing operation in a *usine* is more efficient than that of the earlier household-based processing operation—more fish can be processed by fewer people. The comparison is awkward, however, in that the operations are so dissimilar.

For example, much of the past processing work was relatively passive but necessary "caretaking" of the fish, and done in conjunction with numerous other essential household tasks. It seems inappropriate to compare the "efficiency" of the economic adaptation of such as a household, part of which included processing fish, with the efficiency of a factory that specializes in processing fish.

With rationalization of the inshore fishery, some men, who might once have become or remained fishermen, have assumed jobs in the *usines* and thereby may have deprived women of jobs. However, processing fish was not exclusively women's work in the past; thus development has not altered the traditional sexual division of labor. Most of the jobs in the region's *usines* are already held by women. In comparison to the region, Saint-Simon is unusual in having so many men relative to the number of women involved in processing work (13:20). I cannot explain this anomaly.

The important question regarding the men holding jobs in the *usines* is not whether they assume jobs that women might traditionally hold as fish processors, but whether these men hold jobs that women would traditionally have difficulty acquiring in any case—that is, management jobs and positions of some authority and responsibility.

7. For a discussion of women's changing participation in the fishery of Newfoundland outports, see Antler (1977).

8. Similarly, women's increased participation in the labor force is a questionable measure of economic growth in the Shippegan area.

9. The number of income-reporting men increased by slightly more than two times during the same period (20,665:9,580).

10. I estimate that women married between 1960 and 1970 will have an average of five or six children, compared to the average of ten children borne by women married before 1940.

11. Where there is a long tradition of women's employment outside the home, this ambivalence may not exist. For a discussion of a positive accommodation to outside employment involving women in fishing villages of the Iles-de-la-Madeleine, Quebec, see Muir (1977).

12. An example may help suggest the problems in disentangling the two domains. Inshore fishing, as carried out by kin-related crews, largely comprises "activities performed within the realm of the localized family unit" and, in that sense, would be considered part of the domestic domain. Development strategies contribute to the reduction of the number of men in the inshore fishery and to their increased number in other jobs, performed in the public domain and with nonkinsmen. Thus, it might be argued that development alters the domains in which some men have worked, drawing them from work in the domestic domain to work in the public domain. Such an argument emphasizes the activity of fishing per se and ignores other important activities associated with fishing, including selling the catch; purchasing of bait, boat, and equipment; and dealing with various government officials. These activities are very much within the public domain. Indeed, on closer examination, the two domains in complex society are intertwined much as they are in technologically simple societies. In the latter, kinship articulates the activities of the two domains; in the former, the political economy permeates home and work worlds.

13. Although one woman from Gloucester County has achieved recognition as a result of her union involvement and has (unsuccessfully) run for political office as an independent candidate, women do not seem to occupy the formal leadership positions in local associations, other than those connected with church and school. This does not deny that women may affect political affairs through other than formal means. Furthermore, the potential for political activities in church and school should not be dismissed

or overlooked, as perhaps has been the case in the past because they were predominantly women's domains. Unfortunately, my data do not permit assessment of the influence on political life exercised by women informally or through church- and school-based activities.

14. It may be the case that employed women are simply energetic people who maintain high levels of activity, and it is for this reason that they often have larger gardens than do women who do not work outside the home. The interpretation I have suggested, however, is that working women also devote themselves to household work, such as vegetable gardening, in an attempt to prove (to themselves and/or their neighbors) that, even though they are employed, they do not shirk their domestic work. If the latter is the case, it again indicates the centrality or priority of the domestic role over peripheral, public work roles for these women.

15. This can be a problem even in predominantly rural regions like the Shippegan area.

16. For discussions of pragmatic reasons for involving women in development, see Boserup (1970), Human Resources Development Division (1975), and Germain (1976-1977).

REFERENCES

ANTLER, E. (1977) "Women's work in Newfoundland fishing families." Atlantis 2, 2: 106-113.

BELSHAW, C. S. (1974) "The contribution of anthropology to development." Current Anthropology 15, 4: 520-526.

BOSERUP, E. (1970) Woman's Role in Economic Development. London: Allen & Unwin.

BOSSEN, L. (1975) "Women in modernizing societies." American Ethnologist 2, 4: 587-601.

BROWN, J. K. (1970) "Economic organization and the position of women among the Iroquois." Ethnohistory 17: 151-167.

BUVINIC, M. (1976) "A critical review of some research concepts and concerns," pp. 224-243 in I. Tinker et al. (eds.) Women and World Development. New York: Praeger.

Community Improvement Corporation Planning Department (1968) Northeast New Brunswick, Outline Community Plans, Shippegan. Fredericton, New Brunswick: Author.

DAHRENDORF, R. (1969) "On the origin of inequality among men," pp. 16-44 in A. Béteille (ed.) Social Inequality. Harmondsworth, England: Penguin.

DIXON, R. B. (1976) "Measuring equality between the sexes." Journal of Social Issues 32, 3: 19-32.

EVEN, A. (1970) "Le Territoire pilote du Nouveau-Brunswick ou les blocages culturels au développement économique." Thèse pour le doctorat en économie du développement, Rennes.

FRIEDL, E. (1975) Women and Men: An Anthropologist's View. New York: Holt, Rinehart & Winston.

FRIEDLANDER, J. (1975) Being Indian in Hueyapan: A Study of Forced Identity in Contemporary Mexico. New York: St. Martin's Press.

GERMAIN, A. (1976-1977) "Poor rural women: a policy perspective." Journal of International Affairs 30, 2: 161-172.

HARDING, S. (1975) "Women and words in a Spanish village," pp. 283-308 in R. R. Reiter (ed.) Toward an Anthropology of Women. New York: Monthly Review Press.

Human Resources Development Division, African Training and Research Center for Women, United Nations Economic Commission for Africa (1975) "Women and national development in African countries: some profound contradictions." African Studies Review 18, 3: 47-70.

LEACOCK, E. and J. NASH (1977) "Ideologies of sex: archetypes and stereotypes." New York Academy of Science Annals 285: 618-645.

MATTHIASON, C. J. (1974) "Introduction," pp. xv-xxi in C. J. Matthiason (ed.) Many Sisters: Women in Cross-Cultural Perspective. New York: Free Press.

MUIR, M. (1977) "Professional women and network maintenance in a French and an English Canadian fishing village." Atlantis 2, 2: 45-55.

RAPP, R. (1979) "Anthropology." Signs 4, 3: 497-513.

REITER, R. R. (1975) "Men and women in the south of France: public and private domains," pp. 252-282 in R. R. Reiter (ed.) Toward an Anthropology of Women. New York: Monthly Review Press.

ROGERS, S. C. (1975) "Female forms of power and the myth of male dominance: a model of female/male interaction in peasant society." American Ethnologist 2: 727-756.

ROSALDO, M. Z. (1980) "The use and abuse of anthropology: reflections on feminism and cross-cultural understanding." Signs 5, 3: 389-417.

SANDAY, P. R. (1974) "Female status in the public domain," pp. 207-222 in M. Z. Rosaldo and L. Lamphere (eds.) Woman, Culture and Society. Stanford, CA: Stanford University Press.

SCHMIDT, S. (1976-1977) "Political participation and development: the role of women in Latin America." Journal of International Affairs 30, 2: 242-260.

SEALY, N. (1974) "Ethnicity and ethnic group persistence in an Acadian village in Maritime Canada." Ph.D. dissertation, Southern Illinois University, Carbondale.

SEALY, N. (1979) "Acadian women: economic development, ethnicity, and the status of women," pp. 123-135 in J. Elliott (ed.) Two Nations, Many Cultures: Ethnic Groups in Canada. Englewood Cliffs, NJ: Prentice-Hall.

SMACK, A. C. (1977) "The impact of modernization on women's position in the family in Ghana," pp. 192-214 in A. Schliegel (ed.) Sexual Stratification: A Cross-Cultural View. New York: Columbia University Press.

SMITH, R. T. (1956) The Negro Family in British Guiana: Family Structure and Social Status in the Villages. London: Routledge & Kegan Paul.

Statistics Canada (1961, 1971) Ottawa: Census of Canada.

WADEL, C. (1973) "Now, whose fault is that? the struggle for self-esteem in the face of chronic unemployment." Newfoundland Social and Economic Studies 11, St. John's, Memorial University of Newfoundland.

PART III
SOCIAL POLICIES AFFECTING WOMEN

6

WOMEN AND LAW

Land Tenure in Africa

KATHERINE S. NEWMAN

Law affects many areas of women's life in modernizing countries. The political status of women is affected by rights to vote or hold public office. Women's social and economic status depend, in part, on family law, especially rights in marriage, divorce, and inheritance. But alongside these aspects of legal "position" is another important facet of the law which, we argue, is even more basic to women's status: rights to land, for agriculture is of overwhelming importance in most developing nations. Consequently, laws governing access to land and control over the fruits of agrarian production remain the primary determinants of a woman's income, long-term economic security, and social status.

In this chapter I will look at the relationship between land law and women's status, focusing in particular on the ways in which systems of land tenure have affected the livelihood of women in sub-Saharan Africa.[1] We will take a historical approach from the precolonial era to the present in order to show how changes in land tenure have resulted in changes in the status of African women. This will provide a basis for understanding the situation of women in many contemporary African societies, as well as a basis for evaluating current policies regarding land tenure in terms of their likely impact on women.

INDIGENOUS SYSTEMS OF LAND TENURE

One is often tempted to consider the social conditions of precolonial Africa as somehow static and unchanging, primarily because the word "traditional" is often used to distinguish the customs of indigenous peoples from those imposed upon them by foreign powers. However, African institutions were, in fact, undergoing considerable change prior to the era of European contact. Legal traditions, including those governing the rules of ownership, inheritance, and usufruct (use) rights, were themselves altered in the face of social change induced by native movements. Yet, one could reasonably argue that by the dawning of the nineteenth century two dominant forms of subsistence technology were in use in Africa, each with its own varieties of land tenure rules. Ester Boserup (1970) terms these two systems "male farming" and "female farming."[2]

Of the two, female farming was by far the more widespread. It involved the use of the hand hoe in conjunction with a pattern of shifting cultivation. The land was cleared, mainly by men, and then planted, cultivated, and harvested, mainly by women. The bulk of the labor in such a subsistence system is provided by women. After several seasons of use, the land must be left fallow for a considerable period of time and new areas cleared for planting. Hoe horticulture thus requires large tracts of land and low population density.

The customary rules governing access to land in female farming societies recognize the technological imperative of long fallow periods. Usufructory rights (exclusive rights to cultivate land and to keep the harvest) over virgin lands are established when an individual or family brings it under cultivation. Land that has already been under cultivation is allocated to members of a descent group on the basis of family membership. Land allotments are usually made by the oldest, usually male, member of the descent group and are regarded as lifetime rights with certain limitations. In most African societies, this land remains the "property" of an individual or a family as long as it is under active cultivation. When it is abandoned these "individual usufructory rights revert to the comprehensive 'corporate' or lineage group" (Parsons, 1971: 15). This process of "reversion" of rights to the corporate group provides for the orderly control of large areas of land, against the claims of other land-using groups.

Individual access to land is a matter of birthright and of family membership. However, the nature of access only vaguely resembles Western notions of freehold land tenure. Each individual has the right to expect at least a subsistence income in agriculture and thus the use of a plot of land. However, individuals cannot sell any portion of family land (Barrows, 1973: 3). They have exclusive use-rights over the acreage alloted to them, within the constraints of customary laws governing the proper use of subsistence resources, which vary from tribe to tribe. These rights remain in force for the duration of the title-holder's life, and can be transferred to his rightful heirs.

Apart from providing the rules of access to land resources, a tenure system is a means of providing social security. Every individual is guaranteed access to some part of his or her descent group's land, although not necessarily to any particular piece (Barrows, 1973: 3). The right to earn a living from agriculture remains the individual's to claim, whether or not he or she resides in the village, regardless of the length of his or her absence. Thus, every group member is secure in his or her expectation of a "survival opportunity" (Parsons, 1971: 14).

Are men and women equally secure under such a system of "communal" land tenure? The answer requires an examination of both inheritance rules and the nature of marital obligations with respect to land. Customary law regarding succession varies among the many tribal groups. However, inheritance of usufruct rights tends to form a pattern along descent lines.

Patrilineal systems of inheritance are generally based on one of three different schemes: (a) *lineal inheritance*, whereby a man's land rights may be passed directly to his sons upon his death; (b) *lateral inheritance*, whereby rights may pass to brothers before "descending" a generation to the sons; or (c) *house-property complex*, whereby rights devolve upon sons according to which land their mother cultivated. This last system of inheritance is often found in polygamous patrilineal societies (Gluckman, 1950).

Women do not figure very prominently in any of these patrilineal inheritance systems, for a woman never fully controls the land she has worked, regardless of the extent of her contribution or her responsibilities toward family livelihood. Nor does she inherit land under any of the three patterns above.

Matrilineal societies reckon descent through the female line; however, inheritance practices of matrilineal cultures vary. In many cases, women do not inherit land at all. Instead, land passes either from a man to his brothers (members of the same matrilineal descent group) or to his sister's sons. In both of these forms of inheritance women are excluded from legal control over land belonging to their lineages. Yet they are generally the chief source of labor with which lineage land is cultivated.

There are, however, examples of societies that are matrilineal in terms of descent, but where inheritance of usufruct rights over land is bilateral—that is, where land rights devolve upon sons, daughters, and in some instances wives. The Tonga, who live in both Zimbabwe and Zambia, are just such a people. Men and women were equally eligible to inherit lineage land; in fact, "many women had considerable holdings in the valued river land which they had received through their lineages" (Colson, 1963: 142).

Land belonging to a woman by virtue of matrilineage membership was hers to control, quite apart from the authority of her husband. She could pass lineage land to her children or to other members of her lineage without consulting her husband. She could refuse to share crops raised on this land with her husband or his cowives. Her control over this land could not be affected by divorce or widowhood. Women, like men, were independent cultivators of lineage land they had inherited.

However, women were also responsible for cultivating land to which they had a more limited claim. When they married, Tongan women were obliged to work their husbands' land. A woman's rights over land allocated to her by her husband were of a very different nature than her rights over the land of her own lineage:

> Land allocated to a woman by her husband was always subject to his control. He could dictate her use of it. At any time he could resume a portion of her fields to give it to another wife or to his children. On divorce or widowhood, a woman lost her right to use such land, although she could remove the crops which she had tended [Colson, 1963: 146].

Colson reports that, under these circumstances, Tongan women preferred to marry men from their own neighborhoods, for they could continue to cultivate their own inherited lands while fulfilling marital obligations to cultivate their husbands' land. This way, a woman was less vulnerable in case of divorce or a husband's death.

Tongan men "owned" both the land they inherited and land they cleared. Though land tenure rules precluded a man from passing inherited land to his wife or his children (who were not of his matrilineage), he could dispose of cleared land as he wished, to his wife, sons, or daughters. His lineage could not reclaim this land upon his death (Colson, 1963: 150). Thus, men were able to pass the benefits of their land-clearing labor on to their dependents.

Clearly, Tongan women had some independent security against their husbands' claims. Yet, since women had little opportunity to acquire full rights in new fields by clearing bush land, their land-holding opportunities were not equal to those of men. Benefiting directly from the land to which they held title by lineage membership depended at least in part on remaining near these inherited fields after marriage. Moreover, their ambiguous claims to land allocated by their husbands meant female labor power could be invested in land only partially female controlled and vulnerable to the claims of a husband or his matrilineage.

From the above, it is clear that although women played a significant role in subsistence cultivation in these traditional "female farming" societies, they generally had less formal control or legal standing with respect to land than did their male counterparts, even in matrilineal societies.

Does this mean that the lot of women was precarious? The answer is both yes and no. Access to the basic means of production under customary law was often a function of a woman's tie to a man. While unmarried she was attached to the land her mother cultivated, that is, to her father's or her brother's land. When she married, either she gained access to her husband's land or she remained associated with her brother's land. If she became widowed or divorced she lost most of her land. Consequently, Suellen Huntington (1975: 1008) has argued that women in these societies were dominated by men:

> The major and obvious implication is that "female farming systems" are male-dominated and serve male interests. . . . Men get their wealth, their livelihood, and their leisure from women's labor. . . . Polygyny and high bride-prices may recognize the economic worth and productivity of women, but both also serve to perpetuate male power, authority and wealth.

Yet, the dependency of men upon women for labor power indicates that the situation was not so unequal as it appears simply from examining the "legal position" of women. A man's land was of little use to him without the labor of his wives. He had little incentive to seek divorce, and considerable incentive to provide what was due to his wife under customary marriage law. Among the Barotse of Northern Rhodesia, for example, a man was obliged to give each of his cowives at least one garden. Failure to do so was grounds for divorce, and carried social stigma (Gluckman, 1972).

A second point should be considered in evaluating women's land rights in precolonial Africa: As long as land was in plentiful supply, lineages could afford to be somewhat lax in enforcing the rules of landownership. Moreover, women could often get sons or other males to clear land for them, thus establishing new tracts of land under their own control. In fact, with abundant land, people did not worry much about fine points of land "ownership," since it was so easily available. This does not mean there were no land tenure rules, but rather that an individual's primary concern was good standing in society, since access to land would follow directly from membership in social groups (Colson, 1976: 11).

In summary, the land tenure positon of women in precolonial areas was ambiguous. In female farming systems women lacked legal ownership but typically had de facto access to land that they farmed. However, we will see shortly that the technical principles of customary land law became more important with the onset of colonial rule.

COLONIALISM AND THE REORGANIZATION OF LANDOWNERSHIP AND CONTROL

European conquest of Africa began in earnest in the mid-1800s, though there had been trade for several centuries. Administrative policy for the African colonies was very much a function of the "mother country's" ultimate aims. Thus we shall examine two different kinds of colonies: "white man's countries" (to use Lucy Mair's phrase), those areas of East and South Africa attractive for European settlement, and "indirect rule countries," those colonies principally in West Africa considered unsuitable for European residence. Since land policy differed in these two kinds of colonies, the rights of women to agricultural resources are best understood by discussing them separately.

LAND POLICY IN "WHITE MAN'S COUNTRIES"

Reserves. In the Union of South Africa, Kenya, and Zimbabwe, white immigration was stimulated by moderate climate and opportunities for intensive cash cropping and mining. The most fertile lands were set aside for European settlement, while the indigenous populations were resettled into "native reserves." Reserves were "either not suitable for intensive cash crop production and/or were isolated from transportation facilities for evacuation of products" (King, 1974: 45). The reserves provided insufficient land resources to support the subsistence needs of the native populations.

The reserve system kept Africans from competing against Europeans in cash crop markets; thus whites had a virtual monopoly over export trade. But Europeans controlled far more land than they could cultivate themselves (Van Zwanenberg, 1972: 8-9). Inefficiencies of settler agriculture were due largely to inadequate financial resources, technological problems of farming Kenyan land, and an almost permanent shortage of labor. The reserve system was one attempt to attack the labor shortage problem. Since reserve land was neither fertile enough for continuous crop cultivation nor sufficiently large to produce enough food for the natives, they had little choice but to leave for wage labor. Moreover, having to pay taxes in cash further pushed natives into wage labor in the European sector. In much of East and South Africa,[3] men left the reserves to enter the cash economy, while women generally remained behind. Since male wages were insufficient for family support, the major responsibility for subsistence production fell on the women. While this was traditionally a woman's task, they now had to work the land without the previous level of assistance from men in land-clearing and other "heavy" labor tasks.

The cash-wage economy lowered the status of female cultivators compared to that of their male counterparts who used advanced methods of agricultural production in the export sector. Women's subsistence cultivation continued to rely on handheld hoes and fallowing cycles. Thus, the greater productivity of male workers supported colonial prejudices against women farmers. The productivity gap was exacerbated by the general decline in the reserves' soil quality. Rising population (due to public health measures), and limited land resources placed a great pressure on the length of fallowing periods, and the shorter fallow cycles that resulted sped soil deterioration in the reserves.

Customary rules of land tenure that were "designed" for areas with bountiful land resources had the effect of exacerbating land shortages when their operation was continued in the limited area of the reserves.

> With no new land available, farms were subdivided among multiple heirs . . . so as to give each person access to the several types of farmland required traditionally. Today many possess rights to scattered plots of such small size that it is difficult to support families or even to farm many of the plots [Armstrong, 1966: 2].

The previous section on customary tenure noted that although an elaborate system of inheritance rules and marriage rights in land existed in the agricultural tribes of sub-Saharan Africa, they were only strictly enforced in areas where land had value because it was in limited supply. As land became scarce under colonialism, these rules tightened up, which had the ultimate effect of placing women, particularly those detached from men through divorce or widowhood, in a more precarious position.

In many cases, rules of land tenure began to alter in favor of men, who were, at the same time, gaining the upper hand in the emerging cash-wage economy. Even where women previously had a good deal of autonomy and security in access to land, their legal rights to agrarian resources began to diminish. Writing about women in South Africa, Simons (1968: 261) noted:

> We can be certain . . . that women now have fewer rights in land than before the change [to European rule]. Whether a wife, divorcee, widow or spinster, a woman could hold arable land in her own right and in some, if not all tribes, assert her claims in court against an intruder on her garden plot. Now that there is an acute scarcity of land, a woman's rights are subsidiary to those of the men.

Relocation. In addition to establishing reserves, general economic development plans in Kenya, Zimbabwe, and South Africa often called for relocating African tribes in order to gain access to prime lands or to improve a region's productive potential. Resettlement schemes frequently disturbed traditional land tenure patterns, and this too increased the vulnerability of women.

For example, between 1955 and 1958 the "Kariba resettlement program" moved about 52,000 Valley Tonga to make way for a hydroelectric dam. This relocation scheme forced the Tonga to "exchange" the rich soil and good water supply of the Zambezi plain for hill territory with only sparse arable land (Colson, 1963).

Resettlement destroyed existing lineage rights in land. Thus, in the new area individuals responsible for the initial bush clearance could establish claims to landownership. Given the traditional division of labor, men claimed most of the land in the new territory. Consequently, the way women gained access to land shifted rapidly from the traditional mix of kinship links and husbands' allocations to nearly complete dependence on the largesse of husbands who had cleared land. In three Valley Tonga villages, women's dependence on their husbands rather than on kinsmen for land grew by at least 20 percent after they moved to the new territory (Colson, 1963), and access to land via kinship decreased markedly. At the same time, land access for men shifted from kinsmen to overwhelming reliance on ownership rights based on land-clearing.

Clearly, this forced resettlement had serious consequences for women, for land held by women through marriage was not an autonomous source of agricultural livelihood. Moreover, since arable land was scarce in the new territory, kinsmen were unlikely to be able to share land with female members of their lineages. Women's economic position as a result became increasingly more vulnerable:

> Although land has been allocated to men with regard to the number of wives they have, this does not mean that the wives have become the owners of such land. Since the husband has the responsibility for clearing the fields, the Valley Tonga concede him the rights of ownership. Few women, except widows and divorcees, have had fields cleared for them by other men and only they can claim undisputed ownership. The rest hold land only at the pleasure of their husbands. If they seek a divorce or separation, they also vacate their fields. . . . Widows, unless they have received a field in gift from the husband, are also likely to be deprived of land [Colson, 1963: 151].

Individualized Land Tenure. Europeans were aware of agricultural problems on the reserves. During the 1940s, for example, Kenyan Ministry of Agriculture officials suggested converting reserves from customary land tenure to individualized freehold tenure (Sorrenson, 1967). They felt that introducing English concepts of alienable land would increase agricultural investment and productivity, thus alleviating some of the pressures. Consolidation of land holdings was proposed as the most sensible method of dealing with estates fragmented into noneconomical parcels.

The Swynnerton Plan, put into action in 1953, set the stage for transforming the customary cultivation system via land registration, consolidation, government investment, and agricultural modernization. It became the foundation of Kenya's land policy (Sorrenson, 1967: 220). European-style land reform was also introduced elsewhere in East and South Africa.

Generally speaking, individualized landownership made women more dependent on their husbands because, following European traditions of landownership and title, land titles were nearly always registered to the male "head of household," even in polygamous families. While women retained certain customary rights to cultivate a portion of their husbands' land, after land registration they no longer had an independent claim to the land apart from their marital ties. Women were often left to work the land allocated to them by husbands who were engaged in wage labor off the reserves. Women were, therefore, without the benefit of any legal protection:

> In the Bikita Reserve in Rhodesia, a female farming area, the land reform completed in 1957 allocated the land to men and widows only, but not to married women. This meant that 23% of those who received

> land were absent men, who worked as wage laborers outside the region, while their wives lived as cultivators in the Reserve. The position of the women became precarious, because the men could—and often did—divorce and marry other women, in which case their former wives were deprived of the land they had considered their own . . . since they had cultivation rights in it.
>
> European administration made a similar transfer of land from women to men in the Union of South Africa. In 1893 a proclamation in the Transkei denied the right of each wife of a polygamist to have her own plot and introduced the rule of "one man one plot" with the result that the wives not only had to cultivate in common the land belonging to their husbands but lost it to his male heirs after his death [Boserup, 1970: 60-61].

In conclusion, each of the kinds of land reform measures (reserves, resettlement, and individualized land tenure) introduced by the colonial powers in the white-settler-dominated colonies had a negative impact on the ability of female farmers to retain any independent claim to land resources. Women were left in a far more dependent role than they had previously enjoyed.

WEST AFRICA

In contrast to the regions just discussed, West Africa was deemed generally unsuitable for white settlement because of poor climate, malarial infestation, and similar unhealthful conditions. Colonization in the West was therefore undertaken for the purpose of stabilizing and monopolizing trade between African dependencies and the "mother countries." This was to be accomplished through the installation of colonial governments and the promulgation of tax and labor laws designed to "stimulate" African peasant production of cash crops for European markets. It was therefore the opposite of policy in the settler-dominated colonies of Kenya, South Africa, and Zimbabwe, where natives were actively prohibited from engaging in cash-crop production.

African men were obliged to pay taxes in European currency. This forced them to abandon subsistence cultivation, usually to their wives, and concentrate on crops that would earn enough money for the required taxes. Where the "incentive" of taxation failed to produce the crops European governments desired, peasant producers were ordered to cultivate export crops on pain of imprisonment (Crowder, 1968: 347). This occurred most often when crop prices fell so low that it was not profitable to raise them, and many peasant producers reverted to the subsistence economy. Compulsory cultivation of cotton in Upper

Volta, for example, was seen as a remedy to the apparent "unwillingness" of natives to "work" at cash cropping.

Colonial governments in West Africa also called on Africans (mainly males) to perform compulsory labor on public works, including the railroads, telegraph systems, roads, harbor facilities, and government buildings. These compulsory assessments fell most heavily on individuals classified as not gainfully employed, that is, generally those not involved in producing *cash* crops. Poor working conditions and high mortality rates on forced labor projects, particularly in the French territories, were additional incentives for the African farmer to abandon the subsistence sector and concentrate on the export cash-crop sector.

Several general consequences followed from these policies. First, West Africa slowly developed from a diverse and fairly self-sufficient subsistence economy to a series of export enclaves. Africans became dependent on imported food products purchased at inflated prices. Areas such as Gambia and Senegal, once producers of abundant rice, were forced to import rice in great quantities once these export-inducing tax and labor laws had taken hold (Crowder, 1968: 274).

Second, the colonial economic system in the West led to massive migration from relatively underdeveloped areas where cash crops were not successful to areas where they could be raised, shipped by rail or road, and sent on to major markets. Fertile regions received most of the colonial government investment in transport and communications networks. European governments completely neglected barren regions when developing economic infrastructures. Since people had to pay taxes regardless of which kind of territory they came from, natives of cash-crop-poor areas were forced to seek wage labor in the richer regions. Thousands of African cultivators left Mali, Upper Volta, the poorer areas of Senegal, and Hausaland to work in the mines and cocoa farms of coastal Nigeria, Southern Ghana, and the Ivory Coast.

A third important change in these areas of relative prosperity was a shift in landownership patterns. British, and to a certain extent French, land policy in West Africa recognized customary land tenure patterns. Neither power attempted to interfere with kin-based or "communal" systems of landownership and use. However, where coffee and cocoa production were successful enough for peasant producers to realize healthy profits, systems of tenure began a gradual shift toward alienation.

The more valuable land became as a commodity, the more land was taken into cultivation. Large tracts of forest and brush land were cleared and planted with coffee and cocoa, causing land shortages for subsistence cultivation and an increasing tendency toward a "market" in land among rural African capitalists. Traditional mechanisms for "loaning" land, previously reserved mainly for family members, began to be opened to strangers. *Isakole*, a symbolic gift traditionally given for the right to use a piece of land in Southern Nigeria, began to change into rental payment for a long-term lease agreement in exchange for either cash or its in-kind equivalent. Outright sales of land became more common as the cash-wage economy intensified. Thus, emergence of the export economy pushed traditional systems of land tenure away from the customary practices of nonalienable group land to alienable land under individual title. This occurred without significant intervention of the colonial rulers. Rather, it developed from the introduction and penetration of capital into West Africa, which preceded colonial rule, but which intensified in the twentieth century.

Colonization in West Africa affected women differently, depending on the extent to which the areas they lived in were incorporated in the developing cash-export economy. For our purposes it will be helpful to distinguish between the subsistence/labor-supply zones and the export zones, the former referring to those areas considered unsuitable for cash cropping and therefore useful as a source of migrant labor, and the latter referring to areas targeted for intensive exploitation of the land for the purpose of raising cash crops.

The experiences of women in the subsistence/labor-supply zones were not unlike those of women in the East and South African reserves. Large numbers of able-bodied men were absent from the "labor zones," having migrated to the cash-export zone. Women were left behind to take care of family lands and to raise the next generation of agricultural and industrial workers. Men were responsible for paying taxes for themselves and their wives. Since only men had access to a cash income, subtle changes in family authority became evident in the homelands. However, female access to agrarian resources, principally land, remained much the same as it had been prior to colonial rule. Lacking the reserve system, West Africans in the nonexport zones experienced far less artificial land scarcity than their East African counterparts. Thus the "commoditization" of land and the attendant changes in the customary systems of "communal" land tenure did not take place to the same degree in the subsistence zones (Crowder, 1968). The status of women altered to the extent that they were not part of the migration experience which gave men more geographical mobility. Moreover, men had cash, a symbolic and material manifestation of incorporation into an economic system in which women of the subsistence zones had little part beyond reproducing the male workforce. Nevertheless, the land tenure system of these areas was far less affected than in the export zones, to which we now turn.

The overall effect of West African colonial "development" policies on the female farmers of the export zones was to diminish their control over land and in many cases destroy the market positions they had held prior to colonial rule. Mona Etienne's (1980) study of the impact of colonial domination on the Baule of the Ivory Coast is a useful example. Prior to the establishment of French control, the Baule depended on shifting cultivation of the yam for basic subsistence. The sexual division of labor, as expressed through the marital bond, brought men and women together in a mutually dependent system of yam production and distribution. Men cleared the land and prepared it for cultivation; women planted, tended, and harvested the crop. The husband formally owned the yam crop, though he was bound to give his wife a proportion of the yams she produced to support herself and her children. Women, on the other hand, had usufructory rights over the yam plots. Following the yam harvest, female cultivators used these land rights to produce cotton, which they then transformed into thread. Men (generally their husbands) used this thread in weaving cloth, a highly valued trade item. Coth was, however, a woman's domain. She controlled cloth marketing, though she was required to give her husband a portion of it in recognition of his contribution. Yam production and cloth "manufacture" therefore mirrored each other insofar as male/female production and distribution rights were concerned, and resulted in a mutual dependency between men and women.

French intervention in the Ivory Coast economy broke this reciprocal dependency in the agrarian sphere. Etienne details a host of induced developments which eventually undermined the livelihood of Baule women.

First, French demand for cotton imports increased. Thus, cotton, which might ordinarily have gone onto the Baule domestic thread market, was diverted into the international arena. Baule had to pay taxes either in cash or in cotton. Cash could only be obtained through employment or export production. The consequences of these constraints for Baule women were serious: Their market position was severely eroded and, since men were responsible for the payment of their wives' taxes, female control over the cotton crop greatly diminished.

Second, the downward spiral in the status of female farmers among the Baule was exacerbated by the French emphasis on the male role in agrarian economy:

> Just as the colonial administration—when it demanded that more cotton be produced—had addressed its demands to men, early and later agricultural experts and their male extension agents, when they introduced new techniques, addressed their teaching to men. It is, therefore,

> not surprising that cash-crop cotton, like other cash crops, became the man's domain [Etienne, 1980: 227].

Boserup (1970: 54-55) has made this point for other colonial territories: European development policy ignored African women except as assistance for their husbands. Thus, the policies of taxation and cash-crop development gave men control of the cotton economy, previously women's source of economic independence.

Two related developments made matters even worse for Baule women. First, cocoa and coffee were also introduced as cash crops. Cocoa is a perennial crop, a fact that played havoc with the nature of the tenure system, for in the past the usufruct rights of men and women revolved around annual crops and allowed both sexes to control crops raised and harvested at different times of the year. However, with cocoa, capital investment and potential cash profit were involved, and men had a stake in laying permanent claim to land they previously controlled only part of the year. Land had become a valuable commodity in its own right and grew increasingly scarce as more productive land was taken into cash-crop cultivation. Without introducing any radical legislation, the "natural" economics of colonial capitalism had brought about a shift toward individualized land tenure. We have seen that this development brought increased vulnerability to women in many parts of East and South Africa; the same was true for West Africa (Etienne, 1980: 228; Boserup, 1970: 58).

CONCLUSION

We have now examined the impact of colonial policies on the land rights of women in three regions of sub-Saharan Africa. In concluding, some general observations about the processes we have described will be helpful.

In the precolonial era, women and men tended to work as "partners." A man's formal control over land was of little value without the labor contributions of his wives, daughters, and sisters. Women's land access rights were, by and large, subordinate to men's. Yet these formal rules had little substantive effect while land was plentiful and female labor power was a critical factor in the subsistence economy of shifting cultivators. Formal rules became significant when colonial rule was established and land became scarce because of the reserve policy in the East or because of its increased value due to cash cropping in the West. When scarcity occurred, one of two things happened: Either formal rules of land tenure were activated, usually depriving women of land if they were not "connected" to men, or the rules themselves altered in the direction of land alienation and freehold tenure. This hurt women because they were generally unable to amass sufficient capital to participate in land markets.

Colonial authorities did little to protect women's land rights, since they actively encouraged male dominance over their farming wives. The land, taxation, and labor policies of the colonial governments combined to transform African women from fairly independent cultivators to rather dependent laborers in the subsistence zones. Thus, at independence, women lagged behind men in numerous ways: They had far less experience with the cash economy, less education, less technical training in "modern" agricultural methods, and had suffered a serious loss of social status. While men had suffered a great deal under colonial rulers, they emerged from the era of imperialism in a somewhat better position than their female counterparts.

THE INDEPENDENCE ERA: HARD CHOICES

National movements for political independence brought an end to the colonial period in most of sub-Saharan Africa during the 1960s. However, colonial policies had left deep marks on African societies, principally in the form of narrow export economies, marked social and economic inequalities, and communities disrupted by migrant labor. The new nations of Africa have had to cope with the debilitating effects of these changes, along with major crises in food production, exacerbated by staggering rates of population growth.

Efficient use of land resources has been seen as one important key to solving these problems. Land tenure reform is often viewed as a high priority for increasing productivity of African agriculture. Ironically, African nations have tried some of the same land policies as their former colonial rulers to address contemporary land use problems. Not surprisingly, they have encountered many of the same difficulties we described in the previous section, particularly concerning women's access to land.

Mechanization of agriculture is regarded as a major means of boosting productivity. Yet the capital investment is so great that availability of credit is a significant constraining factor. Customary systems of land tenure, it has been argued, are major stumbling blocks in obtaining credit. Lending institutions are unwilling to provide investment capital without security of ownership, something not provided for in communal systems of land tenure. As a result, many African countries have pushed forward with plans to individualize landownership, consolidate fragmented landholdings, and thereby encourage investment in long-term improvements.

Developing countries are aware of the potential pitfalls accompanying the transition from customary to individualized forms of tenure. Most serious is the creation of a landless class and the loss of the social security land provides in traditional land "ownership" systems. Proponents of individualized tenure suggest that these problems will eventually be solved by increased industrial development, which should follow from improved agricultural exports. Landless peasants will be absorbed in the burgeoning urban economies; social security will eventually be provided through pension plans and other devices common in advanced industrial societies.

There is considerable doubt that this long-term vision will be actualized. Industrial development is at least forty years away from being able to absorb the number of people left landless by the turn toward individualized land tenure (Parsons, 1971: 59; King, 1974: 23). Even if we grant the need for reforms of land tenure systems, we must ask what effect these efforts might have on African women. Surprisingly enough, despite the recognition that women are a significant source of labor power in the agrarian sector, the literature on land reform rarely poses this question.

As we have seen, when land becomes a commodity on the open market, women are seldom able to benefit. The legacy of colonial rule, which left women overrepresented in the subsistence (noncash) sector and underrepresented in the cash economy, is such that contemporary efforts to create land markets threaten to dispossess rural women from their source of income.

Possibly these women will be absorbed into a growing agricultural wage labor force created by the enlargement or concentration of landholdings. However, an examination of the relative wages of men and women in the agrarian sector reveals considerable gaps. Kenyan women receive 40 to 50 percent less than their male colleagues both on smallholder farms and on the agricultural estates where wages are governed by collective agreements. These differentials are justified by growers on the grounds that male tasks (bush/land-clearing, digging, and so on) are more taxing physically than female tasks (picking, planting, and weeding). Though one can argue that female tasks require more dexterity and skill and therefore deserve equal compensation, the growers' interest in maintaining a cheap labor force makes wage equalization unlikely.

For the moment, the absorption of displaced peasant women into the agricultural labor force will not provide them with an income adequate for self-sufficient support. At most, agrarian women's wages will modestly augment family incomes. Where these alternate sources of income are not available to women, land consolidation and mechanization may result in eliminating women from economic activity entirely (United Nations Economic Commission for Africa, 1975: 52).

What are the prospects for the absorption of landless women in the urban areas? The data are far from encouraging. It appears that educated women who have some professional training have little trouble finding employment. But these are a small minority of the African female population; statistics show that boys far outnumber girls at all levels of schooling, with the most dramatic gap at the secondary and postsecondary levels (Mickelwait et al., 1976: 17-18, 21).

The urban employment experience for uneducated African women is not encouraging. The Kenyan situation is fairly typical:

> In 1969 only 25,800 women were employed in the formal sector in Nairobi as against 138,800 men. In all Kenyan towns, 36,400 women were employed in this sector as against 267,000 men. [ILO Report, cited in Palmer and Von Buchwald, 1980: 22].

Women are less readily absorbed than men, in part because they are less educated, but mainly because "severe unemployment tends to reinforce and extend sex-typing of tasks in a newly emerging economic sector" (Palmer and Von Buchwald, 1980: 22). Dual labor markets restricting men and women to particular occupations with large wage differences have developed in both the rural and the urban economies of postcolonial Africa.

This suggests that the position of agricultural women in African societies must be dealt with directly, rather than by relying on either agricultural wage labor or urban industrial employment to provide enough income to promote the independence of women. In countries predominantly dependent on agrarian production, this means that access to land will remain a major consideration.

Direct government intervention by land legislation protecting women's rights to land inheritance and control is needed in most African countries. High courts and legislatures in Tanzania, Kenya, and Ethiopia (among other countries) have had the opportunity to rule on the rights of women to land against the rights of husbands, sons, and uncles (Jones, 1979). The courts tend to take one of two approaches: They rule in favor of the male's formal rights to "ownership" of the land (over the female's usufructory rights under traditional law), or they provide for sex-blind policies of land access that tend to discriminate against women who are unable to meet minimal conditions of land improvement. Nevertheless, that courts in some of these countries (such as Tanzania) have argued that "the age of discrimination based on sex is long gone" is a hopeful sign that the rights of women in inheritance, marriage, and divorce with respect to land are being seriously considered.

Even if legislatures and courts in African nations formulate legal protections for women regarding land access, additional government intervention will be necessary to make female control of land economically feasible. In the absence of effective market mechanisms, rural development programs will have to provide women with the credit and capital improvements needed in order to make efficacious use of the land they have. Cooperative societies, which have a long tradition of female involvement in West Africa, can provide women with support in the form of centralized marketing facilities, child care, and other necessary underpinnings of successful agricultural activity. Concerted efforts to boost the position of women in the agricultural sector are more likely to be successful where the control of resources can be effectively exercised by women—that is, through cooperatives or collectives that receive government support. State intervention, I would argue, is required to ensure that women are incorporated into developing economies on a full and equal basis.

If there is a lesson to be learned from this review of the developments in land tenure systems in Africa, it is this: Colonialism institutionalized sexual inequalities in access to the most basic resource, land. Fundamental differences between the opportunities available to African women and their male counterparts derived from the land and taxation policies imposed during this period. Correcting the damage that was done to women's status during the colonial period of African history is a major challenge for independent African nations.

NOTES

1. When we speak of women in sub-Saharan Africa, we are referring primarily to women in the non-Islamic (so-called Black African) societies. The property rights of Islamic women differ markedly from the cultures discussed in this paper and would therefore necessitate a separate treatment.

2. While "female farming" refers to patterns of shifting cultivation where the bulk of the labor power is provided by women, "male farming" refers to a form of agricultural technology in which permanent cultivation of fields is made possible through the use of the plow. This latter system of cultivation is generally associated with a high male labor contribution and a correspondingly low involvement of women in the food production process. The former system is found predominantly in sub-Saharan Africa and is, therefore, the subject of consideration here.

3. Our discussion of the reserve system refers primarily to those colonies in East and South Africa where European immigrants came in large numbers with the intention of developing these areas for their own benefit. We recognize that in many areas of East Africa (e.g., Tanzania, Uganda) large-scale European immigration did not occur and economic development was accomplished by native hands under policies initiated and enforced by European governments. In this respect, Tanzania and Uganda resemble

more closely our description of the West African colonies, where peasant production for export was encouraged and indeed demanded.

REFERENCES

ARMSTRONG, C. "Land usage and land tenure in sub-Saharan Africa: a brief review of some developments in agricultural areas," pp. 1-14 in Proceedings of the Third Graduate Academy. Los Angeles: University of California, Los Angeles, Graduate Student Association.

BARROWS, R. (1973) "Individualized land tenure and African agricultural development: alternatives for policy." Working Paper 85, Land Tenure Center, Madison, Wisconsin.

BOSERUP, E. (1970) Woman's Role in Economic Development. London: Allen & Unwin.

BUELL, R. (1928) The Native Problems in Africa. New York: Macmillan.

COLSON, E. (1963) "Land rights and land use among the Valley Tonga of the Rhodesian Federation: the background to the Kariba Resettlement Program," pp. 137-156 in D. Biebuyck (ed.) African Agrarian Systems. Oxford: Oxford University Press.

——— (1976) "The impact of the colonial period on the definition of land rights." Berkeley: University of California. (unpublished)

CROWDER, M. (1968) West Africa under Colonial Rule. Evanston, IL: Northwestern University Press.

ETIENNE, M. (1980) "Women and men, cloth and colonization: the transformation of production-distribution relations among the Baule," pp. 214-238 in M. Etienne and E. Leacock (eds.) Women and Colonization: Anthropological Perspectives. New York: Praeger.

GLUCKMAN, M. (1950) "Kinship and marriage among the Zori of Northern Rhodesia and Zulu of Natal," in A. R. Radcliffe-Brown and C. D. Forde (eds.) African Systems of Kinship and Marriage. London: Oxford University Press.

——— (1972) The Ideas of Barotse Jurisprudence. Manchester, England: Manchester University Press.

HUNTINGTON, S. (1975) "Issues in woman's role in economic development: critique and alternatives." Journal of Marriage and the Family 18: 1001-1012.

JONES, C. (1979) "Woman's legal access to land." Detroit, Michigan. (unpublished)

KING, D. (1974) "Land reform and participation of the rural poor in the development process of African countries." Working Paper No. 101, Land Tenure Center, Madison, Wisconsin.

MICKELWAIT, D., M. RIEGELMAN, and C. SWEET (1976) Women in Rural Development. Boulder, CO: Westview Press.

PALMER, I. and U. VON BUCHWALD (1980) "Monitoring changes in the conditions of women—a critical review of possible approaches." Geneva: United Nations Research Institute for Social Development.

PARSONS, K. (1971) "Customary land tenure and the development of African agriculture." Working Paper No. 77, Land Tenure Center, Madison, Wisconsin.

SORRENSON, M. (1967) Land Reform in the Kikuyu Country: A Study in Government Policy. Nairobi: Oxford University Press.

United Nations Economic Commission for Africa (1975) "Women and national development in African countries: some profound contradictions." African Studies Review 18, 3: 47-84.

VAN ZWANENBERG, R. (1972) The Agricultural History of Kenya. Nairobi: East African Publishing House.

7

WOMEN IN COMMUNIST COUNTRIES

Comparative Public Policy

BARBARA JANCAR

This chapter is a review of the policies of communist one-party states that influence the status of women. Consensus regarding the number of elements involved in public policy-making is somewhat elusive (Lowi, 1964; Wade, 1972; Anderson, 1975), but basic components may be reduced to five: problem formation, formulation of alternatives, policy adoption, policy implementation, and policy evaluation. Since this covers some 60 years of policy-making in the Soviet Union and 30 in Eastern Europe and China, I will divide the discussion into two time periods: (1) the postrevolutionary phase, when new regimes consolidate their power and undermine the old society's foundations, and (2) the maintenance phase, when communism is institutionalized and generally accepted, if not always desired, as the established political system. While it is doubtless overly simplistic to date the dividing point, for the sake of a reference point I consider the end of the First Five-Year Plan and the 16th Party "Victory" Congress the beginning of the USSR's maintenance phase. Eastern Europe's postrevolutionary phases ended in 1956, when communist power became permanent. In China the situation is less clear-cut. Mao's death is a likely division, but for women 1959 or 1960 is a more likely beginning for the maintenance period; research suggests no new departures in approach or solution to women's problems after that.

This chapter will look at communist policies toward women within the context of these five policy-making elements and two time frames. The focus will be on elements of problem formation, implementation, and evaluation in the maintenance phase. Eastern Europe and the Soviet Union will be emphasized, since data are most available for them.

THE POSTREVOLUTIONARY PHASE

PROBLEM FORMATION

Woman's economic enslavement in the home was the central impediment to her liberation, according to classical Marxist thought and subsequent Marxist-Leninist ideology. The roots of her exploitation were (1) she was her husband's property, and (2) household economic division of labor so oppressed her with menial tasks that she could not enter industrial society to earn an independent income.

The first comprehensive Soviet policy statement on women was at the First International Communist Conference of Working Women, held concurrently with the Second Comintern Congress in 1920. The economically oriented statement defined communist policy goals for women as: bringing women from the home into the community, ending peasant households that kept women subservient, providing equal educational opportunities for women, mobilizing women for political work, developing communal services to alleviate housework, and providing work conditions able to "satisfy the particular needs of the female organism and also the physical, moral and spiritual needs of the woman as mother." (Pravda, 1920). The statement suggests the communist policy's secondary goals for women. Initial policy aimed at ending women's inferior status in marriage and actively involving women in political work and the building of a new society.

This first policy statement reflects the dualism that permeates all future policy on women. From the first the emphasis was on "*okhrana byta i truda*," preservation of home and work. It clearly identifies women's special physical and material needs. Neither male needs nor even a male role in integrating women into industrial society is mentioned. Women alone had to change their behavior to achieve their emancipation. This defect in problem formation pervades all policy-making by communist one-party states.

POLICY FORMULATION AND ADOPTION

Without exception, all communist countries in the postrevolutionary phase adopted virtually identical policies, as Table 7.1 shows. Women were given equal civil and political rights. Special provisions were enacted protecting women's health at work and outlawing work that might endanger their ability to reproduce or might seriously injure their health. Laws established day-care centers and gave women pregnancy leave. Party resolutions encouraged women to acquire even more than basic education. Quotas were established in vocational and other schools (Vyshinski, 1951), and women were urged to try men's jobs.

Simultaneously, traditional customs were assaulted. This effort was less revolutionary in European Russia and Eastern Europe than in China. Secular marriage and divorce were decreed. In the USSR and China abortion was legalized almost immediately after communist victory. In Eastern Europe the legislation was much later. The 1924 RSFSR Criminal Code outlawed polygamy, bride-price, and child marriage. In 1927 traditional Moslem courts were divested of legality and prohibited from interfering in the spheres of property, the family, and other relationships. Penalties against survivals of "the tribal order" were severe. Special decrees were enacted to promote equality among the sexes, including women's rights to initiate divorce and have equal witness at court (Massell, 1974). In China the 1950 Marriage Act, the major postrevolutionary legislation, made marriage a matter of public interest for the first time and gave women the right to divorce (Meijer, 1971). In Central Asia and China, mainly, women used the new court system for filing divorce actions.

Organized religion came under attack in all communist states. Persecution, depending on strength of religious affiliation, was most severe in Russia, Poland, and Hungary, and probably least severe in Yugoslavia, although terror was and still is used against believers in Croatia particularly. In general, the assault on traditional values and the disruption of traditional family life had begun in Eastern Europe during World War II. Communist legislation merely continued the process.

IMPLEMENTATION

Initial communist policies were revolutionary and comprehensive. In fact, they promised more than they could deliver; generally policy could only be partially implemented. Assaults on the traditional family ended with retreat by the Party and government in Central Asia and China. Lacking an organized infrastructure and with

Table 7.1. Laws and Regulations Affecting Women in the Soviet Union, Eastern Europe, and China

Legislation	Date of Legislation								
Postrevolutionary Phase	**USSR**	**Bulgaria**	**CSSR**	**GDR**	**Hungary**	**Poland**	**Romania**	**Yugoslavia**	**China**
Secular marriage and divorce	1918	1944	1948[a]	1950	1947	1947	1946	1946	1950
Family law	1918	1944 1949	1950	1950	1947	1947	1946	1946	
Equal rights	1918	1944	1948	1950	1947	1947	1946	1948	1947
Protective labor legislation, protection of women	1922	1945	1948	1950	1947	1947	1946	1949	
Child care	1918	1944	1948	1950	1947	1947	1946	1948	
Social insurance	1919 1925	1944	1948	1950	1947	1947	1946	1948	
Abortion permitted	1920	1956	1953	1956	1953	1955	1948	1950	1960
Maintenance Phase									
Change in marriage and divorce laws, family law	1968 1936 1944	1966							
Abortion proscribed	1936 1944	1973	1973	1968			1967		
Abortion reinstated	1953	1975		1972					
Extension of social legislation, family allowances	1971		1971	1972	1969		1970	1973-74[b]	

Table 7.1 (Continued)

Extension of education				1965 1972					
Extension of protective labor legislation			1961 1960	1966 1967				1974	1973
Reinstatement of civil rights	1971		1968						
Extension of child-care facilities, protection of motherhood	1971	1972	1970	1969	1969		1970	1973-74[b]	
Rulings on recruitment of women into administrative positions		1970			1970		1973[c]	1974[b]	1972[c]

SOURCE: The data for this table have been gathered from many sources; the reader is referred to the bibliography in Jancar, *Women Under Communism* (Johns Hopkins University Press, 1978), where the data were first published.

a. Czechoslovakia, Poland, Hungary, Germany, Romania, and Yugoslavia all had secular marriage before the Communists came to power. The laws went into effect after World War I. For example, Czechoslovakia's law was passed in 1919.

b. The laws were passed at the republican rather than the federal level. The same is true in the case of recruiting women into administrative positions.

c. Party decrees rather than regulations.

an uncomprehending population, marriage and divorce laws occasioned widespread suffering both collectively and individually. In Central Asia women were lynched for defying custom and family. In China irate husbands murdered wives seeking divorce. Wives running away from home had nowhere to go; their families rejected them and they turned to suicide. Young couples wishing to marry without family sanction were accused by villagers of promiscuity and also turned to suicide (Chinese Documents Project, 1955). Second, where the Party actively mobilized people politically, men filled Party positions. In the interests of gaining adherents, the regimes were unable to pursue the goal of female emancipation unreservedly, even if they so wanted. The result was retrenchment in favor of prevailing family customs and male economic and political dominance. In China, whenever a campaign to advance women's status went too far, retreat followed. In Mao's China this is seen in 1953, 1959, after the commune disaster, 1969, after the Cultural Revolution, and again at Mao's death.

Similarly, no regime was able to establish an adequate network to implement communal services. Day care and eating and catering facilities were rare except in the largest cities. Divorce, leaving women to bring up children with little state assistance, was quickly discouraged, especially in China. The main movement of women into the economy was of unskilled, illiterate women into unskilled jobs. Pay was low and conditions hard. As a result, women were burdened with home and job cares. Without exception, communist domestic policy has given industrialization priority. The search for capital, technology, and industrial labor relegated other objectives to second place, including advancement of equality for women.

EVALUATION

(1) Communist policies were generally successful in raising the status of women, if numbers are any indication. By the onset of the maintenance period, percentages of women in the labor force, education, and government administration were, on the average, higher than in comparable noncommunist countries. Women penetrated jobs formally considered male domains, such as medicine, law, and engineering. In all communist party states, female literacy rapidly reached male levels. By 1970 women's educational level equalled that of men in Poland, the USSR, and Hungary. Day-care centers and child-care facilities were more extensive than in almost any noncommunist country. Pregnancy leave and benefits for women and children were also, on the average, superior.

Results of communist policy in the initially less-developed areas of Central Asia and China were even more remarkable. Women in

Tashkent told the author their freedom would not be possible without communist power. In China, women's oppression is associated with the "bitter past," and women are told they "hold up half the sky." Although still lagging in top posts, women appear to enjoy considerable equality with men at work.

(2) Although postrevolutionary policy of communist leaderships won impressive gains for women, it also had unforeseen consequences. Since no communist regime was able to provide the infrastructure necessary to ease housework, women were working what is now known as "the double shift." Women acquired four roles in communist society: wife, mother, housekeeper, and wage earner; only the last was paid (Sokolowska, 1963). A second consequence was feminization of job categories with women locating in middle level jobs. Where women took formerly "masculine" jobs, men moved out to higher status positions (Jancar, 1977). Thus, although in most communist one-party states, Yugoslavia and Cuba excepted, women made up half the labor force, they were not much better represented at the top political, social, and economic levels at the beginning of the maintenance period than were their Western counterparts.

A third consequence in the industrialized countries was a sharp drop in the birthrate. While negative demographic trends in the 1960s and 1970s in Eastern Europe and the USSR cannot be wholly explained by policies toward women, there is little doubt they contributed significantly to weakening women's desire for large families. In sharp contrast, the birthrate in developing communist states remains high. The Cuban fertility rate is among the highest for communist countries, but it is accompanied by a relatively high infant mortality rate (United Nations, 1974). Chinese campaigns to lower the birthrate began to show results by the early 1970s, when it was announced that annual population growth had slowed to 1.1 percent.

(3) Women have been both victims and beneficiaries of communist public policy in the postrevolutionary period. While every regime considered women's status important, it was never valued itself but instead seen as a means of implementing policies of greater priority, the economy being first. The huge task of modernization posed problems of mobilizing a primarily manual labor force. Peasants and women were the main sources of labor, and women, having a higher illiteracy rate, took the lower-paid and lower-status jobs. Almost equal in priority was the consolidation of communist power through development of citizen loyalty to the new regime. To accomplish this it was necessary to dismantle old habits, behaviors, and loyalties. Emancipation of women from family and custom helped by weakening family

ties from within and encouraging women to replace husbands' authority with that of Party and state. However, since the regime's emphasis on industrialization precluded providing ways to ease life at home, women were caught between traditional home routines and new job identities. New drudgery merely supplemented the old; women had to pay a high price for "liberation."

THE MAINTENANCE PHASE

Consequences of what initially seemed progressive and farsighted policy-making posed serious questions for communist leaderships. Sociological research into the problems of working women and the family in Eastern Europe and the Soviet Union began in the 1960s and was endorsed by Chinese leaders in 1980. Western communist research continued at a rapid pace during the 1970s, providing a relatively complete picture of what has become "woman's place" in industrialized communist society. Data showed widespread discrimination against women in pay and job status, a weakening of family life, and a continuing perception by men and women that women are inferior. While women may have achieved de jure equality with men, de facto equality appeared a long way off. These problems, combined with the negative demographic trend, occasioned a shift in policy-making focus regarding women in Eastern Europe and the USSR during the maintenance phase.

PROBLEM FORMATION

Sociological research and Party statements suggest four major categories of policy problems relating to the status of women in Eastern Europe and the Soviet Union from the 1960s on: (1) the demographic problem, (2) the role of the family in contemporary society, (3) living conditions, and (4) the economic and social status of women. Only the fourth category directly concerns upward mobility for women.[1] The issue most frequently discussed in Eastern European and Soviet publications, newspapers, and other published materials are demographic and family life problems. The central concern of these regimes with regard to women since the 1960s has been the declining birthrate. Because economic exploitation has been officially abolished, it cannot be used as an explanation for birthrate decline. Instead, sociologists have turned to public opinion surveys and similar techniques to discover defects in distribution of public benefits to women and to criticize not the premises on which public policy toward women has been based, but the implementation of that policy. Significantly, the values expressed in the statement of the First International Communist Conference of Working Women were never modified by any communist leadership; they remain the cornerstone of public policy toward women.

The Demographic Problem. The two questions most discussed in this area are abortion and the low birthrate. When abortion was legalized in Eastern Europe and the USSR in the 1950s, no advance planning regarding possible impact had been done. The legislation had dramatic consequences, especially in East Germany, Hungary, and Romania (see Jancar, 1978b, for data on abortion). During the late 1960s, East Germany experienced a negative population growth rate, as did Hungary. Of interest is why the abortion rate was and is so high. Two recent Soviet studies provide useful, but incomplete, information.

In Vilnias, a study of female students in higher educational institutions in 1976 found that the ratio of births to abortions *decreased* with student age and year of education until, in the over-24 group in the last year of education, there was 1 birth for 4.25 abortions (Rutkis, 1976: 24-27). A Leningrad study of abortion found that the largest group of women desiring abortions was women with at least one child. The study concluded that "the desire to have a child in the future among women having abortions is more affected by *the presence of children in the family* than by the family's per capita income" (Poliakov and Kovaleva, 1976; emphasis added).

What these studies fail to mention is that abortion has become an effective form of birth control. In some countries, like Bulgaria, contraceptives are virtually unavailable (Anteni, 1978). In others, such as Czechoslovakia, the bureaucratic red tape required to get them is too great a hurdle. In still others, notably Yugoslavia, women seem to prefer abortion to other available contraceptives (Kapor-Stanulovic and Beric, 1974: 129-136). By contrast, although abortions are by no means discouraged in China, they are seen as a last resort, and contraceptives are urged upon the population as the most appropriate form of birth control.

Soviet sociologist Iurii Rurikov (1976) suggests that the multiple factors influencing the low Soviet birthrate may be summed up by the phrase "the price of the child." This includes not only the material standard of living, in his view, but also "the newfelt needs" of women "to express and reveal their capacities." Children are no longer the central value to women, but competitors to the status women achieve at work. Additional factors cited are the workload at home, increased number of "maternal" families resulting from increased divorce and/or extramarital sex, the long hours women work, and, finally, lack of knowledge of how to rear a child.

Bulgarian and Yugoslav surveys (Tsentralno statistichesko upravlenie, 1971; Mihovilovic, 1973) of working women made in the early 1970s confirm the Soviet findings. On the average, the ratio of first births to total live births in Eastern Europe and the USSR has increased from around 20 percent in 1929 to over 40 percent in 1971 (Kaszabov, 1974: 17).

In response to the demographic problem, the industrialized communist leaderships have generally held that three children form the ideal family size and have called for a pro-natalist policy aimed at that goal (Piskunov and Steshenko, 1974). By comparison, the Chinese regime has set a goal of not more than two children per family. All the regimes recognize that the problem is not capable of easy external manipulation, but is essentially one of values and personal attitudes involving a woman's perception of her traditional and work roles.

The Role of the Family in Contemporary Society. The official position in industrialized communist states is that the breakdown of the traditional family (formerly a goal of communist policy) is a major factor in the lowered birthrate. Many studies on causes of divorce, the nature of the family under advanced socialism, or love in contemporary society relate family instability to low natality.

The incidence of divorce has greatly increased in communist countries, except China, the only country since the 1950s with enough consensus for popular pressure to discourage divorce. Traditionally, Catholic Poland has the lowest divorce rate among European communist states, next to Romania, which outlawed divorce in 1966.

Generally, more women than men sue for divorce. The main grounds in virtually every country are incompatability, adultery, and alcoholism. About 47 percent of all Soviet divorces are granted on grounds of alcoholism (Chkalalin, 1974: 80). Alcoholism is now a serious problem among women also, particularly in the USSR. So epidemic has the disease become that it is now given as a major cause of the rising Soviet infant mortality rate (Asian Wall Street Journal, 1980).

Increasingly, communist sociologists link problems of the family to psychological relationships. Moscow's Institute of Social Research conducted a study of family life in the Moscow suburbs in the mid-1970s to derive a static model of a "happy family." They found a high degree of alienation and isolation among families in large apartment complexes, a breakdown of communication between partners, and widely differing expectations about the nature of marriage on the part of each spouse. A Czech sociologist identified the internal dynamics of modern family life on the basis of a community of leisure almost totally divorced from economic and reproductive functions (Fišerova, 1976), while Hungarian sociologist Judit Sas describes the heightened function of the family in satisfying personal psychological needs.

Three interesting points stand out in the European communist analyses of the family problem: (1) While family instability is seen as *positive* for women's assertion of personal independence, it is viewed *negatively* in terms of childbearing and child rearing. The demographic problem has priority over women's independence. (2) Contrary to classic Marxist thought, which posits eventual disappearance of the family, the family is now identified as the unit that must continue; hence the Soviet emphasis on moral education for family life. (3) Since economic exploitation cannot be cited in family decline, nonmaterial factors such as psychopersonal relationships are stressed, and research into how to increase stability of relationships is encouraged.

LIVING CONDITIONS

The literature on inadequate or unimaginative housing is large and cannot be cited fully here. A Czech report indicated that the proportion of dwellings with three or more rooms dropped in the 1970-1975 period because new housing had replaced old. A report to the Hungarian Party Central Committee in 1978 asserted that housing was still the "greatest sociopolitical problem" (Nepszava, 1978). In 1972 Poland's First Party Secretary, Edward Gierek, stated that the housing shortage could not be alleviated, let alone solved, prior to 1990 (Trybuna ludu, 1972). In the Soviet Union, the negative impact of giant apartment complexes on family life has come under increasingly severe scrutiny, and housing is reviewed not just in terms of providing living space but for its attractiveness to young couples as well (Vishnevsky, 1975: 2; Pavlov, 1977: 91-96; Arina et al., 1976: 12). The housing shortage is no longer seen just in terms of living space. It is now thought that housing should also meet certain convenience standards and consider aesthetics. Housing must create community and be suited to family needs now.

Child care and pregnancy benefits are also receiving considerable attention now, although less than housing. The USSR and Eastern Germany probably have the best-developed child-care service networks. But even there, the problem of child care has not been solved, because of the urban bias in locating preschool facilities (Izvestia, 1976: 5; Kuhrig, 1973: 152-154). There is also wide variation in quality of child care, depending on a city's size and geographic location.

Pregnancy benefits and family allowances have become increasingly liberal throughout East Europe and the USSR. Despite public opinion surveys, which clearly show that economics are not the main reason for women not wanting children, the regimes apparently still believe women can, in a sense, be bribed to have more children. Although it is undoubtedly true, as much of the literature claims (Gordon, 1977; Perevedentsev, 1977), that family allowances are insufficient, the trend to have fewer children seen in all industrialized countries suggests that no amount of state payment will persuade women to have large families. In China, economics are used to discourage large families; housing space and rice rations are reduced and free schooling is terminated for the second child.

Vacations and leisure time appear to be a more serious problem in industrialized communist states than child welfare benefits. There is extensive documentation that women have less leisure time. A new issue is family vacations. Socialist policy assures every worker a vacation, but because of difficulties scheduling rooms, the husband and wife have vacationed separately while the children have gone to summer camp. Recently this policy has been under increasing attack for contributing to the breakdown of the family, and Western communist leaders have tried hard to accommodate family units. In China, talks with factory officials indicated that the separate vacation was also a problem there, but that other concerns took priority.

In summary, problem formation regarding living conditions has focused on personal psychological needs as the key factor in raising the quality of family life.

The Economic and Social Status of Women. Woman's status has received consideration in two areas: (1) Women have not advanced far enough and are not paid equally with men; and (2) increased economic and social activity has changed women's values, so that the family is no longer the center of their lives (Rurikov, 1976). The problem formed by the intersection of these dimensions constitutes the main dilemma for communist public policy toward women: how to integrate woman's twin roles of job and home without sacrificing one for the other. No communist government wants women to return to the home, and public opinion surveys show that women do not want to either (Jancar, 1978b). Nevertheless, some researchers blame the woman worker for the decline of the family (Perevedentsev, 1978).

Every communist country except the USSR has publicly admitted that women are not de facto equal with men in job position or social status. "The double shift" has generally been blamed for women's lower status. Researchers glibly assume that when women are not so burdened at home they will be able to devote the time necessary to raise their status. Others suggest educational patterns are to blame. Women must be encouraged to take less conventionally "feminine" studies (Ilieva et al., 1973). Finally, there is recognition that "old attitudes" still inhibit promotion of women to high positions. But the central issue of why male dominance persists has been ignored. The problem is stated simply: Women are unequal because of material conditions existing in society today and because of remaining traditional attitudes. Once material conditions have improved and old attitudes have changed, the problem will be solved.

Summary. First, problem formation in industrialized communist states has focused increasingly on demography during the maintenance period. Woman's status is seen as a secondary issue, mainly important in estimating the "price of the child." Second, women's problems are identified on one hand as psychological and social issues, and on the other as a result of a lack of material stimuli. The deeper psychological and social issues are never addressed. Third, problem formation assumes the original Marxist goals of 1920 are valid. Research has found no attempt to question old goals or concepts or to form new ones. The modern problems of women are perceived as a continuation or extension of problems that existed in presocialist society.

POLICY FORMULATION AND ADOPTION

In the maintenance phase, as in the postrevolutionary (see Table 7.1), all the communist countries have adopted similar policies to solve the problems discussed above. There is little innovation or divergence except for date of adoption and details of legislation or Party decree.

Demography. Policy in all the countries trying to increase birthrates has been to make abortion more difficult, that is, to coerce women into having more children. And all the countries, including China, are developing comprehensive demographic policies combining material and "spiritual" incentives. The USSR seems to have led the way in encouraging reproduction; a Standing Committee on Women's Labor and Everyday Life was established under the Moscow City Soviet to provide "moral and material incentives for women to have children" (Velikanova, 1978). Happily, coercion does not play an important role. A Soviet discussion of demographic policy emphasizes that the aim of a sound demographic policy must be "to create conditions which will not have a negative effect on the generative function of women." The author proposes more public forms of child rearing to influence the demographic behavior of the population (Piskunov and Steshenko, 1974: 27).

China provides evidence that demographic trends can be reversed by a program of mass persuasion and propaganda, combining force, public censure, and peer pressure. Whether the more personalized, individualistic Western communist societies can be so manipulated is questionable. Family planning is slowly being accepted in Eastern Europe: Yugoslavia has the most extensive program, with East Germany and Czechoslovakia not far behind.

The Role of the Family in Contemporary Society. In all the industrialized communist countries, the family has by now acquired legal status as the basic social unit of society. Concern now centers on halting the breakdown of the family. Use of force to keep marriages together has occurred only in the USSR (1936 and 1944; the policy was abandoned in 1968) and in Romania (1966). Elsewhere the effort features positive incentives such as family counseling to keep couples together. Cuba is the only country whose family code requires the husband to share half the housework and family responsibilities. Many recent efforts to strengthen the family have been borrowed from the West, such as counseling centers and computer matchmaking (Velikanova, 1978: 12). Other solutions are derived from the domestic environment, including attempts to substitute state functions for religious rites of baptism, confirmation, marriage, and funerals. This trend has been strongest in the USSR, Bulgaria, and Hungary (Nawka i religiia, 1976: 41-45; Rabotnichesko delo, 1978; Nepszabadsag, 1978).

Living Conditions. The housing situation is being seriously addressed in all the countries, through either Party resolution or national plan. All have taken measures to expand the network of child-care facilities, and many have increased the term of pregnancy leave. Family bonuses have been accepted as an appropriate instrument of family policy; the concern is how to distribute them fairly among different income families. So far, the question of leisure time has yet to be considered at the policy level.

The Economic and Social Status of Women. The most innovative policies are in this area. In 1970 Hungary enacted a pioneering decree requiring that women be brought into higher positions. In 1973 Romania initiated its female executive recruitment program, followed in 1976 by a Party resolution establishing a 25 percent quota for women in all regional, local, and enterprise Party committees. East Germany has been providing special educational opportunities for women seeking promotion at work since 1969. China, under Mao, had several campaigns to mobilize women. During the Cultural Revolution a quota was set for women's participation in revolutionary committees; as recently as 1976 a campaign was launched to place more women in administrative positions. These efforts have largely lapsed with the present leadership's efforts at rapid modernization.

In line with these resolutions, women have been elevated in many politburos. The heads of the National Women's Councils are Politburo members in Romania, Hungary, and Bulgaria. East Germany has not promoted a woman to its politburo, but the chair of the National Women's Organization is a member of the Party Secretariat. Poland and the USSR have been least active regarding women's status. No directives or legislation came from Poland's pioneering research on women's problems in the 1960s. Polish women's political representation is among the lowest of communist countries, although Polish sociologists have told the author that Polish women have the best situation in Eastern Europe.

The USSR's emphasis has not been on women's status as much as on providing more satisfying work conditions for women, including flexible work schedules in industries where women predominate (textiles and food); proposals for shorter working hours; and more vocational training for farm women as well as improving farm machinery to make it safer for women (Literaturnaia gazeta, 1978; Rurikov, 1976; Fedorova, 1975: 55-64). A 1976 health law raises sanitary and hygienic conditions and safety standards in enterprises employing large numbers of women, expands medical services protecting women's health at work, broadens assistance to children, and increases opportunities for women in vocational training (Izvestia, 1976).

Summary. Communist policy formulation during the maintenance phase has increasingly been identified with woman's traditional role.

IMPLEMENTATION

Implementation of demographic policy has not been smooth. Tougher abortion legislation has been particularly difficult to implement, with both women and doctors determined to circumvent the law. In Romania, Bulgaria, and Czechoslovakia, doctors have resented being forced to decide whether a woman should bear a child; illegal abortions have also multiplied (Scott, 1974: 145-147; Romana libera, 1976). Family allowances and loans have failed to achieve their demographic aims, the former because of the small stipends and limited eligibility of the recipients (Acharkan, 1975: 34-41).

Housing and child-care policy implementation has been stalled for economic reasons, not lack of popular support. On the contrary, women have expressed concern about medical services at work and preschools. Research indicates that where women have actively demanded better facilities, the local authorities have generally provided them. Women have also expressed keen interest in shorter working hours and flexible work schedules. Thus, in the area of living and work conditions, women appear to have developed a sense of "clout," perhaps because they know the regime has identified quality of life with the demographic problem.

Another obstacle in implementation has been continuation of academic quotas in the communist educational system. While there might have been some excuse for favoring men over women in Soviet educational policy following World War II, there is no reason for such a policy today. Most regimes are silent on this issue. Apparently, the alteration of quotas to promote men in certain professions had become so widespread that several incidents of it were published in the Bulgarian newspapers (Darzhaven viesnik, 1977; Narodna mladezh, 1977).

Not only are policies not being implemented; in some areas women's status is declining. For example, in 1975 Soviet official statistics noted a drop in the percentage of women holding academic titles and higher academic degrees compared to men, despite a numerical increase in scientific personnel. From 1950 to 1974 the percentage of all female scientific personnel holding the rank of professor dropped from 0.8 to 0.5, while the percentage of junior research associates and assistants more than trebled, from 15.9 to 49.3 (Vestnik statistiki, 1974: 91). A Soviet analysis explains this drop by the amount of time women spend on home and children (Puchkov and Popov, 1976). Women between the ages of 30 and 40 with children must choose between leadership and home.

Women have begun to criticize the implementation of policies on women's status. For example, in a 1978 session of the Hungarian National Assembly, the Chair of the Hungarian National Women's Council declared that "the promotion of women [was] making slow progress," despite official statistics showing that in 1976 35 percent of Hungarian factory managers were women. In Romania a national women's conference held in 1978, the first in twelve years, stressed the need to draw more women into social and public life and to promote them to more responsible positions. The reformed National Women's

Organization of Czechoslovakia set as one of its four main objectives the task of finding out why women were not advancing to high-status positions.

Discriminatory quotas, the failure of women to advance, and demographic demands have meant that women's status has improved very little, if at all, during the maintenance period in communist countries. Policy implementation in all countries, including China, has focused on the birthrate with the stated aim of increasing or decreasing population growth. Clearly, communist policy makers have yet to confront the fact that women have become increasingly concerned with status and that this concern must be met.

EVALUATION AND CONCLUSIONS

(1) In the maintenance phase of policy-making, communist leaderships have moved backward from a revolutionary image of women's liberation to the traditional view of women's role. From an emphasis on political mobilization, work outside the home, and equality with men, the focus has reverted to home, family, and children in all the communist industrialized countries. The change is seen in the return to feminine clothing in all communist states, including China. Woman's place may be in the economy when there is a labor shortage, but her "special" place (to borrow the phrasing of the 1978 Soviet Constitution) is in the home.

(2) Communist policies toward women have become increasingly conservative as leaderships have turned from revolution to the task of maintaining economic progress and political stability. During the postrevolutionary phase, women could indeed act as the surrogate proletariat. Their mobilization to the cause of revolution served to "overturn" the old society as no other means could have, as China so well shows. In the maintenance phase, the revolution is history. Women are mentally put back in the home.

(3) At the present time, women in communist party states may be more radical than the leadership desires. Family is their concern, but surveys show that they have accepted new work roles and intend to keep them. Women have further indicated that they may not be willing to fulfill what *Pravda* called their "demographic roles" by bearing the number of children required. Divorce has been interpreted as an indication of women asserting their rights. Abortion can be considered a similar response (Jancar, 1980). In women's conferences and councils throughout Eastern Europe, women have spoken out against their wages and job positions, and a dissident feminist movement has finally emerged in the Soviet Union.

Thus, as the maintenance phase progresses, women appear to be changing their style. They have shaken off much of their passivity and are beginning to make demands on the political system, if only in areas traditionally labeled feminine (e.g., child care). China is going through a period of such rapid changes that it is unwise to speculate on new roles women there may demand. At present, the official public attitude is conservative, and the centering of national effort on industrialization augurs poorly for changes in women's status in the near future, particularly given China's massive unemployment problem.

(4) Communist policy toward women in the industrialized states lacks substance and direction. The original comprehensive program has given way to piecemeal policy-making oriented to whatever priority the leadership designates. Neither the meaning of equality nor the roles appropriate for women and men have been questioned.

(5) The results of communist policy-making for women raise the important question of the efficacy of imposing status change by fiat. The revolution in women's position at the onset of modernization in China and Central Asia was remarkable. Elsewhere, Jancar (1978b) has posited the theory that degree of modernization and length of time a regime remains in power converge on a threshold beyond which incremental change in status diminishes significantly. The initial movement of women from the domestic environment into the world of work is a kind of change that authoritarian regimes can command with relative efficiency. However, the further advance of women to equal status brings into question the whole structure of values and attitudes upon which the male political power hierarchy rests. In their return to conservative values, the communist leaderships have indicated that they are not ready to put that structure to the test.

(6) If women in communist one-party states are indeed more radical than their leaderships desire, we may expect increasing tension to occur between governments and female clients. Since women (as well as men) are not allowed independent political organization, the tension is unlikely to produce anything like a "women's movement." What it may produce is an increase in women's consciousness of their disadvantages. Consciousness generally lags behind reality. Yet consciousness can guide reality. The evidence suggests that women will continue to find ways to have at least an indirect impact in the communist countries.

NOTE

1. Little can be said about China in this section, because the acceptance of sociological research as a tool of policy-making is so recent and virtually no studies have been published.

REFERENCES

ACHARKAN, V. A. (1975) "The social and legal nature of children's allowances, for low income families." Sovietskoie gosudarstvo i pravo (Soviet State and Law) 10: 34-41.

ANDERSON, J. E. (1975) Public Policy Making. New York: Praeger.

Anteni (1978) #7 (Sofia).

ARINA, O., M. D. STEPANOVA, and N. STEPANOVA (1976) "Literaturnaia gazeta." September 15: 12.

Asian Wall Street Journal (1980) Hong Kong and Singapore.

Chinese Documents Project (1955) "The family revolution in Communist China." Research Memorandum No. 15, January, Lackland Airforce Base, Texas, Air Force Personnel and Training Research Center, Air Research and Development Command.

CHKALALIN, V. (1974) "The family and family relationships under socialism." Sovietskoie gosudarstvo i pravo (Soviet State and Law) 21, 4: 80.

Darzhaven viesnik (1977) March 3 (Sofia).

FEDOROVA, M. (1975) Voprosy ekonomiki (Questions of Economics) 12: 55-64.

FIŠEROVA, A. (1976) "Leisure time of the Ostrava population." Planovane Hospodarstvi 1. (as reported in Czechoslovak Situation Report (30) July 31, 1976, Radio Free Europe Research: 1-12; mimeo)

GORDON, L. A. (1977) "Organization of everyday life." Ekonomika i organizatsia promyshlennogo proizvodstva (Economics and the Organization of Industrial Production) 6: 114-118.

ILIEVA, N. et al. (1973) Izpolzvane na shenskite trudovi resurse v NRB (The Use of Women's Labor Resources in the PRB). Sofia: Partizdat.

Izvestia (1976a) March 26. (Moscow)

——— (1976b) July 23. (Moscow)

JANCAR, B. W. (1977) "The recruitment of women into the political elites of Bulgaria, Czechoslovakia, Hungary and Poland." Presented at the 1977 Annual Meeting of the Midwest Political Science Association, Ann Arbor, Michigan, May 3-5.

——— (1978a) "Women in the Yugoslav National Liberation Movement." Presented at the 1978 Annual Meeting of the Midwest Slavic Conference, Bloomington, Indiana, April 14-16.

——— (1978b) Women under Communism. Baltimore, MD: Johns Hopkins University Press.

——— (1980) "Elite Analysis in Applied Research on Women in Communist Society." Women and Politics 1, 2: 47-64.

KAPOR-STANULOVIC, N. and B. BERIC (1974) "Family planning behavior in Yugoslavia," pp. 129-136 in H. P. David (ed.) Abortion Research: International Experience. Lexington, MA: D. C. Heath.

KASZABOV, V. SZT. (1974) "Bulgaria nepessege szuletesgyakorisaganak kerdeshez." Demografia 2.

KUHRIG, H. (1973) Equal Rights for Women in the German Democratic Republic. Berlin: GDR Committee for Human Rights.

Literaturnaia gazeta (1978) January 4 (Moscow).

LOWI, T. J. (1964) "American business, public policy: comparative studies and political theory." World Politics 16: 667-715.

MASSELL, G. G. (1974) The Surrogate Proletariat. Princeton, NJ: Princeton University Press.

MEIJER, M. J. (1971) Marriage Law and Policy in the Chinese People's Republic. Hong Kong: Hong Kong University Press.

MIHOVILOVIC, M. A. [Principal Investigator] (1973) Reports and Studies: The Influence of Women's Employment on Family Characteristics and Functioning. Zagreb: University of Zagreb, Institute for Social Research.

Narodna mladezh (1977) April 3 (Sofia).

Nawka I religiia (1976) 12 (Hungary).

Nepszabadsag (1978) February 2 (Budapest).

Nepszava (1978) April 23 (Budapest).

PAVLOV, B. S. (1977) Molodoi kommunist (Young Communist) 5: 91-96.

PEREVEDENTSEV, V. (1977) Literaturnaia gazeta (December 28): 13.

——— (1978) "Incompatability." Literaturnaia gazeta (February 15): 13.

PISKUNOV, V. P. and V. S. STESHENKO [eds.] (1974) O demograficheskoi politike sotsialisticheskogo obshchestva (The Demographic Politics of Socialist Society). Moscow: Statistika.

POLIAKOV, I. V. and A. P. KOVALEVA (1976) "Abortions in Leningrad characterized in terms of social hygiene." Sovietskoe zdravookhranenie 12: 43-46.

Pravda (1920) 1721 (Moscow).

PUCHKOV, I. S. and G. A. POPOV (1976) Sociodemographic Characteristics of Science Personnel. Moscow: Statistika.

Rabotnichesko delo (1978 May 23 (Sofia).

Romana libera (1976) December 6 (Bucharest).

RURIKOV, I. (1976) "Why there are fewer children." Literaturnaia gazeta 46.

RUTKIS, E. (1976) "Pregnancy and its outcome among day students in the higher educational institution of Vilnius." Sovietskoe zdravookhranenie (Soviet Health Insurance) 5: 24-27.

SCOTT, H. (1974) Does Socialism Liberate Women? Boston: Beacon.

SOKOLOWSKA, M. (1963) Kobieta pracujaca (The Working Woman). Warsaw: Widez powszechna.

Trybuna ludu (1972) May 11 (Warsaw).

Tsentralno statistichesko upravlenie (1971) Zhenata v stopanskiia, obshchestveniia, Kulturniia zhivot a v semestvoto (Women in Economic, Social and Cultural Life, and in the Family). Sofia: Author.

United Nations (1974) Statistical Yearbook, 81084.

VELIKANOVA, L. (1978) "The family and its members." Literaturnaia gazeta (May 1): 12.

Vestnik statistiki (1975) 91 (Moscow).

VISHNEVSKY, S. (1975) Komsomolskaia pravda (Komsomol Truth) September 19: 2.

VYSHINSKI, A. (1951) The Law of the Soviet State (H. W. Babb, trans.). New York: MacMillan.

WADE, L. L. (1972) Elements of Public Policy. Columbus, OH: Charles E. Merrill.

8

PUBLIC DAY CARE IN BRITAIN AND SWEDEN

A Sociological Perspective

MARY RUGGIE

In the last two decades the number of women working outside the home has increased steadily, and the growth has been greatest among married women with young children. Demands are being made on the state not only to assist in some way in the provision of facilitative services, but also to guide the enormous social changes involved. This chapter explores the responses of two welfare states, Britain and Sweden, within a single issue area, public day-care provision for children.

Since Britain and Sweden are both established welfare states, one might be led to expect considerable similarities in the substance of policies, organizational styles, and kinds and levels of provision in their respective social programs. This is not so, however, either in the issue area to be investigated here or in a number of other areas (Heclo, 1974). The differences between British and Swedish policies for working women can be stated briefly. Policies in Sweden facilitate women's employment more than those in Britain. For example, in addition to the differences in day-care provision, which are discussed below, there are important differences in labor market programs.

Swedish labor market programs effectively link women who want to work not only with available jobs, but, more important, with those jobs that provide greater opportunities for advancement, thus attempting to overcome one of the problems connected with a dual labor market. In Britain there are some similar programs on the books, but they have not been effective, particularly in attacking structural factors in the labor market. Moreover, in Sweden maternity/paternity leave is universal, generous (nine months after birth), can be taken by either parent, and includes leaves to care for sick children up to the age of ten. In Britain the state assures at least a seven-month maternity leave after childbirth, but paternity leaves and any additional or alternative provisions are up to individual employers.

Why do these sorts of policy differences exist? Two obvious explanations concern differences in the demand for women workers in the economies of the two countries, and differences in conceptions of women's roles. Space does not allow a systematic presentation of these two areas of explanation for policy differences. But the fact of the matter is that the impact of the economy and of traditional role conceptions differs in Britain and Sweden. In Britain both the economy and tradition affect women's employment much more directly and intensely than they do in Sweden. In Sweden the state more actively mediates the impact of the economy and tradition on women's employment. Why, then, does this difference exist?

The differences between Britain and Sweden in the policies, organization, and provision of social programs concern, at their most fundamental level, differences in the character of state-society relations. Each nation has developed its own set of responses to the questions of for whom, in what manner, and toward what ends the state intervenes in social relations. Different consequences follow from the form of intervention in each nation. Below, I propose two ideal typical models of welfare state systems as a basis on which to analyze the nature of policy differences in day-care provision in Britain and Sweden. Each model depicts a particular mode of state intervention. As an instance of state intervention, day-care provision reveals, perhaps more than any other policy area related to women's employment, the tension that attends public involvement in the private sector. Child care is closely associated not only with the traditional role of women as mothers and homemakers, but also with the most intimate of private domains, the family. State provision of day-care services may be limited so as not to "interfere" with private family child care. Alternatively, state provision may be substantial and justified as contributing to the economic productivity of the nation. The interpretation that prevails follows largely from the particular configuration of state-society relations that prevails.

Britain exhibits a liberal welfare approach to the problem of day care. This approach is premised upon a conscious desire to maintain the delimitation of public and private realms, with the state being reluctant to intervene in the private sector unless compelled to do so by market failure. When a liberal welfare state does intervene, the depth of intervention and the organization and extent of provision themselves are constrained by a "market rationality" (Dahrendorf, 1968). That is, the proper sphere of state behavior is circumscribed by the functioning of market forces, and the instruments of state intervention are designed to compensate for market imperfections while remaining compatible with the basic principles of market organization. In a liberal welfare approach, eligibility for public benefits is confined to the needy, defined as those for whom market mechanisms have failed. Means tests are often used to select welfare clientele. Services are free of charge for them, but there is a reluctance to make these services as good as could be bought on the free market. Thus, there is a contradiction between, on one hand, the attempt to achieve a substantive goal such as social equality and, on the other hand, the manner and means of state action. The ability to reconcile equality and liberalism remains problematical.

In contrast, the response of the state in Sweden to day-care provision resembles a societal corporatist welfare approach. This means, first, that the "associationally organized interests of civil society [are linked] with the decisional structures of the state" (Schmitter, 1974: 86). In the case of Sweden, a particular coalition of government, unions, and organized business forms a tripartite system. Since the 1930s, with the Social Democratic Party holding power continuously for over forty years, this coalition has built Sweden's welfare state, and its consensus-based decision-making has structured policy in all fields. Second, a societal corporatist approach means that the specific policy goals formulated by interest-group representatives are implemented within the state apparatus, with little or no competition from the private sector. The state determines the timing and mode of intervention which can best supersede the market and reverse undesirable consequences of the market allocation.

These differences have important implications for the character of policy outcomes. The analysis here shows that while policies for day care are determined by a number of interacting factors, the framework of state-society relations is central among them. In other words, it is misleading to place hopes for social change solely in the increasing numbers of women who are working. The connection between women's employment on one hand, and facilitative policies and programs on the other, rests on the extent and depth of state intervention. In Britain policies for working women are characterized by weak and derivative state intervention. A liberal welfare approach prevails, which allows greater rein to traditional conceptions of women's roles and to the free play of market forces. In Sweden state intervention is strong and it mediates the impact of the economy and tradition. Moreover, the societal corporatist approach of the state in Sweden actively articulates policies for women within a national plan for full employment and economic growth.

In this chapter I shall first present the historical background of day care and working mothers in Britain and Sweden, pointing out the similarity in attitudes and provision until very recently. I then turn to the changes that occurred in women's employment in both countries in the 1960s. I briefly describe the new policies that accompanied these changes in Sweden, and the policies that continued in Britain, including the current forms of day-care provision in each nation. The main part of the chapter analyzes the role of the state in shaping day-care provision. Differences between British and Swedish modes of state intervention are examined. Finally, in the conclusion I discuss the consequences for women of prevailing state-society relations.

HISTORICAL CONTEXT

BRITAIN

In Britain the first institutionalized day-care arrangements for children of working mothers developed in the early nineteenth century. These were private and profit-making enterprises (Tizard et al., 1976). Most mothers who worked at that time were poor, and so, by implication and practice, was the quality of care given to their children. There were exceptions, such as Robert Owen's nursery school for the children of employees in his cotton mill in Scotland. In the 1850s another type of nursery setting for young children appeared in Britain: kindergartens, based on the child-oriented techniques of the German educator, Froebel. From their inception, these were enriching educational nursery schools for middle-class children with non-working mothers; they were few in number and mostly private. All in all, the early forms of day care in Britain were in the private sector and embodied a functional and institutional separation between care and education, based on social class.

When the state began to provide nursery facilities, the separation between care and education was maintained. Public-sector nursery schooling emerged well before the turn of this century. But interest in it was brief and it quickly became a financial burden on local governments when free schooling was legislated in 1891. Only a few nursery schools continued to operate thereafter. What we know as day care for children of working mothers, called day nurseries in Britain, became established during World War I. These were simply custodial facilities, pretending to no larger purpose or role than to care for children while their mothers worked in the war effort. Most of the day care facilities were disbanded after the war. The few public programs that continued to operate were brought under local-authority jurisdiction by new legislation. In 1918 Parliament passed the Maternity and Child Welfare Act, giving the *welfare* departments of local authorities the power to establish and maintain day nurseries. At the same time, a separate Education Act gave the *education* departments of local authorities the power to establish and maintain nursery schools and classes. This jurisdictional separation between the two institutions, as well as the conceptions of clientele and purposes of programs that go with the separation, are the main inheritance from the past. The subsequent development of day care in Britain repeats history. The expansion of provision during World War II paralleled that of World War I, and so did the decline after the war. Very little has changed since World War II. The discussion below of current forms of day-care provision in Britain reveals "the extraordinary tenacity of older attitudes" (Shonfield, 1965: 88).

SWEDEN

The first Swedish day nurseries in the mid-nineteenth century were also poorly equipped and strictly custodial institutions for the children of poor working mothers. Sweden was similar to Britain in the way that both the public and private sectors thought about day care and how they provided it. The conception and development of nursery schools were also similar. The few nursery schools that existed by the turn of the century were private and provided part-time educational enrichment for children whose parents were better placed in society. This dualism of institutions and purposes persisted until 1941, when a government commission reviewed the question of day care and preschool (Rosengren, 1973). In the midst of World War II and with the ensuing need for women workers, the commission proposed not only that public day-care facilities be expanded, but also that they be improved. The concern with staff training, program activities, and integrated health and social services was farsighted, and the financial system proposed to assist implementation was supportive. But this interest in day care was short-lived. After the war the quantity of provision declined, because women by and large returned to their traditional roles in the home. But there was no retreat to traditional philosophies regarding day care. Instead, there was continued criticism of the quality of day nurseries, and it was translated into a requirement to change existing facilities. These concerns were coupled with a renewed pedagogical interest in part-time nursery schools. Developments in the 1960s provided the conditions for a meeting of the ways of programs for children and programs for working parents.

RECENT DEVELOPMENTS

EMPLOYMENT

Before 1960, a greater proportion of women, including married women, worked in Britain than in Sweden. This changed during the 1960s. By 1970, 42 percent of married women in Britain were working outside the home, and 55 percent in Sweden. One reason for the increase in women's employment was similar in Britain and Sweden: There were more jobs available, particularly in the expanding service sector, and in health, education, and welfare positions in the expanding public sector. But there was an additional reason for the much greater increase in women's employment in Sweden: a new and far-reaching labor market policy. Labor market policy in Sweden is considered to be a central component of economic policy. The policy nexus as a whole is oriented toward the goals of full employment, productivity, and growth. Labor market programs include training, counseling, employment services, and job creation, all conducted under the National Labor Market Board. Together with constant analyses of industrial trends, these programs attempt to assure that jobs are secure, long-lasting, and personally satisfying. With regard to women, efforts are made to guide them into jobs that are nontraditional for their sex and offer wide opportunities, and employers are encouraged to hire more women, in many cases through financial subsidies (Sandberg, 1975).

Although Britain reorganized some of its training programs in the 1970s, the scope, financial outlay, and success of these and related measures is still far inferior to those of the Swedish (Mukherjee, 1972). Britain also passed an Equal Pay Act in 1970 and a Sex Discrimination Act in 1975, but the effects of this legislation on women's employment position have been mixed and disappointing for the most part (Coussins, 1976).

DAY CARE

We can more fully assess state responses to changes in women's employment in Britain and Sweden in the area of day-care policy, for these policies reveal the "deep structure" of attitudes toward women workers and traditional sex roles. The responses of the two countries are in sharp contrast to each other.

In Britain neither policies nor programs nor provisions for day care have changed at all in the last few decades. The response of the state to changes in women's employment was to ignore it at the level of day care, and thereby implicitly to discourage mothers of preschool-aged children from working outside the home. Only one type of public facility in Britain provides day care for preschool children: the day nursery. Only day nurseries are open from early morning to early evening and on those holidays when most parents have to work. The number of day-nursery places in Britain actually *decreased* between 1960 and 1970, despite the increase in mothers' employment. In 1975 the number of places in day nurseries was still not as high as it had been in 1955. (There are at present about 25,000 places.)

Many mothers delay working until their children reach school age. However, schools are suitable to provide day care only for mothers who do not work full-time or during school holidays, including summers. Public schooling begins early for children in Britain. At age 5 some children attend school for a full day, but most attend part-time. Four-year-old children are also permitted to attend public-sector schools if places are available. While a large number of children do attend nursery classes of some sort in the public sector, it must be emphasized that these facilities alone do not constitute a day-care service for working parents. Their hours of operation are short and inflexible, and, of course, they exclude preschool-aged children.

In Britain the private sector provides both day nurseries and nursery schools. Some of the latter take children from the age of three. There are no reliable figures for the quantity of private-sector provision, but it is estimated that there are far fewer private than public day nurseries and nursery schools.

Most working mothers in Britain use childminders (what we call babysitters) for their day-care needs. Childminders are supposed to register with local-authority departments and have their houses inspected, but it is estimated that most do not. For the most part, childminding is a thoroughly private arrangement. And it is not altogether satisfactory. The quality of care is uncertain (Jackson, 1975; Mayall and Petrie, 1977), and parents whose children are no longer infants have particular worries about the value of this type of care (Bone, 1977).

In Sweden in the 1960s, the lack of day-care facilities and the inadequacy of their institutional features were issues taken up by concerned groups, including industry, the unions, and the press. As is the custom in Sweden, a number of government commissions were set up throughout the decade to investigate aspects of the problem. A change in public policy on day care began to take shape. Finally, to consolidate the various findings within the framework of a comprehensive government approach, a Royal Commission on Child Centers was appointed in 1968. The commission's report, issued in 1972, proposed a revamping of the entire system of day care, based on new conceptions of needs and purposes. These included (1) the recognition that, while all children need some form of preschool, the need for day care itself is directly related to the needs of working parents; (2) recognition of the harm done in the past because of the institutional separation of care and education; (3) a public commitment to meet the preschool needs of children and parents, quantitatively and qualitatively. The Commission's recommendations were formulated into a Pre-School Act, which was passed by Parliament in December 1973. As the local authorities began to act on their new mandates, additional legislation (a Child Care Act) to assist their efforts was passed in 1976 and 1977.

The present system of day care in Sweden consists of two basic types of programs: preschool centers and family day homes. Preschools are either full-time or part-time. They are discussed more fully below. There are virtually no private day-care centers or nursery schools in Sweden. Privately arranged child care does exist in the form of babysitting. However, much of the child care in private homes is also under the auspices of the public day-care system. This is now called the family day home component of child care. The change in the status of persons providing child care in their own homes is a remarkable feature of Swedish day care. A Family Commission reporting in 1965 felt that such childminding was making a valuable contribution to overall day-care provision, especially for infants. The Commission realized that to assure the continuing contribution of quality childminding, reorganization and assistance were necessary. It suggested that childminders be employed by the local authorities, with all the benefits this implies, such as holiday pay and pensions, and all the requirements, such as inspection of premises and training (a 90-hour course in child care). The incorporation of family day homes into the local authorities began in 1966. The local authorities refer parents to available homes, collect the fees (the same scale applies as in preschool), and pay day mothers (at a lower rate than preschool teachers).

One of the most outstanding features of the Swedish day-care system is the recognition that the need for child care continues once children begin school. After-school centers provide care and activities for children aged 7 to 12, whose parents work full-time. The same scale of fees applies as in preschools.

THE ROLE OF THE STATE IN DAY CARE

The different approaches of the state in Britain and Sweden to day-care provision reveal not only different conceptions about women's roles, but also differences in the prevailing form of state-society relations. This section attempts to explicate the underlying rationale in the two systems of day care. The focus is on the role of the state in providing day nurseries in Britain and preschools in Sweden, because these facilities constitute *public day care* in each nation respectively. Two dimensions of the role of the state are distinguished. The first, the determinants of intervention, examines the set of circumstances that are taken to justify the initiation of state intervention. The second dimension, design of intervention, examines the purpose and quality of the day-care program provided by the state.

BRITAIN

Determinants of Intervention. What are the circumstances that trigger state intervention in the area of public child-care arrangements? We saw that the state in Britain first provided public day nurseries during a situation of national emergency. Twice, expanded provision was justified on the basis of the country's need for women to work in the war effort. After both wars, public provision returned to its prewar level. Presumably, women were no longer needed in the workforce, since men had returned to their old jobs. But some women did continue to work, and some working mothers were excluded from those day nurseries that continued to operate. To understand the character and level of postwar day-care provision in Britain, we must distinguish between who is included in public day care and who is excluded.

Bases of Inclusion. The necessary condition for inclusion in public day care is poverty. There is a means test for eligibility. Two other conditions are sufficient for placing children in day nurseries: the mother's illness or some similar incapacity, and a family breakdown, such as divorce. In the latter case, the mother is most likely looking for employment or working. This means, furthermore, that only those mothers who work out of financial necessity, because of a family or market-created breakdown, are accepted as clients of public day-care programs.

The official definition of the state's clientele was formulated by the Department of Health and Social Security (DHSS), which is the main government department responsible for overseeing day nurseries. One

DHSS circular (Great Britain, Ministry of Health, 1968), still operative, delineates the clientele as follows:

> The responsibility of local health authorities should continue to be limited to arranging for the day care of children who, from a health point of view or because of deprived or inadequate backgrounds, have special needs that cannot otherwise be met.
>
> The need for day care may arise from one or more of a variety of circumstances in which the child or family may need help. Priority will normally be given to children with only one parent (e.g., the unsupported mother living with her child) who has no option but to go to work and who cannot arrange for the child to be looked after satisfactorily. Other children who need day care, some for the whole day, others part-time, will include those:
>
> (a) who need temporary day care on account of the mother's illness;
> (b) whose mothers are unable to look after them adequately because they are incapable of giving young children the care they need;
> (c) for whom day care might prevent the breakdown of the mother or the break-up of the family;
> (d) whose home conditions (e.g., because of gross overcrowding) constitute a hazard to their health and welfare; and
> (e) whose health and welfare are seriously affected by a lack of opportunity for playing with others.

Clearly, public day care is intended for a traditional welfare clientele: children who are already social victims because of their family circumstances, or whose mothers are unable to care for themselves, let alone their children. Local authorities vary in the order of priority they give in accepting children (and families). In general, children who are most "at-risk" and in imminent danger of requiring removal from their homes, and those who are subject to parental abuse ("battering") are taken first. Then, as the circular suggests, priority can be given to the single parent (invariably a mother) who has to work. Being in this position, that is, of having to work out of necessity, places single mothers (as well as those married mothers who are accepted) in the category of a welfare client, eligible for public support. In sum, a late nineteenth-century type of paternalistic welfarism continues to undergird the conception of this social service. Its goals and implementation are permeated with some variant of the organizing principles of the Poor Laws: "proper limits" to state intervention, deterrence through stigma, strict classification of users, and a central inspectorate (Pinker, 1971).

Justification for Exclusion. What justifies the exclusion of nonwelfare, "normal" working mothers from eligibility for public day-care provision? The first postwar circular on day-care provision was issued by DHSS in 1945 to explain to local authorities why the majority of wartime day nurseries ought to be closed. It informs us, at the same time, of the state's position on "normal" working mothers. It reads as follows:

> The Ministers concerned accept the view of medical and other authority that, in the interest of the health and development of the child no less than for the benefit of the mother, the proper place for a child under two is at home with his mother. They are also of the opinion that, under normal peacetime conditions, the right policy to pursue would be positively to discourage mothers of children under two from going out to work [Great Britain, Ministry of Health, 1965].

Positive discouragement took the form of not providing child-care services or any other assistance to mothers who were not forced by unfortunate family circumstances to work outside the home. Although it was not stated as such, the policy also applied to mothers of children aged 2 to 5. The same 1945 circular said that local authorities should provide nursery schools and nursery classes for this age group. But the irregularity of such provision, the lack of state commitment to assure it, and the fact that preschool programs are mostly part-time meant that mothers of children aged 2 to 5 were also to be positively discouraged from going to work. Another circular on day-nursery provision was not issued until 1968, and has already been referred to. It did not change substantially the earlier policy statement, except to drop the phrase "no less than for the benefit of the mother."

This policy rests, quite unabashedly, on a conception of the traditional role of women: Mothers ought to be at home raising children. But this is not what the ministers in charge said. They based their position on "the view of medical and other authority." We can only surmise that the reference was to John Bowlby in particular. However, it was little realized at the time that Bowlby's findings, which described the situation of children in residential institutions such as orphanages, were only incidentally related to the actual situation of children in day nurseries (Bowlby, 1951). To this day, the full implications of qualifications of Bowlby's work have not penetrated the thinking of officials at DHSS, who continue to use "medical and other authority" to justify limiting day-care provision.

In sum, state intervention in the area of day-care provision is determined in the first instance by the market-created situation of poverty. The state then intervenes but, as we will see below, not to the extent of actually improving the situation. This is one indication that the state is acting in a derivative capacity, secondarily to the market. Furthermore, the state justifies its exclusion of working mothers from public provision on the basis of a preferred conception of the traditional role of women as stay-at-home mothers. In doing so, the state in effect is practicing a form of sex discrimination. Moreover, rather than upholding privacy and the integrity of the family, state policy interferes with the freedom of families to make choices. And rather than acting as a deterrent to working mothers, the lack of public day care harms the children involved.

Design of Intervention. The conception of the clientele of day care—children whose mothers have no choice but to work—influences the kind of service the state offers. Provision is based on the premise that children who are social victims require the care missing in their own homes. A good way to ascertain what "care" means is to examine the circulars periodically issued by the DHSS. Two circulars, issued in 1965 and 1968, revised the standards and guidelines to be followed in day nurseries; they are still in effect. They go into considerable detail about the physical setting of the day-nursery facilities, the health of the children, and how and what to feed the children. In glaring contrast to the detail on these matters, the amount of space and attention given to requirements in the nonphysical care of children, that is, to their emotional, social, and intellectual developmental needs, is small. These circulars reveal that a narrow conception of care organizes day nurseries.

This conception is due not simply to the fact that very young children attend these public facilities. Indeed, some day nurseries refuse to take children under 2. The conception applies to children aged 3 to 5, who are in the majority in day nurseries. Nor is it due simply to the fact that children are in day nurseries all day and, therefore, presumably require greater custodial attention. It is due to three interrelated factors: the conception of the client of day care as a welfare recipient; the government department responsible for this function, the DHSS, and local social service authorities; and the status and training of staff in day nurseries. The most revealing way of presenting these points is to contrast them with provision in public nursery schools for children aged 3 to 5. Once again, nursery schools do not provide day care. I am comparing two public institutions, both providing services for children aged 3 to 5, but each providing a different service based on different conceptions of clientele and purposes. The comparison highlights the fact that children in day nurseries, already disadvantaged by their family circumstances of poverty, are further disadvantaged by the lower-quality service they are receiving relative to children in nursery schools.

Nursery schools are under the jurisdiction of the Department of Education and Science (DES) and local education authorities. They are staffed by trained teachers who have at least three years of post-secondary school education, specializing in courses in child development, education, and teaching. In contrast, staff certified to work in day nurseries attended vocational colleges, for a shorter period of time, and specialize in courses in health and social services as well as child development. Those certified to work in day nurseries can also work in hospitals or various other nursery facilities, but are limited to the role of aides in any school. Their pay scales are lower and promotions more limited than those of nursery school teachers. These two factors, jurisdiction and staff, make a difference for the quality and kind of service provided for children of the same age in two different institutions with two different purposes for being. In investigating these differences, one London borough, Camden, noted that teachers in nursery schools are much better sensitized than staff in day nurseries to children's total needs, especially the needs of children over 3. Teachers also have a wider range of ideas for interesting and useful activities and are better able to organize both their own time and their classrooms (London Borough of Camden, 1975). Moreover, the DHSS is more financially pressed than the DES, and the latter is not only more generous in supplying materials and assistance, but also has a broader vision of purpose and earnestly encourages experimentation.

Thus, day nurseries and nursery schools differ along a number of dimensions: clientele, staff training, jurisdiction, and the conception that staff and the authorities have of their clients. These differences affect the children involved. For example, children in day nurseries are considered by staff and authorities to be "deprived " because their mothers have had to leave them to go to work. Such attitudes affect the way staff interact with the children. Studies have shown that staff in day nurseries do not talk as much with the children and are not as affectionate as staff in nursery schools. Moreover, the overall "cognitive" content in staff behavior is lower in working-class nursery facilities not staffed by teachers than in middle-class schools (Tizard et al., 1976: 201). The issue at stake ought not to be muddled by the question of whether children aged 3 to 5 need early educational training or whether they are just as well off simply playing. What is at issue is the fact that there is a *difference* between what children in day nurseries do and receive and what children in other preschool programs do and receive, and that those in day nurseries are disadvantaged. The difference is due to different conceptions of clienteles and purposes and not to the amount of time children spend in an institution.

In sum, the design of state intervention follows from the determinants. State intervention is justified by poverty, which requires the mother to work outside the home, or by some other personal emergency situation. By providing for child care in a public institution, the state is allowing parents to stabilize or improve their family situation. But this outcome is by no means assured. The program of day nurseries is not directed at improvement, either for the child or the family, except that it removes the child from possible maltreatment or neglect. Thus, day care is what has been called a residual welfare function (Wilensky and Lebeaux, 1965). The fact that the purpose of day care is not improvement is significant because it contrasts sharply with the purpose of programs for preschool children in other institutions, particularly in public nursery schools and classes. The differences disadvantage children in day nurseries.

The kind of intervention we see in British day-care provision is characteristic of a liberal welfare state. A commitment to welfare determines that the state intervenes; a commitment to liberalism determines how and to what extent it intervenes.

SWEDEN

Determinants of Invervention. State intervention in day-care provision in Sweden changed in the 1960s with the increase in the number of working women, particularly among mothers with young children. Indeed, the state had a large part in precipitating this increase through its economic and labor market policies. The change in policy for day care was not only quantitative. (Between 1965 and 1970 public provision increased more than sixfold.) The change was also qualitative. To present this dimension I focus on the report of the Royal Commission on Child Centers. In 1972 it presented the framework of a holistic, integrated system of child care for Sweden.

The Commission carried on within the conceptual guidelines formulated by earlier commissions, but added greater substance to them. Its task was simplified by the clear set of directives issued by the Ministry of Family Affairs, which established the Commission. These directives clarified at the outset the multiplicity of concerns involved in the issue of day care, stating:

> The responsibility for the upbringing, supervision and care of children rests chiefly with the home. The community has, however, to a great extent undertaken a responsibility in this field, among other ways through the provision of child centers by local authorities. Changes in

> the family structure and living conditions have brought a greatly increased demand for public measures to assist parents with the care of their children. In increasing numbers of families both parents go out to work. For unmarried and divorced parents organized child care is a condition for their ability to support the family by paid work. Child centres also fulfill an important educational function in teaching children group activities under pedagogic guidance [Rosengren, 1973: 18].

Implicit in this statement is the duality that has plagued attempts everywhere to resolve the problem in child-care provision: on one hand, the needs of parents, especially working parents and/or single parents, and on the other hand, the needs of children, both with regard to and regardless of their family situation. This duality of needs is often seen as a conflict, because above all young children need to be with their parents. The Commission, through its deliberations, developed a conception of the clientele of day care that attempted to recognize differing needs within a common framework.

The first step was to establish that the pressing need for child centers arose primarily because of the increasing number of working mothers. In gathering and presenting the relevant data, the Commission made no moral judgments of the data on working mothers. The Commission simply assumed that working parents provide one area of need/demand for child care—indeed, the major one. The Commission recognized that negligent or negative public policy, that is, a lack of child-care facilities, does not prevent mothers from working, but it does harm the children involved. Furthermore, in recognition of the the equality of the right to work, the Commission began to use the terminology "working parents" or "gainfully employed or student parents."

But working parents are not the only clientele of child centers. The second task for the Commission was to elaborate other needs for child care. For this purpose, the Commission shifted its focus of the clientele from the family to the child. First, it was agreed that children with special learning or social needs require preschool programs. Second, the problem of the general need of all children for enriching preschool experiences was confronted. This was especially important because a focus on the "need" for child centers in terms of the family situation alone creates a selectivity and corresponding inequality of access to the services. The Commission dealt with this issue by formulating a general preschool plan. There are two main features of the plan. The first is an integration of all preschool programs. All children are offered the same basic program regardless of their reasons for attending or of the length of time they attend. The second feature is an expansion of preschool, gradually, to accommodate all those who wish to attend. Compulsory schooling begins quite late in Sweden, at age seven. The plan mandated that all six-year-old children be given a place in part-time preschool, and that if more places became available, and certainly as provision expanded, younger children should be given places too. Thus, the Commission intended to do away with the distinctions between selectivity and universality as well as those between care and education. In the section on design of intervention, we shall see how the latter in particular was accomplished.

In sum, the timing of state intervention in this social area was determined in the first instance by an increase in women's employment; second, by the recommendations of government commissions of inquiry; and third, by specific social needs. Three general kinds of social needs were taken as determining the timing, organization, and extent of state intervention: the needs of all working parents; the needs of children with educational, physical, or social handicaps; and the needs of all preschool children for some enriching experiences outside the home. Market forces were not to have entered the picture at all. The category of working parent was to be conceptualized in terms of the principle of equality in the right to work.

Design of Intervention. To fill the three needs for day care as formulated by the Commission, the state established preschools with programs and features that could accommodate all of the needs at the some time. The key concept guiding this multifaceted achievement has been integration. Each child center offers a holistic system of services (health, educational, and social), together with special features for special needs. The needs of children are met within a developmental program of social learning, pedagogically similar for all, but with necessary variations and additions for those attending full-time. The needs of working parents are met through extended hours of operation, as well as through such special features as having childminders attached to the child centers and available to care for sick children if parents do not wish to take time off work.

The most important aspect of this integration of services concerns the elimination of the distinction between care and education, or between full-time and part-time programs. In the past, Sweden had both day nurseries and nursery schools. The implications and consequences of this division were similar to those in Britain. However, one institutional feature in Sweden made it possible to integrate services and purposes. The education department in Sweden has never been involved in preschool programs, except in a consultative capacity and in teacher training. The Royal Commission on Child Centers decided, accordingly, to make all preschool programs part of family and social policy (Thorsell, 1977). This could be achieved primarily because there is no attempt or desire in Sweden to teach preschool children to read or write. There is general agreement among all concerned that children can wait to learn these skills until they are in school. Nor is there any desire to lower the compulsory school age of seven. Thus, the Commission adopted a philosophy of social learning which stresses child development. It is applicable to all preschool programs. A comparison of part-time and full-time preschool in Sweden, therefore, would not yield the same sorts of differences as between day nurseries and nursery schools in Britain.

The integration of preschool programs and facilities is complemented by the consolidation of staff training and salaries. All preschool programs (full- and part-time) are now headed by preschool teachers, comparably trained and paid. The only status differences in child centers are between teachers and aides. Insofar as staff equality within the preschool has been achieved, criticism has shifted to the scale of pay (and status) that increases by the level taught, which makes university professors the highest-paid teachers. In addition, there is criticism of the continuing shortage of male staff in the preschools, despite efforts to attract more men.

In sum, while almost all of the children in full-time preschool and only some of the children in part-time preschool have working parents, there is no difference in the services offered to these two groups of children. The Royal Commission devised a high-quality, egalitarian day-care system, integrating the needs of working parents and their children into the mainstream of a public program. State intervention in the area of preschool provision was to be as legitimate an activity as public provision of compulsory schooling. Moreover, the Commission fully recognized the needs of working parents, and accepted responsibility on behalf of the public sector to assist working parents.

Plans for expanding provision have been ambitious. To help local authorities build new centers and continue to expand provision of services, the financial contribution of the central government has increased considerably. Still, despite a growth unparalleled in other countries, there are simply not enough places in child centers to meet the need, let alone the demand, for day care, especially among working parents. At present, there is a shortage of about 15,000 places. The gap in Sweden's provision of day care has meant that the Commission's ideals are not being met in practice. Two shortcomings in particular are significant. First, only children whose parents work full-time are now given a place in full-time preschool. However, 60 percent of working mothers with preschool-aged children work only part-time. Their needs are not being met by the preschools. They cannot be accommodated fully by part-time preschools if their children are under 4 and/or if their work schedules do not fit part-time preschool hours. Second, parents who cannot be accommodated at all in the preschools (and this includes some full-time working parents) are assisted in finding a place in a family day home. But the differences between the services received in a family day home and a preschool are enormous, and particularly disadvantage children who are no longer infants.

Compared to the extent to which the need for day care is being met in Britain, accommodation in Sweden is laudable. But compared to what the state has defined the problem to be and what it wants to achieve, the results fall short of intended outcomes. The state in Sweden has taken an upper hand in formulating and organizing quality day-care programs. In principle, the determinants of state intervention are closely connected with the design of intervention—the programs meet the needs of working parents and their children without discriminating on the basis of different kinds of "need" for day care. In practice, full quantitative provision has not been forthcoming, and has created a tighter set of criteria for eligibility than intended. This consequence contradicts Sweden's labor market policy, which is intended to assure freedom of choice in decisions about work, including part- or full-time employment for mothers of young children. Constraints in expansion have hampered the coordination between labor market and day-care policy.

CONCLUSION

BRITAIN AND SWEDEN COMPARED

Among the many meanings of the term "welfare state," there is "a central core of agreement" that it implies "a state commitment of some degree which modifies the play of market forces" in the attempt to achieve a greater measure of social equality (Wedderburn, 1965: 127). The state in Britain intervenes reluctantly in the area of day-care provision. Intervention alleviates the consequences of market forces in particular cases, rather than generally redirecting these forces, and it compensates for inequality rather than achieving greater equality. The same is true of the relationship between state intervention and the forces of tradition. Traditional conceptions of the role of women have far greater impact in shaping government policies for women in Britain than in Sweden. In the balance of relations between state and society in Britain, the state is secondary to more dominant forces in society, which, in this case, are the market and tradition.

The state in Sweden actively seeks to control market forces and to change traditional attitudes about women's roles. Market considerations are certainly not absent from state considerations, but the "fiction of the self-regulating market" has been dispelled (Polanyi, 1944). In Sweden the success of day-care policy, indeed of the position of women in general, stems from the integration of these concerns into the broader policy nexus of national plans for full employment, economic growth, and productivity. There is a greater equilibrium in the balance of state-society relations in Sweden. A social coalition of government, business, and labor reigns (no matter which political party holds office), and decision-making among the tripartite partners is highly consensual. However, as we have seen, despite a blurring of the division between state and society, a fundamental tension continues to create disjunctures. The inability to meet the goals for day care is but one example of a stagnation in the contemporary Swedish welfare state. In an attempt to overcome stagnation, the state is intervening to an ever greater extent (in the case of day care, by assuming from local authorities more of the responsibility for implementing the programs). Thus, any "backlash" in the Swedish welfare state may be due as much to a crisis of legitimacy directly related to the authority of the state as to the heavy burden of financing social programs (Wilensky, 1976).

IMPLICATIONS FOR WOMEN

The implications of this analysis go beyond the immediate and obvious relationship between day-care provision and women's employment. I have shown that state assistance to working women may be shaped by factors other than the entry of women into the labor market. The situation in Britain is a case in point. Women's employment, and particularly the employment of mothers with young children, has increased at an unprecedented rate in Britain. There is a demand for women workers in the labor market; women are filling vacancies in traditional female jobs in clerical, teaching, and nursing positions; they are not, therefore, taking jobs away from men. And yet, policies for women workers, such as day care, are not coordinated with economic policies. Market forces (which lead to poverty and other forms of stratification) and traditional conceptions of the role of women shape policies for women workers. This is particularly evident in day-care policies, as presented here; it is also true of labor market policies, such as for training and employment services, and even of the Sex Discrimination Act (which basically implies that if employers would stop discriminating, women's position would improve). In sum, in Britain the state acts in a derivative capacity, secondary to more dominant social forces. Future policies must recognize these constraints and seek to deal with them directly, in order to go beyond the limited level of success that has been achieved thus far.

The case of Sweden offers an alternative model of state-society relations, within which women's chances are improved. An active state directing social forces, such as we see in Sweden, signifies that a transformation of the liberal paradigm has occurred. The state in Sweden actively encourages the entry of women into the labor market. Women's employment is an integral feature of labor market policy as well as economic policy for full employment and growth. Moreover, in Sweden women are integrated into the category of workers, and workers as a class have gained a central position in policy considerations. These facts are at the base of policies for women. In Sweden progress in women's equality has been achieved through the active role of the state in controlling the inefficient and inegalitarian stratifying forces inherent in a laissez-faire society, including the conception of women as stay-at-home mothers. In these two cases, then, the status of women follows from the prevailing forms of state-society relations.

REFERENCES

BONE, M. (1977) Pre-school Children and the Need for Day Care. London: Her Majesty's Stationery Office.

BOSS, P. (1973) "Day care for the preschool child: policy and practice in England and Wales," in P. Roby (ed.) Child Care—Who Cares? Foreign and Domestic Infant and Early Childhood Development Policies. New York: Basic Books.

BOWLBY, J. (1951) Maternal Care and Mental Health. Geneva: World Health Organization.

COUSSINS, J. (1976) The Equality Report. London: National Council for Civil Liberties.

DAHRENDORF, R. (1968) "Market and plan: two types of rationality," in R. Dahrendorf, Essays in the Theory of Society. Stanford, CA: Stanford University Press.

DARLING, M. (1975) The Role of Women in the Economy. Paris: Organisation for Economic Co-operation and Development.

Great Britain, Ministry of Health (1965) Circular 5/65. (mimeo)

——— (1968) Circular 37/68. (mimeo)

HECLO, H. (1974) Modern Social Politics in Britain and Sweden: From Relief to Income Maintenance. New Haven, CT: Yale University Press.

JACKSON, B. (1975) "Childminding," in Barrie Knight (ed.) Report of the First National Conference on Childminding. Cambridge, England: National Educational Research and Development Trust.

London Borough of Camden (1975) Report of the Working Party on Provision in Camden for Pre-school Children. (mimeo)

MAYALL, B. and P. PETRIE (1977) Minder, Mother and Child. London: University of London Institute of Education.

MUKHERJEE, S. (1972) Making Labour Markets Work: A Comparison of the UK and Swedish Systems. PEP, Broadsheet 532, January, London.

PINKER, R. (1971) Social Theory and Social Policy. London: Heinemann Educational Books.

POLANYI, K. (1944) The Great Transformation. Boston: Beacon.

ROSENGREN, B. (1973) Pre-school in Sweden. Stockholm: The Swedish Institute.

SANDBERG, E. (1975) Equality is the Goal. Stockholm: The Swedish Institute.

SCHMITTER, P. (1974) "Still the century of corporatism?" The Review of Politics 26.

SHONFIELD, A. (1965) Modern Capitalism: The Changing Balance of Public and Private Power. London: Oxford University Press.

THORSELL, S. (1977) "Pre-school in Sweden." Current Sweden 55 (March).

TIZARD, J., P. MOSS and J. PERRY (1976) All Our Children: Pre-school Services in a Changing Society. London: Temple Smith/New Society.

WEDDERBURN, D. (1965) "Facts and theories of the welfare state." The Socialist Register.

WILENSKY, H. (1976) The "New Corporatism," Centralization and the Welfare State. Beverly Hills: Sage Publications.

——— and C. LEBEAUX (1965) Industrial Society and Social Welfare. New York: Free Press.

PART IV

WOMEN AS AGENTS OF SOCIAL CHANGE

9

RURAL WOMEN AND DEVELOPMENT PLANNING IN PERU

SUSAN C. BOURQUE

KAY BARBARA WARREN

The impact of national policy on rural populations can be studied from various viewpoints. One can examine national policy as it reflects the state's development goals and its agenda for controlling local populations. One can study the direct and indirect consequences of the implementation of national policy. And one can focus on rural perceptions of and responses to national initiatives. The analysis of policy is further complicated by the broader social and political context of national programs for directed change; that is, the history of state expansion, the importance of nonelected representatives of national bureaucracies in local affairs, and the longer-term currents of change that have incorporated rural populations into cash economies and transformed rural class structures and modes of production.

This chapter explores development policies in Peru during the twelve-year period of 1968-1980, examining the political climate in which national policy developed, the operation of programs directed toward rural women, and the responses of rural women to national policy. Our principal goal is to document the significance to women of national and local initiatives in the context of changing national policies and local priorities.

Our consideration of development policy deals with a period of significant state expansion into rural affairs accompanied by pendular swings in Peruvian national politics. President Belaúnde Terry's reformist, civilian government, which came to power in 1963, was interrupted in 1968 by the "Peruvian revolution," a military-directed period of political and economic experimentation that included the displacement of traditional landed elites through agrarian reforms, the reorganization of production to establish a mixed national economy, and the restructuring of school systems and local governments. The military argued for a development model that was neither capitalist nor socialist, seeking to forge an independent alternative for countries straining to weaken their economic dependency on the West. By 1975, however, the revolution had foundered economically, politically, and in terms of popular support. The military decided to yield to pressures for a return to civilian rule, and after a constitutional assembly and a national election, Belaúnde Terry was returned to office in 1980.[1]

These political changes have important implications both for development goals and for the organizations mobilized to implement programs. To trace their consequences for rural Peru, our analysis includes data on two national development organizations: *Cooperación Popular*, a general self-help organization reintroduced by the current civilian government, and *ACOMUC*, a private, voluntary group, focusing on women's needs, that is attempting to survive the transition from military to civilian rule.

THE NATIONAL ORGANIZATION OF DEVELOPMENT PROGRAMS: COOPERACION POPULAR

When Fernando Belaúnde Terry won the 1980 presidential elections with a healthy 45 percent of the popular vote in a field of fifteen candidates, the sense of political déjà vu was enormous, particularly as Belaúnde began to reappoint members of his previous government and to reinstitute programs developed during his first administration. Prominent among the resurrected programs is the self-help community development organization called Cooperación Popular. Despite a troubled political history, this organization is well-remembered for a wide range of rural development projects such as the construction of roads, dams, irrigation works, clinics, and schools. Belaúnde has announced that in the new administration Cooperación Popular will have not only his personal attention, but also that of his wife, Violetta Correa. Her participation has been singled out by Belaúnde himself as marking an important difference from his earlier administration.[2]

Violetta Correa's willingness to be associated with Cooperación Popular is not merely a symbolic act by the President's wife to show support for her husband's programs. Correa has demonstrated her intention to pick and choose among the range of roles available to her and to use her decisions to make strong public statements. For instance, she has declined the presidency of the national public assistance and charity board, an honorary position traditionally bestowed on the President's wife. Instead, Correa insisted that a distinguished professional social worker be appointed to the post, pointing out that this woman had spent her life creating programs to deal with the problems of child and infant care. The President's wife emphasized both the significance of these social issues and the fact that there were professionally qualified women to appoint to such a post.[3]

Correa's decision to become involved in Cooperación Popular appears to signal the importance of the organization to development planning for the new government and the active role she intends to play in it. Cooperación Popular is a political instrument of considerable potential. Belaúnde's congressional opposition during the previous regime (the APRA-UNO coalition) recognized the political significance of Cooperación Popular and blocked its funding until they were awarded organizations (the department development boards) which they could use for similar purposes. This time Belaúnde's party controls both the presidency and the congress; hence the political potential of Cooperación Popular is enormously increased.

Cooperación Popular is a good starting point for a consideration of some of the issues surrounding the process of development and its impact on rural women. The challenges that an organization such as Cooperación Popular must meet in order to be effective in local projects demonstrate the tensions, conflicts, and competing interests in rural areas. These difficulties also help us identify the persistent cultural, economic, and political problems that confront Peruvian policy makers as they envision and weigh development options.

The first obstacle confronting development planners and policy makers will be constructing a comprehensive and accurate picture of women's situation: their labor force contributions, child and family responsibilities, and the present constraints on their full social and political participation, such as restricted educational and health services. An accurate assessment of women's roles and needs in each of these areas is critical for viable rural development strategies.

The statistics on rural Peruvian women are sobering. The National Statistical Institute (INE) estimated the rural female population at

2,700,000 in 1978; some 1,869,000 of these women were above 15 years of age. In 1972, 43 percent of the women over 15 were illiterate, and 69 percent of the illiterate women were rural dwellers. Women represent 63 percent of the country's monolingual Quechua or Aymara speakers. Their infant mortality rate reaches 165 per thousand and their life expectancy is 50 years. The average number of children born per rural woman is double that reported for urban women, or 8.5 versus 4.5 (Hernandez, 1980: 5-12). Given this statistical picture, what development policies make sense? To answer that question we need to move beyond the macrostatistics and examine the lives of rural women themselves.

Rural women's labor force participation has been an especially elusive area of study for statisticians, and shortcomings in our understanding of their roles have resulted in inadequate policy. Women's role in agriculture has been severely underestimated in Latin America. In the Andes, work tends to be organized among family units, and women play active roles in most aspects of agricultural production. As Deere (1977) demonstrates, this participation has been underreported in the census due to poorly constructed census questions, the timing of the survey, and the cultural values of the census takers.[4] The cost to women of underestimating their role in agricultural production has been high. Because their roles in economic production have gone unrecognized, development projects have not been designed to include them. For instance, agricultural extension services have been directed to male heads of households, who, consequently, become the primary recipients of new skills, techniques, tools, and any available credit. So too, the Agrarian Reform of 1969 restricted participation in agrarian cooperative structures to heads of families, a status assigned primarily to men; thus these reforms failed to protect the interests of widowed women adequately.

DEVELOPMENT PROGRAMS FOR WOMEN: THE ASSOCIATION FOR COOPERATION WITH THE PEASANT WOMAN (ACOMUC)

Another consequence of underestimating women's roles and responsibilities in agriculture has been that many programs developed for women fail to serve their needs or suffer from serious organizational weaknesses. ACOMUC, the Association for Cooperation with the Peasant Woman, demonstrates both difficulties. Chartered by the military government in 1972, this organization originally consisted of volunteers associated with the Ministry of Agriculture and attached to agrarian reform zones throughout the country. The wives of officials in the Ministry of Agriculture and Agrarian Reform volunteered to work in their husbands' zones, securing from the ministry access to available social workers, extension agents, cars, and gasoline. The first ACOMUC programs emphasized artisan activity for the international tourist trade, women's cooking repertoire, and sewing skills. In practice, such programs were accessible only to upper-strata families of the peasantry. Poor peasant women were unable to participate because their agricultural responsibilities demand heavy time commitments for work in the fields and the care of family livestock. In contrast, women from wealthier peasant families were able to attend because their participation in agriculture focuses on the preparation of meals for wage laborers and they have more discretionary time available for new activities. Moreover, the skills taught in ACOMUC programs could be developed, by women with access to capital and sufficient time, into supplementary income-generating work.

In 1977, ACOMUC was reorganized under the leadership of a Quechua-speaking sociologist and received international financial assistance from U.S. A.I.D. The program took a new direction by providing focused training for 130 ACOMUC volunteers, and the ACOMUC staff developed pilot outreach courses with the potential of reaching approximately 2,700 peasant women for training. The project is located in an area containing 18,000 peasant families and 10,000 women in the economically active workforce.

A closer examination of an ACOMUC program in the sierra shows how this organization responds to peasant women's needs. In one project in the late 1970s, a group of thirty peasant women, accompanied by infant children, were brought together for a ten-day ACOMUC-sponsored workshop. They participated in minicourses designed to help peasant women with their multiple roles as mothers, agricultural workers, and income producers for the family. After sessions on such topics as food and nutrition, craft production, animal husbandry, and health, the women were asked which subjects would be most useful for future programs in rural communities. The peasant women overwhelmingly selected women's health as a critical issue for their lives. Significantly, the sessions on health had included information on human physiology and birth control methods. At the end of this workshop, the participants returned to their home communities to organize women's committees for a new round of classes that were to be offered locally over the course of several months.

There has been some resistance to the ACOMUC program from peasant men. In one instance women returned from a workshop and began to protest women's lower daily wages and their exclusion from decision-making in a local cooperative organization. The women were denounced and the ACOMUC program identified as a source of outside agitation by local men. The ACOMUC staff had expected some resistance and had prepared itself to help the women weather the outbursts from critics. The present ACOMUC leadership harbors few romantic illusions about either material conditions or relationships between men and women in the rural sector. The organization is mindful of the need to develop strategies which effectively address the problems of women's subordination and yet do not pit one segment of the peasantry against another.

The present leadership of ACOMUC perceives two major restrictions on the impact of their development program. First, there is a tendency to see the organization and its program in the light of the initial leadership, as untrained wives of government officials with little appreciation of the reality of peasant women's lives and needs. The present leadership feels they have dramatically reoriented the organization so that it is accurately attuned to rural realities and allows peasant women the opportunity to define priorities for themselves.[5]

In addition to ACOMUC's problems with its image, the organization still suffers from its dependence on the vagaries of Peruvian politics. While ACOMUC is legally recognized and registered as a private, nonprofit, and nonpolitical organization, its first president was the wife of an army general who served as the Minister of Agriculture. Through formal agreements with the Ministry of Agriculture, ACOMUC received technical and logistical support and recruited its workers (in addition to the volunteer wives of military officers and Ministry of Agriculture bureaucrats) from among the technical employees assigned to the agrarian reform zones. Thus, ACOMUC has been dependent on the Ministry of Agriculture for most of its personnel and equipment. The Ministry, for its part, has been happy with ACOMUC's efforts, since it otherwise dedicates little energy to women's programs.

Despite a continued positive response from the Ministry of Agriculture, ACOMUC's fate under the new Belaúnde administration is problematic. Since ACOMUC is strongly identified with the previous military government, it suffers all the negative evaluations presently directed at that government. ACOMUC leaders are hopeful that there will be a place for them in future reorganizations of the Ministry of Agriculture and the Agrarian Reform. For their part they are willing to work with any state agency, including Belaúnde's Cooperación Popular. However, the willingness of the Belaúnde administration to continue a program identified with the previous regime is uncertain. The ACOMUC leadership has hopes of taking their case directly to Violetta Correa.

While the organizational challenges facing ACOMUC are serious indeed, the staff reports that rural women have responded very positively to their programs. They find that peasant women are open to the courses and anxious to learn. This enthusiasm runs contrary to prevailing assumptions that rural women are closed toward outsiders and conservative, if not resistant, to efforts directed at social change. The reaction of rural women to the ACOMUC program suggests that previous assumptions about women's attitudes toward change may have ignored rural women's assessments of the meaning of development programs for their own lives. There is now ample evidence that women resist changes that they perceive (correctly or incorrectly) will undermine their own sources of independence or their control over vital resources (Babb, 1976; Bourque and Warren, 1981; Nash, 1976; Rubbo, 1975). Certainly those development programs that identify men as the recipients of benefits at the expense of women are likely to be viewed with some suspicion by rural women. The complexity of women's assessments of such programs is evident when we move from a consideration of national-level policies to an examination of rural women's efforts to set their own development priorities and solve their development problems.

RURAL WOMEN'S PERCEPTIONS AND ACTIVISM IN LOCAL PROJECTS: THE COMITE FEMININO IN CHIUCHIN

What social forces shape rural women's perceptions of development alternatives and their activism in local projects? To answer this question, we turn to a case study of one central Andean community, the town of Chiuchin, located at 8000 feet on the western slopes of the Andes in the department of Lima. Chiuchin is a small trade and tourist center of 250 inhabitants serving as a regional focus for entrepreneurial activities, postprimary education, and rural outposts of national bureaucracies for two districts of highland communities. Economically and socially, the town is an important way station between subsistence-oriented peasant communities and the urbanized coast, which lies a day's travel away by bus or truck. In the mid-1970s a cross-section of local women talked among themselves about organizing a women's committee—a *comité feminino*—to work for their agenda of development projects. In their perceptions of development alternatives, these women were caught up in a complicated calculus of (1) their own development goals, (2) the realization that the male-centered power structures of the town favored increasing ties to urban, coastal resources as a primary development strategy, and (3) the limited implementation of national development programs in rural regions.

Chiuchin women outlined a distinct set of female development priorities; at the same time they affirmed a range of goals shared by the town as a whole. In informal meetings at a general store, they singled out electricity, a sewage system, and a paved plaza among other priorities and discussed which women might be counted on to press women's priorities at town meetings. The women had become frustrated with their men's laggardly pace in addressing the questions to which women attached the greatest importance. It was evident that the men did not share their particular priorities and appeared resistant to women's attempts to organize around such issues. Even though some of the women were especially noted for commercial success and independence, they were reluctant to press their own cases, on one hand, because they anticipated male ridicule and resistance and, on the other hand, because they were concerned about the potential fallout that confrontations might produce for their businesses.

During the 1970s, the development projects selected at the town level were largely those aimed at building networks to the urban coast to increase contacts with key officials and to open opportunities for migrating family members. These kin become key network members in new urban ecological niches. In Chiuchin, new school buildings, soccer fields (where male migrants and townsmen celebrate their common background in sports competitions), and government programs for the distribution of scarce commodities became the focus of community energy. Each project was conceived as directly or indirectly facilitating strategic migration or strengthening political connections between local businessmen and coastal officials. Other projects that more directly involved women's work—because they would facilitate child care or improve working conditions while women completed their double day of business and domestic work in the evenings—were given short shrift in town decisions about the allocation of scarce resources for local development.[6]

The maintenance of distinctive female priorities and their compromise—which was a very conscious, situational choice—make sense when one realizes that these women have decided to stay in the countryside and resist the pull of migration at the same time that they carefully prepare their children to become successful migrants. Rural women often express distaste for the cash basis of life in urban centers and stress the relative security of agricultural production. Underlying these attitudes is the fact that women migrants lose central economic roles and important sources of control in the household when they migrate. In most rural communities, women administer family storage, allocate staples throughout the year, and are able gradually to accumulate capital in the form of livestock. In cities they lose all of these sources of income and independence.

However, women also understand that rural-urban interactions and network-building are critical cross-class strategies for increasing access to scarce resources and coping with rural economic uncertainties. Women are very aware of the potential of networks of extended kin to broaden access to resources outside their immediate environment. In fact, women maintain their own rural trading networks between Chiuchin and the outlying agrarian communities for the exchange of labor, agricultural produce, commercial goods, access to education for their children, and mutual support. These cross-class networks have given women an important alternative to relying unilaterally on town power structures to meet their development needs. Women know that new rural-coastal forms of networking will be crucial to the educational and employment options for their children, many of whom will be forced for economic reasons to migrate to coastal cities.

Women's analysis of the costs and benefits of political mobilization around their own priorities has not been a static one. After pouring their individual energies into the town's development projects through much of the 1970s, the women decided in 1979 to organize as a comité feminino. The women then sponsored raffles and other money-making activities centered on the participation and vacation mood of the visiting Peruvian tourists. They made enough money during the first season to buy the plumbing for a public toilet, an important change, since no homes in Chiuchin have toilets or sewage. They also encountered the male resistance they had feared. Three men in particular were quite outspoken about women's interference in town affairs. However, the women carried the day when a young man, now a Lima university student, whose mother was a member of the women's committee, defended the women and insisted that they be allowed to continue with their organization and take part in community discussions. It seems particularly appropriate that a son, who benefited from women's awareness of the importance of rural-urban networks for education, would be the defender of the women's committee.[7]

But even after male resistance abated, the women encountered another difficult obstacle: their own limited time. Much of the women's business activity is geared to the national tourist trade; their boarding houses, shops, and restaurants are busiest during the tourist season and the demands on their management of commercial, agricultural, and domestic responsibilities are great. Taking on added public activities at the busiest point in their own economic cycle proved an extraordinary strain.

MIGRATION AS AN OPTION FOR RURAL WOMEN

The creation of rural-urban linkages has become an increasingly important development strategy for rural men and women as a result of high rates of migration to the urbanized coast since the 1960s. In addition to being part of the strategic choices that rural citizens must make, migration also poses critical problems for political leaders at the national level, since central government policy toward the rural areas affects the choices that citizens make about migration. This is true not only in the obvious issues surrounding agrarian reform, but also in choices central governments make about the expansion and improvement of the educational system and the provision of social services in the countryside. The presence or absence of such facilities as well as their perceived quality influence rural migration decisions. To date Peruvian governments have not been successful in checking or even slowing rural-urban migration.

Migration in Peru has been dramatic and is physically evidenced in the growth of squatter settlements ringing Lima. In the 1940s squatter settlements represented less than 1 percent of Lima's population. By 1972 this figure had become 25 percent and by the 1980s approached one-third of the urban population (Collier, 1976).

While both men and women migrate, the experiences for each in the city are different. In Peru men migrate more frequently than women and are more likely to move without children and families. Like men, women find their first jobs through kin networks, but women have a narrower range of occupations available to them. Chaney (1977) reports that in Peru both male and female migrants aspire to factory jobs. Despite long hours and difficult working conditions, factory jobs offer social security benefits, sick pay, and paid vacations. The manufacturing sector of the Peruvian economy, however, is unable to absorb all the workers seeking employment, and female migrants are less likely than male migrants to be hired for such jobs. Over time both the number and the percentage of women employed in manufacturing have declined. In 1940 women represented 56 percent of the economically active population in manufacturing; by 1961 this figure had dropped to 28 percent, and by 1972 to 25 percent.[8] This drop in female employment in manufacturing occurred simultaneously with increased female migration to cities. Chaney points out that as a consequence of this shift in sex patterns in manufacturing, not only are women forced out of the industrial labor force, but they are also pushed into the least attractive jobs in the service sector. In countries like Peru where the absorptive capacity of industrial manufacturing is limited, men who cannot find work in this limited sector tend to secure the better-paying jobs in the service sector. This dynamic in the sexual division of work drives women "into the lower echelons of the tertiary section, and specifically into domestic service" (Chaney, 1977: 41).

Women seldom move out of the service sector: Those who start as domestic servants—the most common occupation—will remain domestic servants. Upward mobility out of this sector is rare.[9] If a woman becomes pregnant and loses her position as a domestic servant she will most probably move laterally into the ranks of the street vendors. Women are estimated to constitute 62 percent of Lima's 75,000 street vendors (Centro de Información, Estudios y Documentación [CIED], 1980). The number of women engaged in this activity is graphically apparent in the crowded streets of Lima and is regularly decried in the Lima press. Street vending allows women to keep their young children with them, takes very little capital to set oneself up in business, and requires the skills and expertise that women bring with them from the rural areas. This is a precarious living at best, and one particularly subject to arbitrary government intervention. For instance, just prior to Belaúnde's inauguration the government carried out a major campaign to rid the center city of the street vendors so that Lima would look its best for the international visitors attending the inauguration.

As the above discussion suggests, the process of migration can leave a woman doubly disadvantaged. Women have limited earning power in the urban, coastal economy where, moreover, they lose the degree of independence and control that they may have previously exercised in the rural area through their vital participation in agriculture and stock-raising. Furthermore, women's restricted access to cash is less apparent in the rural areas because the overall economy is not as heavily monetized and alternative forms of exchange exist. Consequently the balance between rural development and the options available in the urban area is complex for those who find themselves disadvantaged in terms of health and educational services in the rural sector, but with limited options in the urban cash economy (Bourque and Warren, 1981). Rural women's strategies to date in towns like Chiuchin have been to forge ties to the urban areas, sending off their children to be educated, but maintaining their own links to subsistence farming through the maintenance of family land in the sierra.

CONCLUSIONS

Returning to the initial questions we posed about the impact of national-level policy on rural women's development strategies, we ask how the new administration is likely to affect women's lives. Belaúnde has indicated that the new Cooperación Popular will have an urban as well as a rural focus, reflecting the demographic shift that has occurred in the twelve years between his administrations. Whether this means that rural self-help development projects will become secondary to the new urban focus is an important question. In addition to the issue of the regional allocation of funds, the central fact remains that Cooperación Popular is an instrument that Belaúnde will use to broaden his popular support. Consequently, Cooperación Popular is bound to be an intensely political organization used in national power contests.[10]

Cooperación Popular will be located at the heart of ongoing controversies and conflicts in a realm where women, both historically and in the present day, play extremely limited roles (Chaney, 1980). In the elections for the 1978 constituent assembly, of a total of 1,200 candidates, 95 were women. Of the 1,124,281 votes cast in Lima, only 14,233 were cast for female candidates, and only 2 female representatives were actually elected. There are now 12 women in the National Chamber of Deputies (similar to the U.S. House of Representatives), 6 from Belaúnde's Acción Popular, as well as 2 female Senators (one from Acción Popular). Women represent a very small proportion of the unionized workers in Peru. Even in the primary and secondary schoolteachers' union, where women constitute approximately half the membership and have been active participants in protests and strikes, only one woman sits on the national executive committee (Hernandez, 1980).

Thus, while Violetta Correa's presence in the new Belaúnde team holds out some hope for attention to development strategies that would deal with women, her impact will be circumscribed by the overwhelming male dominance of the political system.

Whether dealing with women involved in traditional agricultural activities or with women in commercial enterprises, Peru's development policy must recognize that women have complex analyses of local development priorities as well as substantial economic responsibilities critical for the functioning of their families. The balance they strike among their responsibilities is often fragile; hence a new baby or the loss of a mother's or sister's assistance may overtax their survival strategies and make it virtually impossible to take on additional tasks. At the heart of understanding rural women's development perceptions, activism, and needs is the comprehension of the range of their economic roles and the critical nature of their contributions for the survival of the family unit.

Policy makers must identify the most appropriate unit to use in development planning for rural women. They must be attuned to the different priorities of men, women, children, families, communities, transcommunity rural networks, and rural-urban networks. Policy makers will need to know where the interests of one of these social units conflict with those of another, which unit is the proper focus for a given program, and what will be the consequences of a decision not to incorporate certain units in the definition and implementation of projects.

Related to this issue is the question of how high a priority the new government will give to problems that particularly affect rural women. Expanding women's participation in local development and national social life depends on the willingness of government policy makers to attack illiteracy, to provide the option of determining the size of families, and to integrate women in the cash economy and national economic life.

Belaúnde's Cooperación Popular is predicated on the notion of self-help: Communities provide the labor for public works projects and the government provides the technical expertise and heavy materials. In conception, it assumes a more grass-roots, eclectic orientation, rather than the top-down, centrally planned policy of the previous military government. As suggested throughout this chapter, such an approach will elicit different, and at times conflicting, responses from various groups in the rural sector. Whether this self-help philosophy will imply new possibilities for participation—particularly for groups that managed to become organized for the first time under the military government, such as ACOMUC or the comité feminino[11]—or will become the justification for the "benign" neglect of rural women and their development issues, remains to be seen.

NOTES

1. For detailed discussions and evaluations of the "Peruvian Experiment," see Lowenthal (1975) and Palmer (1980).

2. Belaúnde made this quite explicit during the swearing-in of his cabinet the evening of his inauguration by remarking, "You remember my last democratic government. This new government will have a difference: we are, Violette and I, a team at the service of the people" (El Comercio, July 20, 1980: 12).

3. Such appointments are common in Latin America. They function to demonstrate that public charity and assistance are properly the care of women yet identified with the largesse of the chief of state.

4. For further discussion of the problems inherent in census data, see the "General Report on the Seminar Women in the Labor Force in Latin America," prepared by the Instituto Universitario de Pesquisas do Rio de Janeiro (1980). See Deere and León de Leal (forthcoming) for a full analysis of the variations in rural women's labor force participation.

5. The ACOMUC data are based on interviews conducted with ACOMUC's leadership in the summer of 1980 and reports made available through the office of U.S. A.I.D./Lima. The data from Chiuchin are based on fieldwork reported more fully in Bourque and Warren (1981), and data collected by Bourque in 1980.

6. See Bourque and Warren (1981) for a fuller discussion of local-development decision-making.

7. This is not meant to suggest that education and coastal experience invariably result in more open, egalitarian responses from men. Mestizo norms and the experience of women in the squatter settlements suggest that women find severe limitations on their community political participation in urban settings. For further information on women in squatter settlements, see CIED (1980).

8. Data are adapted from the Peruvian National Census and reported in Villalobos (n.d.).

9. See Smith (1973) and Chaney (1977) for further discussion of the issue of mobility and the conditions of domestic servants.

10. The attempt to garner popular political support by sponsoring public works projects is not unique. The military made such an effort through the creation of SINAMOS in the early 1970s.

11. The military cannot claim responsibility for the organization of the comité feminino. The roots of that organization go back to the first Belaúnde government. However, the climate of participatory rhetoric that the military government fostered until 1975 and the opening up of the political process to competing groups after 1977 may have influenced the fledgling efforts of the Chiuchin women.

REFERENCES

BABB, F. (1976) "The development of sexual inequality in Vicos, Pero." Special Studies Series No. 83, Council on International Studies, State University of New York at Buffalo.

BOURQUE, S. and K. WARREN (1981) Women of the Andes. Ann Arbor: University of Michigan Press.

Centro de Información, Estudios y Documentación [CIED] (1980) Presencia de la Mujer en las barriadas. Lima, Peru: Author.

CHANEY, E. (1977) "Agripina: domestic service and its implications for development." Presented at the First Mexican-Central American Symposium on Research on Women, Mexico, D.F., November 7-10.

——— (1980) Supermadre: Women in Politics in Latin America. Austin: University of Texas Press.

COLLIER, D. (1976) Squatters and Oligarchs: Authoritarian Rule and Policy Change in Peru. Baltimore: Johns Hopkins University Press.

DEERE, C. (1977) "The agricultural division of labor by sex: myths, facts and contradictions in the northern Peruvian sierra." Presented at the Joint Meeting of the Latin American Studies Association and the African Studies Association, Houston, Texas, November 2-5.

DEERE, C. and M. LEON DE LEAL (forthcoming) Women in Agriculture: Peasant Production and Proletarianization in Three Andean Regions. Washington: ILO.

HERNANDEZ, F. (1980) "El problema de la mujer." Mujer y Sociedad 1, 1: 5-12.

Instituto Universitario de Pesquisas do Rio de Janeiro [IUPERJ] (1980) "General Report on the seminar Women in the Labor Force in Latin America." Rio de Janeiro: Author.

LOWENTHAL, A. [ed.] (1975) The Peruvian Experiment. Princeton, NJ: Princeton University Press.

NASH, J. (1976) "A critique of social science roles in Latin America," pp. 1-21 of J. Nash and H. Safa (eds.) Sex and Class in Latin America. New York: Praeger.

PALMER, D. S. (1980) Peru: The Authoritarian Tradition. New York: Praeger.

RUBBO, A. (1975) "The spread of capitalism in rural Colombia: effects on poor women," pp. 333-357 in R. Reiter (ed.) Toward an Anthropology of Women. New York: Monthly Review Press.

SMITH, M. (1973) "Domestic service as a channel of upward mobility for the lower-class woman: the Lima case," pp. 191-208 in A. Pescatello (ed.) Female and Male in Latin America. Pittsburgh: University of Pittsburgh Press.

VILLALOBOS, G. (n.d.) "La madre trabajadora: el caso de las obreras industriales." Centro de Estudios de Población y Desarollo, C.E.P.D. Series C, No. 1, Lima, Peru.

WOY, S. (1978) "Infrastructure and participation in Peru: SINAMOS," pp. 189-208 in J. Booth and M. Seligson, Political Participation in Latin America, Vol.1: Citizen and State. New York: Holmes & Meier.

10

WOMEN'S ORGANIZATIONS AND SOCIAL CHANGE

The Age-of-Marriage Issue In India

BARBARA N. RAMUSACK

The minimum legal age at marriage for women in India has been the focus of controversy and legislation for over a century. In a recent article, Geraldine Forbes (1979) has outlined the evolution of this issue and has ably argued that efforts to raise the age at marriage through legislation have implied a symbolic commitment to modernity but not necessarily to improving the status of women in India. Although some might contend that too much has already been written on this topic, this earlier propaganda and research provide a valuable foundation for an investigation of different questions about the relationships among groups and individuals seeking amelioration in the social status and legal rights of women. More important, it

AUTHOR'S NOTE: I wish to acknowledge with gratitude the support provided by an American Institute of Indian Studies Senior Research Fellowship and a grant from the Taft Fund of the University of Cincinnati for research in India in 1976-1977, and by a Summer Stipend from the National Endowment for the Humanities for research in England in 1979. I am also most indebted to Geraldine Forbes for her generosity in sharing her research materials with me.

supplies data for an analysis of what occurs after a legal right is established and of the ability of women to exercise the newly guaranteed right.

This essay will concentrate on the passage of the Child Marriage Restraint Act of 1929 and on the efforts to promote its effective implementation. It will consider the problems that arise in a campaign to improve the social and physical conditions for women through legislative change in a colonial environment. They include (1) the most productive sequence of activities in promoting social reforms—education of public opinion, legislation to provide a legal framework, associations formed to initiate and support change, and alternate social institutions for those willing to change; (2) the manner in which definition of goals influences the content and effectiveness of legislative remedies; (3) the delegation of responsibility for implementation of laws regulating private spheres of life; (4) the role of women's organizations; (5) the use of external allies such as male social reformers and international organizations, especially feminist ones; and (6) the impact of nationalism and imperialism in a colonial setting on the struggle for women's rights.

LEGISLATIVE REFORM

In the early decades of the nineteenth century, some British administrators and missionaries and a few Indian male social reformers cooperated to improve the social and legal status of Indian women. They were most appalled by customs that affected the lives of women most directly and so secured legal sanctions prohibiting infanticide, which was primarily practiced on female babies, and *sati,* the sacrificial death of a Hindu widow on her husband's funeral pyre. Their campaign to ameliorate the condition of women who survived such practices proceeded more slowly and focused on the education of women and the advocacy of widow remarriage. Closely linked to these issues was the custom of child marriage, which precluded much education and produced substantial numbers of Hindu child widows but not child widowers, since men were allowed to remarry. In 1850 Pandit Isvara Chandra Vidyasagar, most noted as a proponent of legislation permitting widow remarriage among Hindus, was one of the first to write about the evils of early marriage and to urge his associates to combat this custom by personal example. He wanted them to pledge not to marry daughters before 11 and sons before 18, to educate daughters, and to remarry widowed daughters (Bose, 1960: 141-142). Vidyasagar was able to obtain the Hindu Widow Remarriage Act of 1856, but his idealistic effort to end early marriage produced little impact.

The revolt of some Indian soldiers and civilians in 1857 moderated the pace of social reform sponsored by British administrators. It was not until the 1880s that the debate over child marriage was revived, through Behramji M. Malabari, a social reformer from the minority community of Parsis, in the Bombay area. In 1884 Malabari published a series of *Notes* which called for attacking the problem through government policies and propaganda. Universities were to prohibit married students from taking examinations, the government was to give preference to hiring unmarried men, and education departments were to insert material in textbooks describing the ill effects of child marriage. Malabari's great skill was as a propagandist; he combined graphic personal accounts with statistics from the Census of 1881 to highlight the deleterious impact of child marriages on young girls and their children (Heimsath, 1964: 148-153). There were over two hundred responses to his *Notes* but no consensus on a solution. After a negative response from the British Government of India, Malabari shifted his campaign to England, where his lobbying efforts were reinforced by a series of articles in *The Times* describing the mental and physical consequences of the early consummation of marriage (The Times [London], 1886-1890). British feminists added their support through the National Indian Association in Aid of Social Progress and Female Education, founded by Mary Carpenter in 1871, and through journal articles. Millicent Garrett Fawcett, the leader of moderate suffragettes, argued for legislative remedy, claiming "our law, and the strictness and certainty with which it is carried out, help to form or reform the conscience of the native populations on these matters" (Fawcett, 1890: 718). Malabari's crusade, pressure from prominent factions and individuals in London, and the support of Indian male social reformers combined to influence the British colonial administration to amend the Indian Penal Code in 1891, changing the minimum age of consent for sexual intercourse from 10 to 12.

Meanwhile, social reform proved to be a divisive issue among Indian nationalist leaders. Liberal moderates such as M. G. Ranade supported this legislation as restoring ancient customs and permitting the education of women, but others, such as B. G. Tilak, protested against this governmental interference in such a private sphere of social relations. Tilak argued for the primacy of political reform over social change and claimed that social change would take generations of struggle and would be more effectively implemented when India was independent. Tilak also realized that there was more popular support for the orthodox Hindu position, that females should marry before puberty, and he was anxious to build a political base on this widespread opposition (Cashman, 1975: 47-63).

Although the age-of-consent debate appeared to link nationalist politics with social reaction, the actual legal measure was still a compromise. It set no minimum age of marriage but rather sought to eliminate the most harsh physical consequences of early marriage by prohibiting consummation before the age of 12. Even so, this legal protection was of limited value, since it did not address the problem of enforcement. Who was to bring action against the guilty party? The young girl who was forced into premature sexual intercourse had no advocates among relatives or friends to plead her case and few means to repair the physical or mental consequences of the illegal act. A highly defective legal sanction had been accepted by British and Indian social reformers as better than no change at all.

The inadequacy of the 1891 legal action had long been apparent, but concern about it became prominent only in the 1910s and 1920s. Annie Besant, the British theosophist, feminist, and supporter of Indian nationalism, attacked child marriage as producing lowered vitality, pervasive nervous diseases, and premature old age, and proclaimed the voice of God in Nature as the basis for a change in Hindu marriage customs. She, like Malabari, buttressed her argument with figures from the Census of 1911 and by appeals to the selfishness of men who were ruining themselves and their sons by contracting early marriages (Besant, 1913: 49-76). World War I prompted concern about the physical conditions of recruits and reinforced Besant's plea to men to end child marriage, at the very least because of its physical consequences for the sons of extremely young mothers.

In 1921 the League of Nations held a conference on the traffic in women and girls for immoral purposes. The conference recommended the increase of the minimum age of consent for single women to 21 in order to limit this traffic. An Indian representative to the League urged that 21 be changed to 16 and apply within marriage (Gupta, 1925). Meanwhile, the Indian Councils Act of 1919 had enlarged the franchise among Indian males and had significantly increased Indian representation in provincial and central legislatures. The colonial administration declined to sponsor any legislation on the age of marriage, but now several Indian social reformers had been elected to the Central Legislative Assembly, and they could take the initiative. Several private bills were introduced, but all were routinely defeated. In 1927 Hari Singh Gour proposed a bill raising the age of consent to 14 within marriage and 16 outside marriage. The Indian government appointed a select committee on this bill, and shortly thereafter Rai

Sahib Harbilas Sarda introduced a Hindu Child Marriage Bill, which sought to impose minimum ages at marriage.

On 25 June 1928 the Indian government appointed an Age-of-Consent Committee chaired by Sir Morapant V. Joshi, a Brahman lawyer from Berar and former Home Member in the Central Provinces. The only women on the committee were Mrs. M. O'Brien Beadon, a British physician, and Rameshwari Nehru,the wife of Brij Lal Nehru. Accompanied by nine volumes of evidence, the Age-of-Consent Committee report advised that 42 percent of the Indian female population married before 15, and that most evidence indicated that consummation occurred with little regard for the physical age or maturity of the female. The report recommended a comprehensive approach, with 15 as the minimum age at marriage and 21 as the age of consent and compulsory registration of births and marriages (Indian Government, Central Publication Branch, 1929a: 95-97).

Once again the actual legislation represented a significant compromise. Sarda's earlier bill was extended to all communities and was passed on 1 October 1929, with the support of the votes controlled by the colonial administration, as the Child Marriage Restraint Act. It set 14 as the minimum age at marriage for females and 18 for males, did not mention the age of consent, did not mandate the registration of births and marriages, and provided a cumbersome procedure for complaints, which was designed to prevent false accusations. Furthermore, there was to be a six-month delay before the act came into effect on 1 April 1930.

THE LOBBYING NETWORK

Before considering the implementation of this act, it is necessary to examine in greater depth the coalition of groups and individuals who lobbied for and influenced the shape of this legislation. First, there were the Indian male legislators who confronted government reluctance and active opposition from orthodox Hindus and Muslims, socially conservative Indian legislators, and ambitious political leaders. The reformers were frequently Brahmans and from areas that were not the leading centers of nationalist political activity: Gour was from Central Provinces, as was Joshi, and Sarda was from Ajmer-Merwara, the British enclave in the Rajputana area of princely states. They were responding partly to stimuli from outside India and partly because of their desire to eliminate social evils, which they perceived as preventing female education and reducing the strength of the Indian struggle for freedom. Some Indian leaders outside legislative politics supported their general goals. Most notable was Mahatma Gandhi. In the pages of *Young India* (26 August 1926) Gandhi argued that legislation "may be good for bringing a minority to book" but that only enlightened public opinion could cure a popular evil. He was not against legislation but wanted greater attention to the cultivation of positive popular support. Gandhi (1935) would later state that the campaign against child marriage was "preeminently women's work."

During the contest over the Age-of-Consent Bill in the 1880s, the only female voices of support were those of British women physicians, missionaries, and feminists. This controversy, however, stimulated the development of local women's associations in the Bombay province, where the debate stimulated by Tilak was most heated (Everett, 1979: 60-61). By the 1920s there would be three all-India or interregional women's associations that endorsed raising the age of marriage as one of their main objectives. The earliest was the Women's Indian Association (WIA), organized in Madras in 1917 by two British theosophists, Dorothy Jinarajadasa and Margaret Cousins, with Annie Besant as its president. The WIA called for reform in its journal, *Stri Dharma,* and at its meetings (Everett, 1979: 72, 147).

The next advocate was the National Council of Women in India (NCWI), founded in 1925 as a coordinating body for five provincial councils in Bombay, Bengal, Bihar and Orissa, Burma, and Delhi. The NCWI was based in Bombay and was affiliated with the International Council of Women. In her presidential addresses Maharani Chimnabai Gaekwar of Baroda emphasized the need to campaign for an increase in the age of marriage and consent until there was a revolution in social practices (NCWI, Biennial Report, 1927: 13). In 1929 she viewed the Sarda Act not as a victory but as an opportunity to permit better education for women and greater equality within wedlock (NCWI, Report of 1928-1929: 20). On the provincial level, however, there was less support for the Sarda Act among NCWI members. Dhanvanthi Rama Rau, a former college teacher, Kashmiri Brahman wife of an Indian member of the Indian Civil Service, and later champion of birth control, recorded a discouraging experience. During the legislative session in 1927 when Sarda introduced his bill, she tried to enlist the active support of the NCWI in Simla, the summer capital of the Indian government. Rama Rau was dismayed when the wife of one senior British official argued that she and other British could not support such a bill, since "the Queen's Proclamation, issued when India became part of the British Empire [1858], stipulated that there should be no interference with the religious rites and practices of the people of the country under British rule" (Rama Rau, 1977: 153).

The third champion was the All-India Women's Conference (AIWC), which was initially called together in 1927 by Margaret Cousins to formulate more appropriate educational programs for women, but quickly expanded into a permanent association addressing social as well as educational goals. The AIWC leadership included elements of the NCWI, since the Maharani of Baroda was also its first president, and of the WIA, since Jinarajadasa and Besant, as well as Cousins, were active. The AIWC soon emerged as the largest and most comprehensive women's organization in India and as the most active feminist proponent for legislative reform of the age of marriage, since it identified early marriage and *purdah,* the seclusion of women, as the major constraints on the education of women. Like their male allies the AIWC ably performed lobbying tasks that focused on the colonial administration and the Indian and British legislators. They formed a standing committee on the issue; sent deputations to the Viceroy, Lord Irwin, and to the Age-of-Consent Committee; attended debates in the Central Legislative Assembly; and met individually with key legislators (Cousins and Cousins, 1950: 449, 459; Forbes, 1979: 414). It is difficult to assess the impact of their efforts or those of the WIA and the NCWI, but they clearly demonstrate the symbolic importance of this issue to Indian women's associations and their growing ability to utilize the techniques of interest-group politics.

External concern about the age of marriage and consent was not confined to the League of Nations conference on traffic in women and children. The most dramatic foreign intervention was the publication of *Mother India* by Katherine Mayo, an American journalist who had already produced books on the Pennsylvania state police and the Philippines. Mayo (1927: 20-21) claimed that it was dissatisfaction with the lack of knowledge about India on the part of the average American that had sent her "to India, to see what a volunteer, unsubsidized, uncommitted, and unattached, could observe of common things in daily human life. Leaving untouched the realms of religion, of politics, and of the arts," Mayo would confine her inquiry "to such workaday ground as public health and its contributing factors." She began her attack on the age-of-marriage issue in an early chapter entitled "Early to Marry, Early to Die," but the negative effects of this custom are an undercurrent throughout her book. That this volume was surely one of the best sellers of 1927-1928 in the Anglo-American world is attested to by its repeated printings (nine between July 1927 and August 1928) and the numerous copies available in used bookstores (ten in one shop alone during 1980 in Cincinnati, Ohio). Mayo was considered shocking by her contemporaries because she explicitly discussed sexual relations between husbands and wives at a time when they were only beginning to be discussed with candor in print in Anglo-American culture and were hardly mentioned in India (Corbett-Ashby, 1978). Indian political leaders and British sympathizers attacked Mayo for her negative analysis of the Indian capacity for self-government, and some charged that her work was encouraged by the colonial administration, which was in the process of reviewing the constitutional progress of India under the 1919 Indian Councils Act (Jha, 1971). Many reviewers in Britain thought that Mayo's factual material appeared accurate but that she looked only at the negative or shocking aspects of Indian culture.

Mayo's book had a profound impact on Eleanor Rathbone, an English feminist who read it during her summer holiday in 1927. Rathbone had succeeded Millicent Garrett Fawcett in 1918 as president of the National Union of Societies for Equal Citizenship (NUSEC), the successor to the moderate faction of the suffragette movement in Great Britain. Since the franchise had been won, Rathbone had been working for the "new feminism." She argued that women should not concentrate solely on removing the remaining inequalities between men and women but that women should "demand what we want for women, not because it is what men have got but because it is what women need to fulfill the potentialities of their own natures and to adjust themselves to the circumstances of their own lives" (Stocks, 1949: 116-117). In the domestic arena, Rathbone sought organizational support from NUSEC for her proposal for family allowances paid in cash directly to mothers. This scheme sought to improve the economic position of women and the quality of care for children, but not to change dramatically the role of women in society (Lewis, 1975: 9-11; 1980: 169-172). Rathbone also tried to increase British feminist interest and participation in international feminist groups and issues.

In October 1927 Rathbone called a conference at which 35 organizations were represented to discuss the problems described in Mayo's exposé. Lord Lytton, the brother of Constance Lytton, the radical feminist, himself a former governor of Bengal, moved for a resolution emphasizing the responsibility of British women for Indian social problems. It was also decided that NUSEC would sponsor a survey of the actual conditions in India and would use questionnaires as one part of the survey. A second element was to be a handbook that would "present in a convenient form to British readers the main facts concerning women in India and the various reformative activities at work" (Caton, 1930: v).

It has not been possible to locate a copy of this questionnaire or of the responses to it. As secretary of the AIWC Kamaladevi Chattopadhyaya cautioned, "We must realize the entire consequences of a responsible body like the All-India Women's Conference taking such a step as cooperating with an organization outside India for the purpose of a survey" (AIWC, 1929). Her sentiments were just one indication of the growing resentment of Indian women toward the involvement of foreign women in the age-of-marriage and other social issues. Rathbone tried to clear the air by inviting six Indian women, including Lady Dorab Tata, the president of the NCWI, and Hannah Sen, a Bengali Christian educator, to tea at her home near the Houses of Parliament in late summer of 1929. Rathbone felt that this session removed most sources of distrust, and she continued to pursue a multifaceted attack on child marriage. She arranged a letter to *The Times* (12 September 1929), which was signed by numerous British women's organizations and prominent individual women; published an article in *Hibbert Journal*, "Has Katherine Mayo Slandered 'Mother India'?" (1929); and planned a conference at Caxton Hall on 7-8 October 1929 for British women's organizations interested in Indian social reform. In her *Hibbert* article Rathbone (1929: 213) acknowledged that "the attitude of this Conference [AIWC] of Indian women drawn from all parts of the country—their uncompromising demand for better education and denunciations of the 'sheer iniquity' of child marriage—shows that the spirit of reform is alive among them." But Rathbone went on to say that many owed their first coherent knowledge of the terrible facts to the American stranger, although British women shared with British men the responsibilities for their rule over India. Thereafter, many Indian critics, male and female, viewed Rathbone as sympathetic to Mayo and unaware of the efforts of Indian reformers.

The Caxton Hall conference, which was chaired by Rathbone, was the scene of an emotional confrontation between Rathbone, the dedicated but didactic veteran feminist, and Dhanvanthi Rama Rau, now in London while her husband was attached to the Indian Statutory Commission. Rama Rau had once sought the assistance of the wives of British officials in India, but now she was angered by Rathbone's stress on the responsibility of the British women for the extermination of social evils in Indian society. Further inflamed because all the speakers were British women, most of whom had never been to India, Rama Rau (1977: 171-172) advised that "educated Indian women were working in every province of their country to eradicate social evils and outmoded customs." She added that Indian women "were sure we could be more successful than any outsiders, especially those ignorant of the cultural patterns of our social reformers." After this rebuke, Rathbone retreated. She resigned as editor of the proposed handbook, ostensibly because of her new career as a Member of Parliament being elected in May 1929 as an Independent from the Combined English Universities constituency. The handbook was published under the title, *The Key of Progress*, a phrase used by Sir John Simon, the chair of the Indian Statutory Commission, to describe the importance of women's education in India. Rathbone's name was mentioned only once, in the preface.

ENFORCEMENT, OBSERVANCE, PROPAGANDA

Most accounts of the age-of-marriage issue proceed after 1929 to discuss the agitation surrounding the Hindu Code bills of the 1950s which were to raise the age-of-marriage question again. The need for an age-of-marriage act in 1978 indicates that legal reform alone cannot solve the problem of early or premature marriages. Thus it is important to examine in greater detail what happened after the passage of the 1929 act. On the village level, Charlotte Wiser has noted that when she tried to start a discussion on the provisions of the Sarda Act, village women were indifferent and more interested in talking about the reported death of a young child devoured by locusts (Wiser and Wiser, 1963: 74).

In the political sphere, Indian attention was drawn to the civil-disobedience movement launched by Mahatma Gandhi with his Salt March in April 1930. The British establishment, under the guidance of Lord Irwin, arranged the Round Table Conference in London in November 1930 as a channel for debate over future installments of constitutional reform. Most Indian legislators and nationalist leaders now concentrated their energies in one of these two arenas. Many of the most active Indian feminists also became involved in nationalist political agitation or in village uplift work, frequently in response to appeals from Mahatma Gandhi.

Meanwhile, the Sarda Act did not come into effect until April 1930. Eleanor Rivett, principal of a girls' missionary school in Calcutta and vice-president of the national YWCA, reported to Rathbone that "there was at least some expectation on the part of parents that the law, once enacted, would be enforced; therefore they must act speedily, rather than evade the law" (Rivett to Rathbone, 3 August 1930; see Rathbone, 1929-1935). This observation was substantiated by the Census of 1931, which recorded a startling increase in married women under the age of 15 among both Hindus and Muslims, compared to the 1921 census. Those parents need not have rushed the marriages of their children, since the act was not vigorously enforced.

There were obvious defects in the drafting of the legislation, since action could not be brought until after the marriage had taken place, and the magistrate had to wait until someone brought the complaint and pledged 100 rupees as security. The lack of compulsory registration of births and marriages was another major liability. Even more discouraging were efforts by conservative factions to amend or repeal this relatively mild act (Subbarayan to Rathbone, 23 June 1931; see Rathbone, 1929-1935).

In Madras, a coalition of women's groups that included the local branch of the AIWC, the WIA, the YWCA, and the Indian Ladies' Samaj held a public meeting on 25 July 1931 to protest the weakening amendments to the Sarda Act and to the Madras Act for the Suppression of Brothels and Immoral Traffic in Women and Children. Besides resolutions of protest and demands for strict enforcement of existing legislation, the meeting called on the youth and women in every district to establish Sarda committees, which would educate public opinion and report violations of the act (Rathbone-Reddi, 1931; see Rathbone, 1929-1935). Similar resolutions against amendment and for conscientious enforcement were passed by the NCWI at its biennial meeting on 17 March 1932 (NCWI, Third Biennial Report, 1930-1932). Muthulakshmi Reddi, the honorary general secretary of the WIA and the first Indian woman to be nominated to sit in a provincial legislature (Madras), advised Rathbone that the WIA had also agreed to provide any complainant with a loan of 100 rupees for the required security to promote the reporting of violations (Reddi to Rathbone, 29 July 1931; see Rathbone, 1929-1935). The AIWC established vigilance committees to monitor the enforcement and the observance of the provisions of the 1929 act.

In England these efforts of Indian women's associations appeared to be too limited in scope to official and some private observers. Eleanor Rathbone entered a continuing and often acerbic correspondence about the enforcement of the 1929 act with the Secretary of State for India in London, who held ultimate responsibility for the British governance of India. Wedgwood Benn, the Labour Secretary of State, asked Rathbone early in May 1930 to understand that any indication that the British government was "insisting on a rigorous application of the new law, or indeed bringing any sort of pressure to bear, [would] add incalculably to the embarrassments of the Government of India and all the local provincial Governments, and do much to hinder the return of a calmer atmosphere we all wish to see." (Benn to Rathbone, 15 May 1930; see Rathbone, 1929-1935). In short, the Indian government would not enforce legislation that would alienate conservative supporters or possibly inflame nationalist challengers. Rathbone felt much "distracted at the thought of all the wretched little brides who are likely to be sacrificed on the altar of India's political aspiration during the next few years" (Rathbone to Hartog, 26 May 1930; see Rathbone, 1929-1935).

Rathbone now pursued a double-pronged campaign. First she sought to stimulate greater activity among sympathetic individual Indian women and their associations. She wanted to counter the claims of British officials that the Sarda legislation was in advance of Indian public opinion (Willingdon to Hoare, 11 September 1933; see Hoare, 1933; Rathbone to Subbarayan, 16 July 1931; see Rathbone, 1929-1935), and therefore difficult to enforce under even normal political conditions. Second, she continued to be a gadfly to successive secretaries of state, first Benn and then Sir Samuel Hoare, asking thirteen parliamentary questions on this topic. Her attention, like that of Indian political leaders, was also claimed by the Round Table Conferences, and there her major interest was to achieve a significant extension of the franchise among Indian women.

Becoming disheartened by her lack of impact on British imperial authorities, Rathbone carried out a threat to follow the example of Mayo by writing a polemical book. The Englishwoman, however, confined her invective to the indifference of British officials and argued that Muslims were as guilty as Hindus of arranging early marriages. She linked her concern for the age-at-marriage with the franchise issue by proposing that the British Parliament, in its next installment of reforms in India, must "give women themselves the constitutional means, through their status in the new Constitution, of freeing themselves from the evils from which we have so signally failed to free them" (Rathbone, 1934: 77).

At the same time, Rathbone suggested the formation of a single-issue organization, to be called the All-India Society for the Abolition of Child Marriage. Its purposes would be to educate public opinion on the evils of child marriage; to enforce the Sarda Act as far as possible; and to work to strengthen it by amendment (Rathbone, 1934: 98). Rathbone challenged Indian women to provide the dedicated leadership needed for such an organization. More significant, she advocated bolder measures than the passage of "stereotyped resolutions at occasional conferences" or the initiation of "a prosecution leading to a fine which has come to be regarded . . . as a possible slight addition to the normal costs of a wedding" (Rathbone, 1934: 109). She specifically suggested that Indian women's associations dramatize the evils through demonstrations and processions; should spread propaganda through speeches, songs, drama, and films; should use airplanes to scatter leaflets and write slogans in the sky; and that individual women should not attend such early weddings or employ servants or buy from those who had broken the law. Rathbone acknowledged that when similar methods were first used in the women's movement in England, she "disliked and despised them." But Rathbone had come to realize that as long as these methods did not injure innocent bystanders, emotional appeals often had a force lacking in "arguments based on justice, logic, economic necessity, and social hardship." Finally, Rathbone pleaded that "a general uprising of Indian women against child marriage and its sister evils would do more to forward the cause of Indian self-government and to raise the repute of India in the eyes of the world than any other single thing that it is in the power of women to accomplish" (Rathbone, 1934: 114). The English feminist tried to appeal to both the nationalism and the feminism of Indian women. Her view of this agitation as important work for women and her request to move beyond past forms was echoed by Gandhi (1935) when he suggested that the AIWC "descend to the villages" and establish a "personal touch with village women" on this issue.

Now more aware of her ambivalent position and the debatable nature of her proposals, Rathbone sent copies of her book, *Child Marriage: The Indian Minotaur*, to several Indian feminists for their comments. She acknowledged the difficulty of her position as a foreigner but argued that British women must accept responsibility as long as British men continued to rule in India. She also advised the AIWC that she was willing to help subsidize the salary of a paid worker to organize the proposed single-issue organization. Rathbone had hoped that Rameshwari Nehru, who had served on the Age-of-Consent Committee, might be persuaded to head such an association; but Nehru declined because of her involvement in Gandhi's movement against untouchability and in AIWC work (Nehru to Rathbone, 23 August 1934; see Rathbone, 1929-1935).

Rathbone's financial offer was refused by Rajkumari Amrit Kaur, the president of the AIWC, who claimed that they must do such work themselves. Lakshmi Menon, a young lawyer from Lucknow, wrote to Rathbone that some members of the AIWC Standing Committee, including herself, contended that the AIWC should accept help from a sister abroad if they felt no shame in appealing for foreign aid to relieve the victims of a recent earthquake in Bihar (Menon to Rathbone, 13 September 1934; see Rathbone, 1929-1935). The AIWC agreed to appoint a committee on child marriage, which was first chaired by Shareefah Hamid Ali. A social worker and member of the prominent Muslim family of Tyabji in Bombay, Begum Hamid Ali described Rathbone's book as helpful, fair, and forcibly written. She argued, nonetheless, that Rathbone did not realize how difficult it was to take legal action under the 1929 act, especially in rural areas where child marriages were most frequent, and how impossible it was to determine the positive impact of the act, that is, how many child marriages it had actually prevented (Ali to Rathbone, 8 August 1934; see Rathbone, 1929-1935).

In her book Rathbone had suggested some amendments to strengthen the 1929 act, and in 1935 N. M. Joshi, a labor leader and member of the Central Legislative Assembly, approached Rathbone for legal assistance. She obtained a draft bill from two lawyers in London and forwarded it to Joshi with the understanding that her role would be kept secret (Rathbone to Joshi, 23 January 1934; see Rathbone, 1929-1935). Joshi was able to secure Bhubanananda Das, a Congress member from Orissa, as sponsor of the amending act. Rathbone began to lobby for official support of the bill at the India Office on her own initiative while both Muthulakshmi Reddi and the AIWC independently sought her support. This Das bill was enacted in 1938 and enabled the courts (1) to issue injunctions against proposed child marriages when proof of the intention to violate the Sarda Act was brought before the courts; (2) to prosecute on adequate information privately placed before the courts, without the necessity of public discourse and financial security; and (3) to require the husband to make provision for the separate custody and maintenance of the child wife until she was of legal age, when a conviction under the Sarda Act had been obtained (Stocks, 1949: 178-179).

The Das Act seems to have had little impact, as once again Indian political activists were drawn into legislative politics after the passage of the Government of India Act in 1935, which provided for responsible, Indian-controlled ministries on the provincial level. Indian women interested in the child marriage issue became involved in a subcommittee on women's status of the National Planning Commission of the Indian National Congress. Eleanor Rathbone was gradually drawn into the European crises and became a dedicated worker in the resettlement of Jewish refugees from Europe. Legislation and propaganda might have raised hopes for change, but a lack of sustained attention permitted older customs to survive.

CONCLUSIONS

This controversial issue, however, illustrates several factors about social change. Legislation establishing or protecting certain desired norms is usually proposed as the initial step in effecting change. In India prior to 1947 the general pattern was to approach colonial administrators and later legislators to secure appropriate legal reforms. In the case of raising the age of marriage, the people most affected by the legislation were the least involved. In the 1880s and in the 1920s, Indian male social reformers, at first outside the governmental structure and then as legislators, were the principal proponents of reform. There were some British women active in both eras, but Indian women participated prominently only during the 1920s. Their newly emerging associations quickly mastered the techniques of lobbying colonial officials and nationalist legislators, of presenting evidence before official investigative bodies, and of passing resolutions of support at public meetings. Many of the women in these associations had limited personal experience of child marriage, although they were not as distant from its immediate impact as were many of the Indian male reformers and British feminists.

Most of the people active in this campaign recognized that legislation was just the beginning of major change. They hoped that it would have an educative effect and would provide legal support for those individuals desiring social reform but apprehensive about paying the emotional and social costs attached to challenging the accepted practices of caste or community. This realization that the primary role of the legislation would be edificatory might have made the reformers less concerned about the actual provisions of the various bills than they should have been. They were willing to compromise with reluctant colonial officials and social conservatives to obtain any legislation after earlier defeats. It would have been difficult to implement any legislation dealing with such a personal relationship as marriage, but the Child Marriage Restraint Act of 1929 had so many procedural loopholes that it was almost useless as an actual legal sanction.

The British administrators frequently excused their lack of vigorous enforcement by pleading that the 1929 legislation was in advance of public opinion. This defense spotlights the crucial issue of who has the responsibility for educating public opinion or of securing public acceptance of proposed social reforms. The British indicated that

Indians had the primary responsibility, since Indians would be most directly affected by the legislation. Eleanor Rathbone argued that the British officials would pass drastic political legislation if it suited imperial purposes, and so must accept some responsibility for public education on social issues. She was particularly angered that she had been denied the use of All-India Radio for a talk on the Sarda Act because it was deemed a controversial matter (Rathbone, 1934: 96).

Indian male reformers were helpful allies in securing the legal reforms, but appear to have devoted limited attention to propaganda work after the passage of legislation. Women's associations such as the WIA and the AIWC assumed the primary role in this sphere. They were multifaceted, umbrella organizations that focused on social reform across a broad spectrum, and sought unity. They were urban-based and, as both Rathbone and Gandhi urged, had to bridge the gap between themselves and village India, where child marriages were most prevalent. Many AIWC leaders, such as Shareefah Hamid Ali, were aware of this problem, but their organization was in an early stage of development and had limited personnel and financial resources.

It could be argued that a single-issue organization might have produced more positive results. Dhanvanthi Rama Rau (1977: 151-152) helped to form a Child Marriage Abolition Society in 1927, but it appears to have had a brief existence. Two possible reasons are Rama Rau's move to England and the formation of the AIWC. It remains impossible to ascertain how many early marriages the AIWC and the WIA prevented through their vigilance committees and public meetings, but their efforts were not statistically significant. When the AIWC formed its Sarda Committee in response to Rathbone's proposal in 1934, it suffered from the overcommitment of its small band of leaders and the growing insistence on political independence first and social reform second. This situation was made more difficult by nascent communal and generational tensions within the women's movement, which began to divide Hindus and Muslims, and older and younger women, over such issues as the Pakistan movement and birth control.

A single-issue organization might have been useful in two broad areas. First, it might have provided long-term propaganda. In the age-of-marriage campaign, most of the initial propaganda was focused on the government or the educated classes. There was an assumption that legislation and the example of the Western educated elite would encourage reform on other levels of Indian society. There was a need for propaganda directed toward more varied social groups and to explain the legislation once it was passed. Such propaganda might have promoted tolerance for those willing to exercise their newly acquired legal rights, if not outright acceptance of the new norms. The government, which controlled the most resources, left this task to those who had very limited ones, the women's associations. Second, the single-issue organization might have cooperated with other private associations and governmental agencies to form alternative structures for those denied traditional support mechanisms because they had exercised their legal rights. In the instance of early marriage, one goal could have been appropriate educational facilities for the young women who were to be married at the legal age. Schools could have been the substitute for the husband's family as the protector of young women.

International organizations and foreign feminists had positive and negative impacts on the movement for social change in a colonial setting, and might have a similarly ambivalent function in women's movements in Third World countries. Resolutions advocating reforms that bodies such as the League of Nations or the United Nations pass to achieve change in one context, can stimulate the concern of reformers in member nations and possibly serve to enhance the legitimacy and urgency of indigenous reform programs. Polemical exposés, such as Mayo's *Mother India*, are of more doubtful value. They have a positive effect in shaming administrators and legislators, who might then be more sympathetic to legal reforms, but this good might be outweighed by the production of literature denying the existence of the problem or by a reaction against the new legislation.

Foreign feminists like Eleanor Rathbone and international feminist organizations also have an ambivalent, although possibly less adverse, impact on social change. Rathbone viewed India first through the problems of women and attempted to utilize techniques that had proved effective in her earlier social welfare and feminist campaigns in Britain. Her initial efforts to ascertain the reality of conditions in India and to mobilize support among British feminists reflect her desire for an accurate data base and her own organizational network. Her major errors of judgment were her failure to survey Indian public opinion and to assess adequately the previous work of individual Indian reformers and of the Indian women's organizations. Rathbone also did not perceive that her personal "mother knows best" manner could not fail to arouse the antipathy of younger Indian women, who wanted independence from British political control and paternalism in any form. Dhanvanthi Rama Rau wanted the support of British wives in India as allies, but she did not want to serve as a lieutenant in Rathbone's campaign in England. Rama Rau also appears to have transferred her repugnance toward the social conservatism of British memsahibs to the more socially radical, such as Rathbone.

As Rathbone became more aware of the sensitivities of Indian feminists and the quality of their leadership and organizations, she became more effective as an ally. She had the time and resources to conduct research and to interpret its results so that her publicity and lobbying programs would have a sound data base. As an outsider, she, like Malabari in the 1880s, could take a strong stand on a social issue that was controversial and divisive within Indian society. Her position in Parliament and on the Child Welfare Committee of the League of Nations gave her broader arenas in which to propagandize on behalf of Indian women. Here she was similar to Indian male social reformers, like Gour and Sarda, who had access to structures where they could legislate on behalf of Indian women. Still, her proposal for a single-issue organization, coupled with a plea for committed Indian leadership, demonstrates her awareness that effective change would only come on Indian terrain under Indian direction.

Rathbone's efforts as well as those of the Indian women's associations were ultimately thwarted more by the constraints of imperialism and nationalism than by their difficulties in cooperation. The need to maintain themselves in power influenced the British administration to refrain from vigorous enforcement of the Child Marriage Restraint Act and to discourage or prevent the use of government-controlled media and district structure as an educational instrument. The Indian nationalist movement generally argued for political reforms first, increasingly for the winning of independence, and then for social reforms. Nationalist leaders seeking to project an all-India image sought a consensus. Since age of marriage was a sensitive matter, there was some reluctance to devote major resources to it. This emphasis on political goals first set an unfortunate precedent, which assigned a lower priority to women's rights and status.

REFERENCES

All India Women's Conference [AIWC] (1929) Personal communication from Kamaladevi Chattopadhyaya, New Delhi, December 24.

BESANT, A. (1913) Wake up, India: A Plea for Social Reform. Adyar: Theosophical Publishing House.

BOSE, N. S. (1960) The Indian Awakening and Bengal. Calcutta: Firma K. L. Mukhopadhyay.

CASHMAN, R. I. (1975) The Myth of the Lokamanya: Tilak and Mass Politics in Maharashtra. Berkeley: University of California Press.

CATON, A. R. (1930) The Key of Progress: A Survey of the Status and Conditions of Women in India. London: Oxford University Press.

CORBETT-ASHBY, M. (1978) Interview with Geraldine Forbes. (unpublished)

COUSINS, J. H. and M. E. COUSINS (1950) We Two Together. Madras: Ganesh and Company.

EVERETT, J. M. (1979) Women and Social Change in India. New York: St. Martin's Press.

FAWCETT, M. G. (1890) "Infant marriage in India." Contemporary Review 50 (November): 712-720.

FORBES, G. H. (1979) "Women and modernity: the issue of child marriage in India." Women's Studies International Quarterly 2: 407-419.

GANDHI, M. G. (1926) "Curse of child-marriage." Young India (August 26).

——— (1935) "Awfulness of child-marriage." Harijan (November 16).

GUPTA, J. S. (1925) "Children protection bill." Modern Review 37: 270-273.

HOARE-TEMPLEWOOD (1933) MSS Eur E 240/6. London: India Office Library and Records.

HEIMSATH, C. H. (1964) Indian Nationalism and Hindu Social Reform. Princeton, NJ: Princeton University Press.

Indian Government, Central Publication Brancy (1929a) Report of the Age-of-Consent Committee. Calcutta: Author.

——— (1929b) Age-of-Consent Committee Evidence, 1928-29. Calcutta: Author.

——— (1933) Census of India 1931, Volume I, Part I: Report. Calcutta: Author.

JHA, M. (1971) Katherine Mayo and India. New Delhi: People's Publishing House.

LEWIS, J. (1975) "The decline of the organised English feminist movement during the 1920s." Memorial University of Newfoundland, January.

——— (1980) The Politics of Motherhood: Child and Maternal Welfare in England, 1900-1939. London: Croom Helm.

MAYO, K. (1927) Mother India. New York: Harcourt Brace Jovanovich.

National Council of Women in India [NCWI] (1927-1932) Biennial Reports. New Delhi: Nehru Memorial Museum and Library.

RAMA RAU, D. (1977) An Inheritance. New York: Harper & Row.

RATHBONE, E. F. (1929) "Has Katherine Mayo slandered 'Mother India'?" Hibbert Journal 27, 2: 193-214.

——— (1934) Child Marriage: The Indian Minotaur. London: Allen & Unwin.

——— (1929-1935) Papers. Boxes 92 & 93. London: Fawcett Library.

STOCKS, M. D. (1949) Eleanor Rathbone: A Biography. London: Victor Gollancz Ltd.

The Times (London) October 15, 1886; February 8, 1888; September 17, 1888; April 22, 1889; July 15, 1889; December 2, 1889; July 28, 1890; August 20, 1890; September 3, 1890; September 13, 1890; September 12, 1929.

WISER, W. and C. WISER (1963) Behind Mud Walls. Berkeley: University of California Press.

11

SOCIAL FEMINISM IN FRANCE

A Case Study

NAOMI BLACK

This chapter is based on a case study of the *Union féminine civique et sociale*, (UFCS), a Catholic women's organization founded in France in 1925 (Fogarty, 1957: 283; Rollett, 1960). The UFCS has become secularized, shedding clerical advisers and other connections with the Church. In 1981, it continues impressively active.[1] It will illustrate here the way in which traditional women's organizations, armed with the doctrines of social feminism, have been able to develop a political role for women. I shall also be making a more general argument that the beliefs of social feminism have important implications for social change and for development more widely understood. Social feminism and the women's organizations it continues to sustain must be seen as radical because of the policy concerns they produce.

I

Feminism can be defined on both an individual and a group basis. As a social movement, it can most usefully be identified in terms of the

AUTHOR'S NOTE: This chapter was made possible by the kind of extensive assistance given me in the summers of 1977 and 1978 by those in the Paris office of the *Union féminine civique et sociale*. I would like to thank especially Suzanne Vianne, Jacqueline Godet, and Thérèse Doneaud.

consequences of group action. Women's groups should be considered feminist if their activities on behalf of women produce a greater degree of female autonomy. Such a definition includes more than just the groups of women who have joined specifically to change the situation of women. It includes also a range of traditional women's groups like the UFCS, some of which would deny that they are feminist.[2] Such groups' beliefs are "social" feminism, if they derive a public role for women from a conviction that women's private roles are distinctive and of primary importance.

Social feminist groups are often dismissed as conservative. Their older versions sometimes get some credit for being forerunners of the true women's movement, but the surviving examples have attracted little serious attention. Such groups typically refuse any label of "radical," in the sense of anticipating drastic systems change. All too often, their disclaimers are accepted at face value (Albistur and Armogathe, 1977; O'Neill, 1971). If their purposes are not defined in terms of equalizing the situation of women and if their membership is limited to women, then they are seen as parochial and outdated (Dogan and Narbonne, 1955). Any distinctive beliefs they show are then diagnosed as instrumental at best, and at worst as a false consciousness whose function is to maintain existing conditions (Rowbotham, 1974). As society progresses, education and integration into the workforce should soon eliminate the need even for a training ground for the un-self-confident traditional woman (Stott, 1978). Hence the repeated call for the elimination of women's sections or auxiliaries, and the objection to women's commissions or quotas in political parties (Philips, 1980).

Among academic analysts, the dismissal of traditional women's organizations is part of a wider lack of comprehension of the group activities of women. It is now almost two centuries since women's organizations have begun public action on behalf of women. Historians now concede the existence of something called the "women's movement." It is even given partial credit for certain changes in the formal status of women in the industrialized world. There is a continuing tendency, however, to focus narrowly on self-identified feminist organizations that are closely related to the wider patterns of social and political change. These organizations can plausibly be interpreted as mere segments of neglected aspects of more general waves of progressivism (Dangerfield, 1961). Such "equal rights" groups extend to women the logic of various ideological orthodoxies, whether liberal (rights of man—and woman) or Marxist (the consciousness-raising impact of relations to production—or reproduction). The women's movement, understood this way, is an attempt to remove anomalies in the treatment of women as compared to men; it continues or revives as new generations of women perceive inconsistencies of situation that earlier ones overlooked. Equal-rights feminism has often been radical in style, but such feminism had no innovations, in theory or practice, to offer.

In particular, the equal rights feminists tended to create organizations both similar and closely related to the existing political system. Even the violent suffragettes of the British Women's Social and Political Union followed an established British pattern of threatening insurrection and property damage as a means of extending the franchise. Focus on such groups has encouraged a belief that the most significant women's organizations are the ones most like those found in conventional politics, and the key issues are the ones that eventually make their way into normal partisan disputes. The majority of historical studies of women's organizations have therefore focused on the struggle for the vote. More recently, contraception and abortion have attracted attention, while studies of women in the United States show continuing concentration on voting, officeholding, and the battle over the Equal Rights Amendment (Evans, 1977; Rabaut, 1978; Women and Politics, 1980). Such analyses explain the assumption that the women's movement was dead after the acquisition of the vote as well as the surprise when it reemerged into public view in the 1960s (Banks and Banks, 1964). Discussions of the "rebirth" accordingly tend to interpret the new women's movement as a spinoff of postwar organizations and ideologies believed to be more autonomous, such as civil rights and antiwar movements (Hole and Levine, 1971; Evans, 1979).

As to the more traditional organizations, analysts have tended to dismiss or even condemn them (but see noteworthy exceptions: Du Bois, 1978; Lemons, 1975; Liddington and Norris, 1978). My example, the UFCS, has been specifically attacked as an example of a conservative group in which patriarchal ideology has been used to inhibit women's development (Michel and Texier, 1968: II, 88-89). In the 1980s, when the World Synod of Catholic Bishops issues statements condemning divorce and "immoral" contraception, it is understandable that a Catholic women's group might be expected to hinder women's autonomy (World Synod of Catholic Bishops, 1980). But the UFCS is also a social feminist group, whose actual beliefs and programs have been misrepresented by hostile critics. It thus provides a particularly good test of the potentialities of the sort of traditional women's organizations that continue to flourish unnoticed in most parts of the world today.

Like equal rights feminists, social feminists are committed to public action. But for them the logic, the expected consequences, and the specific policy demands are different from those of the better-known branches of the women's movement, as well as from the programs of conventional politics. For social feminists, the basic assumption is that, historically, women as a group and as individuals have different experiences from those of men. There is often disagreement about the innateness, the permanence, and the range of relevance of such differences (Campbell, 1952: 15). But there is agreement about an objectively identifiable distinctiveness. Physiological differences between the sexes are believed to be of continuing importance even when conception and birth can be controlled by women; although not all women bear or rear children, the possibility has made women's lives different from the lives of even the most disadvantaged men. The resulting perspectives and capabilities—customarily excluded from public life—provide a basis for the possible transformation of society as a whole. As bearers of these values, women have an obligation (not just a right) to participate in the larger society. The state becomes an analogue to the family, for which women have traditional responsibility, as well as an extension of the family and a major influence on it (Woolf, 1931, 1938). Finally, social feminism emphasizes policies thought to have been neglected by men. Along with broad preferences for nurturance, cooperation, and peace, social feminists support the use of substantial resources for the more specific needs of women and children, both in the home and in relation to work, health, and education. They also urge serious attention to the control or even elimination of war, and to the related issues of quality of life and international economic cooperation and development.

Thus, for social feminists, women's freedom and activism are vitally important, but for instrumental reasons. Although specific priorities for reform and versions of change are expected to vary over time and space, a drastic change in the social order is intended. Both private and public spheres are to be transformed by eliminating inequality and violence in both (UFCS, 1977).

For Marxist and neo-Marxists, such a social feminist analysis is unacceptable simply because it postulates something other than class as a principle of social organization and social change (Smith, 1977). The conventional liberal rejection is more complex. The very consistency of social feminism over time is taken as an indication of irrelevance rather than as showing how profound a social transformation is implied (Degler, 1965). We may guess also at the impact of commonly accepted notions of development. Ideas about the permanent specificity of female experience contradict the identification of universality as progress. In addition, those hopeful of improving the relatively disadvantaged situation of women are likely to distrust a perspective derived from the patriarchal family, the institution so many see as the key to women's oppression (Heilbrun, 1979).

The philosophical bases of such criticisms of social feminism can be answered, as Elizabeth Wolgast (1980) shows, by a more careful analysis of the notion of "special rights," which allows for a social recognition of needs and services, while recognizing claims for equal rights. The *practical* creation of a public role for women is in itself radical, given the way most known societies exclude women from authoritative participation in public life. Social feminism undercuts such exclusion by extending domestic obligations to include public service. It also provides a specific agenda developed and expanded over time. The items of this program are undeniably political and progressive. It is this agenda that most clearly supports the claims I would make for the radical implications—and impact—of social feminism. The translation of "female" virtues into public policy has produced what we could think of as a transnational feminist consensus. As the UFCS's experience shows, this consensus can make even the members of a relatively traditional women's group active, self-aware, even radical.

For the fifty years preceding World War II, the social feminist program was articulated by an international coalition of women's organizations, the International Council of Women (ICW). First established in 1888, the ICW is still active, though certainly less influential today (International Council of Women, 1973). The ICW is an umbrella group providing an international connection between national coalitions of women's groups of diverse kinds. At the national level, member organizations of the ICW included "associations of women in the trades, professions and reforms as well as those advocating political rights [and] women workers along all lines of social, intellectual, moral or civic progress and reform [and] literary clubs, art and temperance unions, labor leagues, missionary and industrial associations," as well as individual suffrage organizations (International Council of Women, 1966: 12). The motto was the Golden Rule, and the orientation was an increasingly secularized Protestantism, so that Catholic groups could not formally join. But from 1910, these groups had their own World Union of Catholic Women's Leagues, whose membership was reported as 33 million in 1936 (Boy, 1936: 79-86). Other women's organizations with narrower concerns maintained their own separate international networks, such as the International Federation of Business and Professional Women. However, the large majority of these groups, including the Catholics, cooperated with the ICW in international and local campaigns

(Whittick, 1979). The goals of the ICW were deliberately framed to attract just such support, and the documents of the UFCS repeatedly indicate awareness of shared objectives.

The programs of the International Council of Women indicate that the following issues were central to social feminist concerns in the period preceding World War II: (1) equal pay and access to work for women (including women's right to participate in the paid labor force); (2) protective labor legislation applicable to both sexes, as well as factory inspection, including state support of maternity; (3) abolition of the double standard of morality, of state-supported prostitution, and of the international trade in women and children; (4) the vote and all accompanying civil rights for women, including independent nationality; (5) improvement of the situation of workers in the home, both housewives and domestics; (6) support of international arbitration, peace, and international organization (with equal participation by women); (7) consultation of appropriate women's organizations in relation to policy affecting women and children; and (8) an international convention on equal rights. All were justified in reference to the special qualities, capacities, and needs developed by women; all were felt to have high priority. Although the list includes issues such as the vote, more commonly identified with the women's movement, they were not given exclusive attention.

Many of these policies have still been only incompletely implemented. Yet such progress has been made that they have now acquired the status of "motherhood issues"—principles no one dares object to (Commission of the European Communities, 1975, 1978). This was far from the case even in the 1930s, when married women's participation in the paid labor force and in politics was not generally accepted, (Erskine, 1971). Even when the extension of political rights to women was most bitterly resisted, however, such issues were not issues of partisan politics (Morgan, 1975). Today they are still seen as more social than political (Mossuz-Lavau and Sineau, 1980). For the social feminists, these were motherhood issues in the literal sense that their desirability derived from the shared universal experience of actual or possible mothers. Thus, even extremely conventional women could accept them as important. Social feminism then led to a remarkable range of international concerns: cooperation with foreign women pursuing similar goals in other countries, interest and involvement in international organization (women's and also universal), and, finally, a generalized interest in the progress of the international system. Quite apart from the content of their interest, such traditional women must be seen as having moved out of parochialism and apoliticism. Furthermore, we can see truly radical implications in the way that they were applying to politics a new set of holistic standards that questioned reliance on aggression, competition, and inequality.

At this stage, I shall look more closely at the particular social feminist organization that is my example. A brief description of its origins and its domestic policies will be followed by an account of its international involvements. This is where the impact of the organization's social feminism is the most clearly visible.[3]

II

From its founding in 1925, l'Union féminine civique et sociale was supported by some of the more liberal of the French Catholic hierarchy. The R. P. Desbuquois was the first chaplain, and the future Cardinal Verdier drafted the statement of principles (Rollet, 1960: 95-96; Corlieu, 1970). The historian of French social Catholicism, biographer of the UFCS's founder, describes how the groups original members placed themselves: "between a traditional view that confined [women's] horizon too narrowly to the home and a sectarian feminism that isolated them in the name of emancipation by breaking the natural and sacred bonds of the family" (Rollet, 1960: 194). Contrary to what is still commonly believed, there were many feminist groups active in France in the interwar period. The UFCS believed that they were individualist, materialist, excessively egalitarian (denying the principles of hierarchy and authority), and, above all, opposed to the family. In addition, these groups failed to represent the interests of working women, especially married ones with children. The UFCS thus anticipated the criticisms to be made later by the various women's liberation movements. Their own purpose was summed up to their satisfaction in a central principle: "an absolute fidelity to the better understood mission of wife and mother . . . [which includes] the accomplishment of civic and social duties necessary to the common good" (Rollet, 1960: 194). The first publication of the UFCS put it as follows: "If the Frenchwoman votes tomorrow, she must, by her vote, serve the country by protecting the Family." In 1925, the vote was expected momentarily, but it was not acquired for another twenty years. The rationale was expanded as follows:

> The Frenchwoman cannot ignore the great social problems. She must, henceforth, prepare herself to seek the solution to them in the civic arena. . . . The *Union féminine civique et sociale* applies in the civic arena, that will soon be opened to women, its program, which is that of the social Catholics, and it works closely in collaboration with them [UFCS, 20 September 1925].

The UFCS was a Christian Democrat rather than a Catholic Action group.[4] It is best described even in the 1930s as "associated with" and "under the guidance of" the hierarchy (Fogarty, 1957: 283). As Rollet (1955, 1960, 1975) notes, the UFCS competed for the adherence of Catholic women with a very large general Catholic Action women's group directly and orthodoxly controlled by the Church until this day. But the UFCS always intended a wider appeal and a more autonomous structure. By 1945 its key public document, a booklet entitled *La femme au service du pays* ("woman in the service of the country"), had dropped the explicit references of earlier editions to Catholicism and the Church, replacing them by a vaguer "Christianity" (Butillard, 1942, 1945). Documentation of the 1960s and 1970s shows no traces of confessionalism. The first issue of the UFCS's revitalized newspaper, *Dialoguer*, traces the process of secularization, and points with pride to the consistency of social policy shown throughout the changes recorded (UFCS, February/March, 1968).

Mlle. Andrée Butillard, the formidable founder who ran the organization until her death in 1955, certainly saw her work in essentially religious terms. But for her there was no distinction between devotion and lay initiatives. Some of her reported remarks catch this: "Don't get drowned in detail; it isn't our goal . . . and the Lord would not bless it." Her advice to a working woman she was coaching for a public presentation: "Accept in advance the possible humiliation, offer it up for the cause, say a good *Veni Sancte*, and get on with it" (Rollet, 1960: 53, 176).

Led by Mlle. Butillard, the UFCS concentrated on developing leaders within each socially disadvantaged category—women, women workers, working-class wives and mothers. In 1955, Dogan and Narbonne saw the organization's influence as largely urban, and its goal as "the formation of representative elites" (Dogan and Narbonne, 1955: 129). Mlle. Butillard's own public activities had begun with organizing women's unions, first in the provinces with Mlle. Rochebillard, then in Paris, working successfully with home workers. The UFCS at the beginning of its history took up this concern and helped to obtain maternity benefits for women workers in state manufacturing establishments. The more direct link to the foundation of the UFCS was the first organization Mlle. Butillard set up: the Ecole Normale Sociale for training leaders among women trade unionists. That, in turn, had grown out of self-education and leadership classes Mlle. Butillard had helped to set up among the women she was organizing in Paris. Later, the UFCS was to generate at least four more "daughter" organizations that followed up its main interests: a parents' school, a league for restoring mothers to the home, a family association of heads of households, the World Mothers' Movement, and a committee for women in development. All became independent; the last two are still in existence. There seems no doubt that through these groups and its own activities, the UFCS did, in fact, "form" a significant proportion of those women active in politics, particularly at the local or municipal level (Gros, 1975; Renard, 1965). Once the vote had been achieved, a major element in the UFCS's activities was political education directed specifically at women candidates and officeholders. Mlle. Butillard's last creation, three years before her death, was the UFCS correspondence courses for municipal councillors.

At the UFCS, those who worked with Mlle. Butillard speak of her with affection and vast admiration. She is described as a "saint" and as a "revolutionary." Although she herself rejected the terms "feminist" and "suffragist," there seems no doubt both described her and her organization. Certainly, the central concern of the organization was women's autonomous political role. Even before the franchise was acquired, the UFCS reminded women of the possibilities of participation for certain classes of women in France. Since the last years of the previous century women had been acquiring rights as electors and members in a range of professional and other public settings (Albistur and Armogathe, 1977: 392-393). In the third issue of the UFCS's newspaper (January 1926), members were reminded of possibilities for women workers and employees in the Conseils des Prud'hommes, women shopkeepers in the Chambres de Commerce, and certain farm women in Chambres d'Agriculture. Later, the possibilities of cooption onto municipal committees were repeatedly pointed out. In the postwar period, increasing attention and increasing participation related the UFCS members to the range of policy advisory boards and commissions, including those involved with the national plans. When public voting and officeholding became possible for women in France, the earlier obligations to register and vote whenever eligible become all the stronger. Accompanying this was a continually growing series of educational projects. The motto of the organization is "influential because competent" ("influentes parce que compétentes"). And the motivation continues the same, as the activity does, with or without a Catholic underpinning. At the moment of acquisition of the vote (1944), Andrée Butillard reiterated the UFCS's rationale, under the title "feminine task": "This ballot [the Frenchwoman] welcomes . . . joyfully. . . . What must be the ambition of the woman called to this new task? To be and to remain fully herself" (UFCS, December 1944). The feminine task is to be Christian and to be a mother endowed with intuition, moral concerns, and the gifts of the educator. From this follows the duty of acquiring the "competences appropriate to the civic task." Civic society is an extension of the home.

This is clearly a highly political version of social feminism, albeit with an explicit Christian justification. Accordingly, the UFCS had little trouble working with other self-identified feminist groups in the interwar period. It shared the general goals of the ICW, and therefore of the constituent French group, the Council of Women of France (Corlieu, 1959). This was true even though there were specific areas of disagreement: the UFCS's preference for the "mother in the home," its demand for a "family vote," its opposition to divorce and contraception, and its insistence on the maintenance of a formal hierarchy within the household with a male "head." However, the UFCS also emphasized the rights and needs of working women, the primacy of female suffrage, the protection of abandoned and exlploited women and children, and the economic vulnerability of women without legal "majority." As a result, when it came to actual issues of legal change and enforcement, the UFCS's position turned out in practice to be compatible with the wider social feminist consensus.[5] With postwar liberalization and secularization, the organization painfully worked out positions on abortion that allowed for a couple's free choice, and formulated an imaginative view of role-assignment (UFCS 1971, 1972, 1976).

Again, it should be stressed that the UFCS was never under the direct control of the Church. It is nevertheless remarkable how activist and how feminist, despite disclaimers, was the role that it developed for women in domestic politics. Its international role was even more remarkable, however. Here the universalist ideologies and linkages of Catholicism seem to have strengthened the political implications of social feminism. Domestically there was always tension, finally resolved by the UFCS's movement away from confessionalism. Internationally, all the women's groups had to allow for diversity of cultural goals and even of religion, and all together relied for unity on their conviction that "female" virtues were universal.

III

The history of the transnational women's organizations is yet another area waiting to be fully explored. We know that a network of communications has existed since at least the middle of the nineteenth century (Hurwitz, 1977; Evans, 1977; Sebo, 1976). Lacking legitimacy in domestic politics, activist women came to look across national boundaries for mutual support. On the simplest level, their exchanges were informational. The tactics and success of women in other countries could supply examples, encouragement, or warning. This awareness is present in the UFCS from the very start. In April 1926, the UFCS newspaper printed the first of a continuing series on "Women of the World." Belgian women, readers were told, were using the municipal vote to "purify" politics. Still in 1926, there were warnings not to follow the route of Czechoslovakia, where socialist and communist women (atheists by definition) were the most active. The appointment of "Mrs. Norman Wilson" as the first Canadian woman senator in 1930 was noted and the Conservative victory in Britain analyzed in 1931 in relation to the situation of women. A steady flow of information continued, reinforced by exchanges of informal visits, often on the occasion of national or international congresses of women's groups, especially in Belgium, Germany, and Poland. After the war, the UFCS was to note with pride that it was the first French organization to reestablish contacts with German counterparts. The postwar period saw the visits much expanded, along with the twinning of municipalities (the political context in which UFCS members were most active). A strongly pro-Europe stance developed, possibly as a consequence.

In all this it is not easy to distinguish between the characteristic pattern of social Catholic groups—which tend to interact across national boundaries—and the somewhat similar pattern of women's organizations as such, most particularly the social feminist ones. Internationally, the explicit pressure activities of the UFCS were supposed to go through the World Union of Catholic Women's Leagues, in whose meetings Mlle. Butillard was reported to be active. But there are records making it clear that the UFCS was in direct contact with such international bodies as the International Labor Bureau. The World Union of Catholic Women's Leagues participated in the vast campaigns of the other international women's networks, which the International Council of Women coordinated, in part through a Liaison Committee of Women's International Organizations active in relation to the League from 1925 on (Whittick, 1979; White, 1951). These campaigns focused on disarmament, and also on issues of child welfare, the nationality of married women, and the situation of working women, as the Great Depression hardened and women's right to work was under attack. The other major area of concern was what was then called the "white slave trade," the traffic in women and children, as well as the related issue of the traffic in drugs. All these areas were dealt with by League commissions, and the Liaison Committee had as one of its jobs the channeling of representatives of women's organizations into consultative positions. The historian of the League feels these areas of concern (with the exception perhaps of disarmament) were of little importance in the League structure; he concedes, however, that there were some successes, mainly in relation to the "immoral" trades (Walters, 1952). This international coalition, to which the UFCS belonged, however indirectly, was responsible for the League's preliminary reports on the status of women that appeared just before the war; these constitute the links to the establishment of the United Nations' Status of Women Commission, and ultimately to International Women's Year and its consequences.

As noted above, the UFCS did develop its own transnational women's organization, the World Mothers' Movement. Founded in 1947, it seems to have had as its main goal the enactment of a Charter of Rights of Mothers. It currently has consultative status with the Economic and Social Council of the United Nations (category II—on certain topics only) and has been reported involved with international conferences connected to its concerns (White, 1951; Ferraru, 1979). The origins of the organization are to be found in three massive international conferences convened by the UFCS (in 1933, 1937, and 1947). Its motto, coined of course by Mlle. Butillard, is a capsule summary of the UFCS's social feminism: "The mother . . . artisan of human progress."

All these strictly international activities required a good deal of attention but little action from most UFCS members. A more demanding form of international concern related to the foreign policy of France. An organization such as the UFCS necessarily has policy preferences derived from its basic beliefs. From the beginning, these preferences are presented explicitly as a basis for judging public officials. The very earliest statements make support contingent on policy; this is how the vote was to be used. Once the vote had been acquired, each election saw a systematic program outlined as a basis for querying candidates and selecting party affiliation. The UFCS was not enthusiastic about any of the parties, but it was realistic and practical about the mechanics of using the party structure; and foreign policy was a central element.

Even before the war and before the vote, analyses and categorical judgments of foreign policy were frequent in *La femme dans la vie sociale.* A strong interest in peace, disarmament, and international arbitration was constant, joined in due course by concern for the regulation and peaceful use of atomic energy. Peace is always seen by social feminists as the key female value. However, the UFCS's application of this value is remarkably sophisticated. Thus, they only reluctantly approved the Munich Agreements in 1938, pointing to the high "moral and material costs" and the sacrifice of Czechoslovakia

(UFCS, September 1938). The Italian attack on Ethiopia and the Spanish Civil War were both deplored, in spite of fascist support of the Church. Later, France's Indochina settlement was severely criticized, even in the midst of the rejoicing at the end of fighting. These concerns mounted until the end of the 1950s; in 1960 a five-year-old column, "Le Monde en Marche," ("The World on the Move") was replaced by a column on consumer concerns. But even after that date, there was substantial material related to foreign policy in the UFCS publications. Interest in French reactions to Europe and to world economic problems continued to be important.

From the 1960s, a new element of international concern appeared as the UFCS became more attentive to the situation of individual women or specific groups of women maltreated in other countries. Increasingly, often in concert with other women's or family organizations, this group urged the French government to pressure other governments on behalf of women. In the last two decades attention to the European Community has shown a tendency to be included under rubrics such as "civic action" (in relation to the European parliament) or "consumerism" (the economic impact of the Community). Today, attention to immigrant workers continues, as does concern with issues of colonialism and political and economic development. These are long-established areas of UFCS interest, and here the contemporary UFCS is in step with the worldwide trends of social feminism and, more widely, the women's movement.

A related concern of particular interest to a French group was the condition of women in the French empire, along with strong views about France's general policies in relation to dependent territories. The UFCS had many sections in Algeria (thirty are noted in 1975, with the oldest dating from 1930) and others in Morocco, Tunisia, Martinique, Cameroon, and Madagascar. They seem to have been founded by Frenchwomen, possibly the wives of colonial officials. Their main activities concerned native women; a journal in Malgache was published for some time, which suggests the presence of indigenous members at least in Madagascar. Pressure activities of the UFCS certainly played a part in a decree issued by Minister Georges Mandel in 1939 concerning the situation of native women in French territories; this decree, translated into law after the war, abolished the disposition or sale into marriage of minor or unconsenting adult women.

As might be expected, the UFCS had a general, consistent policy on dependent territories. Already in 1932 statements about Algeria and Madagascar struck common themes: awareness of deplorable conditions such as disease and poverty, along with a stress on the need for conversion (religious) and for treating the natives as friends and equals. At this stage, the underlying attitude was one of tutelage; by the end of the war, it had moved to support for self-determination. An impressive position paper on colonialism, drafted in 1938 by Mlle. Georges-Martin, expressed support for native elites and for native customs when not "opposed to human dignity." Among the customs specifically condemned in relation to native women were many still common today: child marriage, polygamy, marriage without the woman's consent, repudiation, separation of a divorced or repudiated woman from her children, and the destitution of aged women. The UFCS also cited, surprisingly, oppressive patriarchy, drawing from their usually supportive historian, Henri Rollet, an indignant footnote saying that they should also have considered the "abuses of matriarchy" (Rollet, 1960: 138-141). In general, the argument was that colonization depended on moral authority, not on force. From this followed consistent criticisms of France's policies or lack of policies in North Africa. In this context the theme of economic development appeared early; aware of the connection, by 1958 UFCS members were told to ask would-be deputies how they would reconcile development needs within France with those of Algeria and the rest of the territories controlled by France.

We should not underestimate the impact of Catholicism on the UFCS's foreign policy stances and on its general views of the world. The group gave a degree of approval to the Franco regime, participated in the family organizations under Vichy, and consistently opposed the Soviet Union. Yet its feminism, if nothing else, modified these opinions. It does not seem ever to have been accused of being collaborationist, a surprising fact considering the hostility it has provoked among feminists of the Left. It is true that there were UFCS *résistantes*, and even a martyr. It is also true that the UFCS showed commendable hostility to such decrees as the ones for eugenic sterilization and euthanasia. The blanket early opposition to "materialist" communism came to be modified by attention to the foreign control of the French party, an issue that is of wide concern in the era of Eurocommunism. It is now admitted that UFCS members can join the Communist or Socialist parties or even stand for office under their auspices. The earliest postwar policy statements attacked fascisms of the Right as well as fascisms of the Left. And both were criticized, not just for their larger social and political stances, but also on the basis of their treatment of women. Perhaps, as social feminists have always argued, exclusion from political power, when coupled with an interest in it, can after all provide a perspective difficult to attain otherwise. The UFCS suggests that such a perspective can even be retained after acquisition of formal access to public power.

IV

Many political analysts, including some sympathetic to the women's movement, have seen social feminism's domestic-based arguments as inhibiting women's role in public life. Such conceptions of role are said to explain why women are allowed to use the vote, but are restricted to minimal participation in the "masculine" fields of financial and defense policy. Maurice Duverger, for instance, feels that such an approach implies that women are "monovalent," and can consequently be kept within certain narrow spheres of capability, while "polyvalent" men have societywide aptitudes and therefore power (Duverger, 1955: 126, 123; 1969). This criticism seems less and less relevant today, even as an explanation of women's conflicting attitudes about their public role. Women are certainly still struggling with the consequences of the transformations of society. However, it is doubtful if a "domestic" sphere can still be said to exist in the modern welfare state which penetrates all areas of life. Nor can any exclusively masculine area of public policy or activity be identified any longer, even if men continue in control. It is beginning to look as if many current problems are transitional, such as the continuing perceptions of sex-appropriate roles, the discomfort with anomalies, and the continuing tendency to see individual women as representative of the whole sex. Positive role models for women are now more common, along with strategies for enlarging the public role of women (Kanter, 1977). The more accurate structural explanations of the continuing disadvantage of women direct attention to historical roots and to the basic nature of human society. In practice, social feminism has tended to work against patriarchal structures by facilitating the group action of women and created a public role with which they could feel comfortable.

Social feminism can thus be seen as mainly positive in its practical impact on public life. But in the long run, it is inadequate on the theoretical level. This perspective praises the "feminine" qualities of endurance, nurturance, intuitiveness, and cooperation. But it is also likely to argue that these qualities are derived not just from women's experience, but from some intrinsically female qualities connected with women's nature and developed through their actual individual participation in activities such as child care and homemaking. This means that males can neither share these virtues nor participate in these experiences in any authentic way. For women, one consequence of such an analysis has been the "double shift" syndrome, which reserves all domestic responsibility for the women, even in childless couples with both members in the paid labor force. Men and women alike apparently continue to feel that domestic responsibilities take priority for women (Commission of the European Communities, 1975, 1978). Even more than segregation within the political and economic arenas, such attitudes and the resulting burdens have restricted women's public participation.

There is a tendency for social feminists to feel that women have a virtual monopoly on the private virtues and competence. For the average woman, this produces an intolerable burden when the demands of the public realm are added. No wonder the result is a very truncated version of economic or political life for most women. For men, the practical consequences have been far less. But the theoretical implications are even more powerful. Even the most rigidly segregationist sexism has always allowed women some areas of competence to which men had no entry. As they became activists, however, social feminists had to argue that the "male" qualities used to justify their exclusion from public life were well within the reach of most women. These included the capacity for abstract and analytic reasoning as well as the ability to speak in public and conduct public meetings. Extended, this argument showed that most women could handle the use of overt power, including force; they could demonstrate physical strength and effectiveness; they could share all appetites; and they could finally take over the active role in sexuality and control of reproduction. An equal rights feminist who sees no essential difference between men and women could eventually opt for the use of technology to overcome biologically based differences in function, arguing for an androgyny new to human experience (Firestone, 1970). But a social feminist will likely end up with a model in which women are demonstrably capable of all that has been traditionally ascribed to men, while they still monopolize the virtues and capabilities derived from women's bodies, shared consciousness, and historical experience (International Women's Year Secretariat, Canada, 1976: 151, the "female chauvinists").

Charlotte Perkins Gilman's *Herland* presents a social feminist utopia or dystopia (1979). There, the maternal principle has produced an all-women society with all the male virtues, including scientific knowledge and physical and martial strength. Parthenogenesis has removed the last vestigial male function. A group of men wanders in. Their only recourse is rape. They are finally expelled from the feminist Eden. Such implications may well explain some of the rejection of social feminism as a long-range ideology. Certainly, it can serve no more than a transitional function, possibly for the transition that is actually in process.

Social feminism continues to provide a marvellous transformational vision for women, however, precisely because it generates what Carolyn Heilbrun (1973: 58) calls the "female hero." Its very inapplicability to men encouraged the woman-only group that seems to be necessary for the development of shared consciousness, as well as for the acquisition of skills and the growth of networks of women and of women's organizations. As cross-national historical research on women's organizations develops, it is possible to see the impact of social feminism in a wide range of settings, operating through groups like the UFCS, the British Women's Co-operative Guild, and the many National Councils of Women (Gaffin, 1977; Strong-Boag, 1976). In the context of the larger web of women's organizations, it will be possible to give a more meaningful interpretation of campaigns such as those for the vote and the Equal Rights Amendment (Lemons, 1975; Liddington and Norris, 1978; Lewis, 1975).

But even more important, particularly in the context of development and social change, is the continuing survival of social feminist organizations. The social feminist rationale seems especially powerful among the women's organizations in the Third World. Even in the older, industrialized nations, many of the new "women's liberation" groups adhere to a philosophy that is close to social feminism's commitment to the identity and superior virtue of women's ways and values (*Questions féministes*, 1977; Morgan, 1978). Although these groups often claim that feminism dates only from the 1960s, they nevertheless constitute important links with surviving social feminist groups and with the important women's organizations of the developing world. Mody and Rogers (1979: 20) point out the ubiquity of women's self-help and self-education groups in the Third World, discussing examples from Taiwan, Java, Malaysia, Africa (Nigeria, Sierra Leone, Tanzania, Gambia), Korea, Guatemala, Honduras, Colombia, and India. They conclude, "Women's groups need to be identified, encouraged and developed to serve as nurseries and laboratories for healthy all-round personality development and socialization into active public roles for women." These are not groups dedicated to transforming the situation of women. But they are committed to notions about the specificity of experiences and needs of women, and they bring into the public realm the familiar programs of social feminist policy preferences. This became very clear indeed at the informal meetings of nongovernmental organizations that accompanied the U.N.'s conferences for International Women's Year (1975) and the Mid-Decade (1980). Here representatives of the women of developing nations agreed on the priority of education, employment, health, and peace (Forum 80, 25 July 1980).

The publicity surrounding the Mexico City and Copenhagen conferences for International Women's Year and Decade has led observers to talk of a split between women of the modernizing world and those of the more advanced, industrial nations. Indeed, this is included in the rhetoric of many Third World women and women's groups. Women's organizations have always disagreed among themselves about priorities and tactics, and about the desirability of specific changes. But a closer analysis will show that, in general, the Third World women are relatively uninterested in arguments about the similarity of men and women. Instead, they accept the social feminist vision of a transformed social order, and of the role in its creation to be played by women, women's organizations, and women's specific values. Their doubts about the importance of legal equality echo past doubts about the wisdom of expecting great consequences from campaigns for the franchise. We may also be reminded of the days when Russian women stressed liberalization or abolition of Czarism, while Indian and Egyptian women had as their priority the end of British rule, and sympathetic British women felt that the political power symbolized by the vote was their own most immediate goal (Stanton, 1970). All agreed, as do organized women all over the world today, that governments do not take sufficiently seriously the needs and the viewpoints of women.

Today, the transnational social feminist agenda for change includes the implications of women's critiques of economic development. This is an extension of both the logic and the specific items of the programs presented by groups such as the International Council of Women in past generations. We have seen how social feminism enabled a group like the UFCS to transmute the constrictions of Catholicism into an activism with worldwide involvements.

The transformation of the role of women has begun. For social feminists, this change will be successful only if it can also transform the whole social order. Organizations with such an impact, and such goals, are radical in the deepest sense. Every study of development must take them into account.

NOTES

1. It is difficult to estimate either the size or the influence of the UFCS today. Dogan and Narbonne (1955: 130) thought there were about 450 UFCS members of municipal councils in 1952. In 1975 a sympathetic account saw 8000 *adhérentes*, and thought the movement had some influence on about 200,000 (Michy, 1975: 55); a later UFCS document put its 1975-1976 membership at 13,000 and the contacts at 350,000 (UFCS, 1977). Every account of Frenchwomen's participation in local politics shows some who were recruited by the UFCS, and even those who attack the group think of it as influential with the government (Michel and Texier, 1968; as a contrast, see Rabaut, 1978: 325,357).

2. Linda Gordon (1977: xiv) defined feminism much as I do: "sharing in an impulse to increase the power and autonomy of women in their families, communities and/or

society." Within the newer groups of the revived women's movement there is a tendency to classify as feminist only those women prepared to claim what is still an inflammatory designation, and only those groups which, founded since the mid-1960s, ground their beliefs in convictions about the "oppression" of women (Gillespie-Woltemade, 1980; Birotheau-Coussy, 1977). In French, where it is often used in a derogatory sense, the distinction "féministe/féminin" (feminist/feminine) seems to carry that loading (Commission of the European Communities, 1978). In 1978, the UFCS classified itself as "féminisme réformiste" (reformist feminism), but put the World Mothers' Movement under the traditionalists, who rejected feminism (1978: 5, 30, 25).

3. Unless otherwise identified, all citations are from the UFCS's newspaper, entitled *Le femme dans la vie sociale*, from 1925 to 1967, and *Dialoguer*, from 1967 to the present. All translations from the French are mine.

4. After the encyclical *Rerum Novarum* directed attention in 1891 to the "condition of the people," particularly the working class, a wide range of lay Catholic organizations developed in Europe under the impetus of figures such as Albert De Mun. In "Catholic Action" or "Christian Action," the laity carried on apostolic work under the close direction of the Church; the emphasis was on the formation of consciences and on preparation for political, social, and economic action, rather than the action itself. Alongside this is "Christian Democracy," where the "laity take over entirely and act on their own initiative and responsibility, though within the normal framework of the beliefs, rules, and practices of the church" (Fogarty, 1957: 4). Christian Democracy includes the UFCS as well as the better-known Catholic trade unions and political parties; in France, all of these groups secularized by the 1960s (Rollet, 1955, 1958, 1975). Catholic Action and Christian Democracy together are usually referred to as "social Catholicism."

5. Today, "pro-family" policies are associated with the Right and with attempts to repeal legislative and practical gains made by women. In interwar France, policy concerning reproduction was represented by the brutal natalist laws against abortion (repealed only in 1974) and there were Depression pressures for the dismissal of women workers. The UFCS favored equal pay and strongly opposed suggestions that married women be barred from the labor force. Active in the campaigns that produced a revised family code just before World War II, they insisted that the formal authority of the male head of households did not limit women's economic or civil capacities. Other UFCS concerns that struck earlier observers as reactionary were shared by the *neutre* feminist groups of the period, and now look like standard feminism: insistence on the rights of abandoned wives; demand for a mother's allowance to be paid directly to the mother; concern about prostitution, alcoholism and alcohol abuse, and venereal disease.

REFERENCES

ALBISTUR, M. and D. ARMOGATHE (1977) Histoire du féminisme français du moyen âge à nos jours. Paris: Editions des femmes.

BANKS, J. A. and O. BANKS (1964) "Feminism and social change: a case study of a movement," pp. 547-569 in G. K. Zollschan and W. Hirsch (eds.) Explorations in Social Change. London: Houghton Mifflin.

BERG, B. (1978) The Remembered Gate: Origins of American Feminism. New York: Oxford University Press.

BIROTHEAU-COUSSY, A.-M. (1977) "Approche d'un mouvement féminin—l'union féminine civique et sociale 1925-1976." Mémoire, diplôme d'Etudes Superieures de Droit Publique, Université de Nantes.

BOY, M. (1936) "Les associations internationales féminines." Thèse, Doctorat-ès-Droit, Université de Lyon.

BUTILLARD, A. (1942, 1945) La femme au service du pays. Paris: Union féminine civique et sociale.

CAMPBELL, O. (1952) The Report of a Conference on the Feminine Point of View. London: Williams & Norgate.

Commission of the European Communities (1975) European Men and Women: A Comparison of Their Attitudes to Some of the Problems Facing Society. Brussels: Author.

——— (1978) European Men and Women in 1978: A Comparison of Their Attitudes to Some of the Problems Facing Society. Brussels: Author.

CORLIEU, D. C. de (1959) "Le conseil international des femmes." Presented to L'association des femmes diplômées d'université, Grenoble, March 7.

——— (1970) Carnets d'une chrétienne moderniste: de 1870 à nos jours. Toulouse: Editions Privat.

DANGERFIELD, C. (1961) The Strange Death of Liberal England, 1910-1914. New York: Capricorn.

DEGLER, C. (1965) "Revolution without ideology: the changing place of women in America." pp. 193-210 in R. J. Lifton (ed.) The Woman in America. Boston: Beacon.

DOGAN, M. and J. NARBONNE (1955) Les françaises face à la politique: comportement politique et condition sociale. Paris: Armand Colin.

DU BOIS, E. (1978) Feminism and Suffrage: The Emergence of an Independent Women's Movement in America, 1848-1869. Ithaca, NY: Cornell University Press.

DUVERGER, M. (1955) The Political Role of Women. Paris: UNESCO.

——— (1969) "Des conservatrices." La Nef 38 (October-December).

ERSKINE, H. (1971) "The polls: women's role." Public Opinion Quarterly 35, 2: 275-290.

EVANS, R. (1977) The Feminists: Woman's Emancipation Movements in Europe, America and Australasia, 1840-1920. London: Croom Helm.

EVANS, S. (1979) Personal Politics: The Roots of Women's Liberation in the Civil Rights Movement and the New Left. New York: Knopf.

FERRARU, A. (1979) "From UNCHE to UNCSTD: aggregate data on nongovernmental organizations with observer status at U.N.-sponsored conferences." Presented at the annual meeting of the International Studies Association, Toronto, Canada, March 21-24.

FIRESTONE, S. (1970) The Dialectic of Sex: The Case for Feminist Revolution. New York: William Morrow.

FOGARTY, M. (1957) Christian Democracy in Western Europe, 1820-1953. London: Routledge & Kegan Paul.

Forum 80 (1980) Copenhagen, July: United Nations.

GAFFIN, J. (1977) "Women and cooperation," pp. 112-142 in L. Middleton (ed.) Women in the Labour Movement. London: Croom Helm.

GILLESPIE-WOLTEMADE, L. (1980) "Feminism as an international metaculture." Presented at the annual meeting of the American Sociological Association, New York, August 25-30.

GILMAN, C. (1979) Herland. New York: Pantheon.

GORDON, L. (1977) Woman's Body, Woman's Right: Birth Control in America. Harmondsworth, England: Penguin.

GROS, B. (1975) Qui sont ces femmes élues dans les Yvelines? Meulan, January.

HEILBRUN, C. (1973) Toward a Recognition of Androgyny. New York: Knopf.

——— (1979) Reinventing Womanhood. New York: Norton.

HOLE, J. and E. LEVINE (1971) Rebirth of Feminism. New York: Quadrangle/The New York *Times*.

HURWITZ, E. (1977) "The international sisterhood," pp. 325-345 in R. Bridenthal and C. Koonz (eds.) Becoming Visible: Women in European History. Boston: Houghton Mifflin.

International Council of Women (1966) Women in a Changing World: The Dynamic Story of the ICW. London: Routledge & Kegan Paul.

——— (1973) "Women and the UN." Produced for the UNESCO Gift Coupon Programme, Paris.

International Women's Year Secretariat, Canada (1976) Women in Canada. Toronto: Decision Marketing Research.

KANTER, R. (1977) Men and Women of the Corporation. New York: Basic Books.

LEMONS, J. S. (1975) The Woman Citizen: Social Feminism in the 1920s. Urbana: University of Illinois Press.

LEWIS, J. (1975) "Beyond suffrage: English feminism during the 1930s." Maryland Historian 6, 1: 1-17.

LIDDINGTON, J. and J. NORRIS (1978) One Hand Tied Behind Us: The Rise of the Women's Suffrage Movement. London: Virago.

MICHEL, A. and G. TEXIER (1968) La condition de la française d'aujourd'hui. Paris: Editions Gonthier.

MICHY, J.(1975) "Les mouvements féminins et les mouvements féministes." Pourquoi 106 (May): 55-57.

MODY, B. and E. ROGERS (1979) "Women's networks and development planning." Presented at the annual meeting of the International Studies Association, Toronto, March 21.

MORGAN, D. (1975) Suffragists and Liberals: The Politics of Woman Suffrage in Britain. Oxford: Blackwell.

MORGAN, R. (1978) Going Too Far: The Personal Chronicle of a Feminist. New York: Vintage.

MOSSUZ-LAVAU, J. and M. SINEAU (1980) "Les femmes françaises en 1978: insertion sociale, insertion politique." Paris: CORDES.

O'NEILL, W. (1971) Everyone Was Brave: A History of Feminism in America. Chicago: Quadrangle.

PHILIPS, M. (1980) The Divided House: Women at Westminster. London: Sidgwick & Jackson.

Questions féministes (1977) 1 (November).

RABAUT, J. (1978) Histoire des féminismes français. Paris: Stock.

RENARD, M. -T. (1965) La participation de femmes à la vie civique. Paris: Editions ouvrières.

ROLLET, H. (1955) Sur le chantier social. Lyon: Chronique sociale de France.

——— (1958) L'action social des catholiques en France [tome II]. Paris: Boivin.

——— (1960) Andrée Butillard et le féminisme chrétien. Paris: Spes.

———(1975) La condition de la femme dans l'église: ces femmes qui ont fait l'église. Paris: Fayard.

ROWBOTHAM, S. (1974) Women, Resistance and Revolution. Harmondsworth, England: Penguin.

SEBO, K. (1976) "The women's movement as a transnational phenomenon." Presented at the annual meeting of the International Studies Association, Toronto, February 26.

SMITH, D. (1977) Feminism and Marxism: A Place To Begin, a Way To Go. Vancouver: New Star Books.

STANTON, T. (1970) The Woman Question in Europe. New York: Source Book Press.
STOTT, M. (1978) Organization Women: The Story of the National Union of Townswomen's Guilds. London: Heinemann.
STRONG-BOAG, V. (1976) The Parliament of Women: The National Council of Women of Canada, 1893-1929. Ottawa: National Museums of Canada.
Union féminine civique et sociale [UFCS] (1925-1967) La femme dans la vie sociale.
——— (1968) Dialoguer.
——— (1971) Dossier: "Les choix: face au droit à la vie." April.
——— (1972) "Note concernant la législation sur l'avortement." December 6.
——— (1976) "Note sur les 'Projets pour les femmes 1976-81.' " June.
——— (1977). Dossier: "Présentation de l'UFCS." March.
——— (1978) Cahier d'Education Civique 45/46: "Femmes et féminisme." July-December.
WALTERS, F. P. (1952) A History of the League of Nations. London: Oxford University Press.
WHITE, L. (1951) Non-Governmental Organizations: Their Purposes, Method, and Accomplishments. New Brunswick, NJ: Rutgers University Press.
WHITTICK, A. (1979) Woman into Citizen: The World Movement towards the Emancipation of Women in the Twentieth Century with Accounts of the Contribution of the International Alliance of Women, the League of Nations and the Relevant Organizations of the United Nations. London: Atheneum with Frederick Mueller.
WOLGAST, E. (1980) Equality and the Rights of Women. Ithaca, NY: Cornell University Press.
Women and Politics (1980) 1, 1.
WOOLF, V. (1931) "Introductory letter to Margaret Llewelyn Davies," pp. xv-xxxix in M. L. Davies (ed.) Life as We Have Known It, by Co-operative Working Women. London: Hogarth.
——— (1938) Three Guineas. London: Hogarth.
World Synod of Roman Catholic Bishops (1980) "A message to Christian families in the modern world." English text printed in the New York Times, October 26.

12

THE CONTEMPORARY AMERICAN WOMEN'S MOVEMENT

ANN BAKER COTTRELL

Women secluded by patriarchy, women without enough to eat, and illiterate women might well ask, as have many American women and men, why middle-class American women, the best-fed, best-educated, seemingly freest women in the world want to fight for their rights, let alone for "liberation." That this movement is taking place in the United States and most Western nations indicates that economic development does not mean a full development with respect to equity for women.

This chapter examines the development of the current women's movement in the U.S.—its participants, organization, issues, and activities—to answer the question of why these women are fighting for change. In this movement we see the diversities among women committed to change, the difficulties encountered in sustaining the movement, and the impact of the movement.

SETTING OF THE CONTEMPORARY AMERICAN WOMEN'S MOVEMENT

Concern with "women's issues" and organizations devoted to them did not disappear with the achievement of suffrage. The League of Women Voters, descendant of the suffrage movement's reform branch, and from the more radical branch, National Women's Party, are still active; NWP has introduced the Equal Rights Amendment (ERA) to Congress almost yearly. Many other, even older, organizations have also quietly and continuously worked to improve women's situation, such as the YWCA, the American Association of University Women, the National Federation of Business and Professional Women, and Sigma Delta Epsilon/Graduate Women in Science. Though there has been continuous concern with women's opportunities and position on the part of these and other groups, during the 1950s and 1960s demographic, economic, and social trends, combined with changing attitudes, created a setting in which many women felt the need for greater collective action to create change.

DEMOGRAPHIC, EDUCATION, AND ECONOMIC PATTERNS

During the 1950s the traditional family was emphasized and the suburban single-family home was the dream for many middle-class families. Family size increased with more third and fourth children, then began to decline in the 1960s. By the mid-1960s the average age of women at the birth of their last child was 27. This left still active women as full-time wives and mothers for husbands and children present only part of the time. The proportion of women who were married similarly declined in the 1960s. At the end of the decade, 35 percent of all women of marriageable age were not married. (Freeman, 1975: 29). Even more significant in terms of reaction to restricted economic opportunities was the increase in female-headed families; between 1959 and 1969 this group increased by two-fifths to 10 percent of all families (Ferriss, 1971: 49-61).

Many observers of the early organizational efforts of the women's movement were baffled because women, they felt, had come such a long way. Yet Ferriss (1971) did not find any significant changes in socioeconomic variables over the previous 20 years to account for it. Both these interpretations are true; in absolute terms the numbers of women getting higher education and going to work increased greatly, but their position, compared to that of men, was not improving.

The number of women in higher education increased visibly during the 1950s. But because the number of men increased even faster, women formed a percentage of students in higher education smaller than that during the Depression. In 1962 women were awarded 33 percent of all B.A.s and M.A.s, compared to 40 percent in 1930 (Dixon, 1971: 428).

Likewise, in absolute numbers, women's participation in the paid labor force steadily increased in the 1950s and 1960s: 33.9 percent of women worked in 1950, 43 percent in 1970 (U.S. Department of Labor, 1980: 3). However, neither the status of work women did nor their pay improved compared to that of men. In fact, segregation of women to "pink occupational ghettos" actually increased. The percentage of women who were clerical workers increased from 52.6 to 72.6 between 1940 and 1968 (U.S. Department of Labor, 1969: 92), and the percentage of professional and technical workers who were women declined (45.5 percent to 38.6 percent) partly because male employment in these fields increased so rapidly.[1] Wage differences reflected this segregation and the greater upward occupational mobility among men, for women's median wage declined from 64 percent of the male's in 1955 to 60 percent in 1965 (Dixon, 1971: 429).

The most startling change in women's labor force participation, given the norms surrounding motherhood, was the increase among married women with preschool children. Of such mothers, 33 percent worked in 1968, compared to 13 percent in 1951 (Oppenheimer, 1973: 85). Particularly significant for the beginnings of the women's movement is that the greatest increase in working women was among well-educated wives in moderate-income families (Chafe, 1972: 218-219). They could see how little their education meant compared to that of men. It is this college-educated group, especially the professionals, to which the women's movement appealed.

SOCIAL AND PSYCHOLOGICAL SETTING

Women did not appear to question their "place" during the 1950s—not openly, at least. Girls were socialized to expect marriage and life as full-time homemakers. To the extent that some women were dissatisfied (25 percent in a 1946 poll wished to be male if reborn; Chafe, 1972: 200), they were encouraged by society and psychiatrists to blame themselves. There were challenges to "women's place," but without an articulated consciousness of categorical discrimination against women, these were quiet and individual.

Through the 1950s and increasingly in the 1960s, women experienced a sense of frustration born of a heightened perception of relative deprivation. In the early 1960s a greater number of young women had grown up with mothers who were not full-time homemakers. In addition, more young women had gone to college or were in college, thus gaining skills, knowledge, and a sense of their own worth. Finally, more women were living on their own and working whether married with children or not. Such women gained a sense of potential (if not always real) financial independence. These factors raised aspirations that clashed with the realities that women were still expected to stay home, at least when children came, and that employed women earned less for the same work than men—even if allowed to do the same work. The sense of relative deprivation in this situation was made even more extreme for the few women in traditionally male professional jobs by their unequal treatment on the job. Thus, by the end of the 1960s many women were frustrated at home, while many others were at work but equally frustrated by limited opportunities, poor pay, unequal treatment, and lack of child care. These women were likely to be receptive to the questions and challenges posed by the new women's movement.

POLITICAL SETTING AND ORIGINS OF THE WOMEN'S MOVEMENT

Two additional factors contributed to the mobilization of women in the mid-1960s: the presence of egalitarian and anti-establishment movements and the existence of communication networks among women. The civil rights, student and counterculture, and peace and antiwar movements set the stage for challenging the way "the system" operated. In the late 1950s and 1960s the demands of Blacks made Americans aware of structural discrimination in culture, institutions, and individual actions. Thus, ideas fundamental to later feminist demands were present, even though recognition of the parallels was widely resisted when feminists initially made their case. The Black movement was important because it addressed general oppression, including psychological and cultural oppression, rather than economic exploitation alone. It also validated the idea of separatist politics in declaring that whites had no place in the movement. The counterculture movement introduced the politics of emotion, which not only admitted but built on the relevence of personal responses and the need for personal freedom.

These movements had an even more direct impact on the origin of the women's movement. Many early leaders of the more radical branch of the women's movement had been politically active in one or more of the others. These women had become used to challenging dominant institutions, questioning societal values, and developing new ideas. Those with the Student Nonviolent Coordinating Committee (SNCC) in the South also found, in Black women, role models for strong, independent women. Consequently they developed skills and an appreciation of their own abilities. This was especially true for those women in Students for a Democratic Society's (SDS) Economic Research Action projects, for they were more successful community organizers than men (Evans, 1979). Yet, within the Left they often experienced sexual exploitation and were generally denied a role in policy formation or leadership. Women in the civil rights movement were particularly sensitive to this discrimination because of constant involvement with that issue. In this respect the catalyst for the current women's movement parallels that of the earlier (nineteenth-century) stage of the women's movement, for many of those leaders had been sensitized by their involvement in the abolition movement. Thus, by the mid-1960s there was a body of politically aware, activist women who were particularly responsive to what came to be called a liberation movement for women (see Carden, 1974; Dixon, 1970; Evans, 1979; Freeman, 1975; Morgan, 1970).

Throughout the 1960s women active in mainstream politics and government were also becoming increasingly aware of women's unequal position and frustrated by lack of change. In 1961, at the urging of women in government, including Esther Peterson, head of the U.S. Women's Bureau, President Kennedy established the National Commission on the Status of Women. Then state commissions were formed. These brought together politically active women to study and discuss women's issues. Into this climate of increased awareness of women's position and their expectation that something might be done came Friedan's best-selling book, *The Feminine Mystique* (1963). The response to this book made it clear that many women were not happy with the status quo. Expectations of change were further heightened by the 1963 Equal Pay Act and especially by the addition of "sex" to Title VII of the Civil Rights Bill in 1964. When the Equal Employment Opportunities Commission (EEOC), established to administer Title VII, did not enforce the bill's sex provision, concerned EEOC employees urged the formation of a feminist pressure group.

In 1966 women on the commissions, congresswomen, and EEOC employees came together at the Third National Conference on Commissions on the Status of Women. These women were disappointed by the general lack of commitment to changing women's status. The fact that they were not permitted to present a resolution asking EEOC to treat sex discrimination as seriously as race discrimination infuriated them; the women present decided then to form the National Organization for Women, NOW (see Carden, 1974; Freeman, 1975; Friedan, 1967; Hole and Levine, 1973).

Thus, there were several conditions in the early 1960s that predisposed a significant number of women to be receptive to a women's movement: objective deprivation, sense of relative deprivation and general malaise, a social atmosphere attuned to inequalities in the American social system, and communications networks among women who shared similar feminist concerns. These factors contributed to development of the new world view and self-concept necessary for women to move from individualized responses to collective action. As long as women conceived of their problems as personal and blamed themselves, collective effort was impossible. A "gender consciousness" was necessary. In the women just described, as well as those later in the 1960s, who were not in these networks, we see a changing attitude that progressed through Werner Landecker's (1963) three levels of consciousness. His description of developing class consciousness applies equally well to gender consciousness. It includes (1) class status consciousness, that is, identification of oneself as a member of a specific social class; (2) class structure consciousness, or perceptions about the nature of the class structure as a whole; and (3) class interest consciousness, the recognition of one's own interests as identical to those of others in the same class, and different from those of a different social class.

In the 1950s women were at the first level. Friedan's *The Feminine Mystique* provided many women the foundation for gender structure consciousness. In addition, a core group of women developed gender interest consciousness because of their experiences with the government (including Commissions on the status of Women and EEOC) and with the New Left. The formation of NOW and, soon after, of the more radical women's groups added an action dimension to the cognitive gender interest consciousness. This is an important distinction to make, for it is possible to develop gender interest consciousness, recognizing that one's interests are tied to those of other members of a group, without making the additional commitment to *do* anything more than lend passive support.

THE CONTEMPORARY WOMEN'S MOVEMENT

ORGANIZATION AND ISSUES

Feminists share a view of women's problems that interprets them as cultural, social, economic and political, rather than personal. However, from the beginning of the contemporary movement there have been several sorts of feminism, differing in specifics of theoretical analysis as well as in organizational philosophy. This is not surprising, given the diverse backgrounds and political experience of the first organizers. Three broad categories of feminists emerged early in the movement: the women's rights branch and the women's liberation branch, which soon divided between radical and socialist feminists.

Women's Rights. The reformist segment of the women's movement is best represented by NOW (still the largest feminist organization), Women's Equity Action League (WEAL, an offshoot of NOW), and the National Women's Political Caucus. Freeman (1975) suggests calling this the "older" branch because it predates the others and because the women involved have generally been older.

NOW was established by highly educated, largely professional women whose experience and expertise was in formal, traditionally structured organizations. NOW, both conceptually and organizationally, was founded as a national, rather than as a localized, grass-roots, organization. It recognized the need for a broad attack on the system, for equality only in economics does not lead to gender-role equality.

Primary emphasis has been on integrating women into the public life of the nation on an equal basis with men; NOW seeks a society in which no distinction is made according to gender and pursues this goal through the 3 "Ls": lobbying, legislation, and litigation. Initially, NOW virtually ignored the personal issues women confronted in the domestic sphere and, unlike the other branches, did not seek theoretical understanding of the origins of women's oppression. More recently it has responded to some of the issues raised by the more radical feminists. Fairly early, local chapters incorporated consciousness-raising groups (a technique introduced by radical feminists). The national organization has also taken positions on personal issues—for example, abortion and lesbian rights. NOW has turned attention to family issues, such as legislation for displaced homemakers or inclusion of the value of unpaid women's work in old-age insurance, pensions, or divorce settlements. The laissez-faire attitude of the national NOW toward local chapters (except in the last phases of efforts to ratify the ERA) also reflects a slight accommodation to the organizational style of the Left.

Women's Liberation. The more radical, younger women activists built their organizations on a more radical political philosophy and organizational style. These women sought complete restructuring of American society in months, or at most, years. Freeman (1979) calls this the "younger" branch because the members are younger and so are the groups. This younger-older distinction is useful, because the branches cannot be entirely associated with issues popularly identified as conservative or radical. The self-identified radical branch, for example, has been more concerned with traditional women's issues, such as marriage and child care (though its views are not traditional), and has been oriented toward service more than political activism (Freeman, 1975: 51).

Within the women's liberation branch there is agreement on the fact of oppression, but disagreement over its nature. The major division is between socialist and radical feminists. The former interpret women's oppression as one facet of the more generic subordination of the proletariat; women's oppression is rooted in the capitalist economic system rather than in male ideology and behavior. Because socialist feminists do not base their analysis on the difference between males and females, some do not consider them feminists.

Radical feminists tend to be more theoretically oriented than the women's rights branch, but are not as tied to existing theory as socialist feminists. Radical feminists build their analysis on the ubiquity of patriarchy: Men oppress women in all classes and all societies, including socialist. While men are seen as the oppressors, most radical feminists agree that their target for change must be gender roles, not men, for men are also dehumanized by the present system. A smaller proportion of radical feminists, however, "identify the agents of our oppression as men. . . . All men receive economic, sexual and psychological benefits from male supremacy" (Redstockings, 1970: 534).

Most radical feminists believe that "personal is political." The organizational manifestation of this is structureless consciousness-raising groups. In these groups, as one activist wrote, "our feelings will lead us to our theory, our theory to our action, our feelings about that action to new theory and then to new action" (Sarachild, 1969: 78). In emphasizing the personal and rejecting formal hierarchy, considered characteristic of male organizations, these women have insisted on completely equal involvement for all group members, often to the point of rotating leadership and giving each member an equal, limited amount of time to speak. The consequence of this organizational style has been the formation of large numbers of small, fluid, and localized groups (Freeman, 1975).

In the mid-1970s lesbian feminism emerged as a distinct focus; lesbians largely separated from other feminists. This, to a degree, is an extension of the radical challenge to male oppression and is also a reaction to perceived rejection by "straight" feminists. The lesbian community, while itself factionalized by class, political, and other differences similar to those in the larger feminist movement (and society), is generally more involved in building a female community and culture than in aspirations to change the larger society.

ACTIVITIES

This and subsequent sections of the chapter will continue to describe developments in the women's movement generally, but where possible will use examples from a case study of the movement in one city, San Diego, California.

The women's rights branch continues to be the main source of lobbying and litigation. Initially pursuing mainly issues of discrimination in job placement and promotion and the goal of equal pay for equal work, it is now raising the more fundamental question of equal pay for work of comparable worth in terms of skill, effort, and responsibility demanded. Along with these issues and the ERA, NOW is also coming to be involved in many issues initially espoused by radical feminists, such as abortion, sexual preferences, and media images of women. Women's rights organizations, in part because of their legislative thrust, continue to be national (e.g., NOW, WEAL, NWPC), though many also have state or local chapters.

The movement has encouraged many traditional feminist organizations to strengthen their stand on feminist issues. The YWCA is a good example of an organization that has become quite active in feminist causes. Several new orgaizations, such as 9-5 (office workers), have their origins in YWCA meetings; and the American Home Economics Association in 1970 demanded an end to sex discrimination in education, business, industry, and government. It supported the ERA and advocated repeal of restrictive abortion laws (Women Today, 1971).

The radical branch of the movement has, from the beginning, placed more emphasis on issues closer to the experience of all women: child care and women's health issues, especially abortion, as well as rape and other forms of violence against women. Their activites are those that can be done by small groups—local women's self-help centers offering education or services, such as abortion counseling, day-care centers, women's health centers, houses for battered wives, bookstores, feminist publications. At first the links between these groups were highly informal, through personal communication, travel, and some newsletter exchange. Some of these local groups at present are becoming more formal and institutionalized; some groups doing similar work throughout the country have developed national organizations to link them—for example, the large (several thousand members, mainly organizations) and active National Women's Health

Network. Its involvement in legislation on a broad range of health issues indicates some blurring of lines between what were originally regarded as women's rights and radical activities.

It is impossible to catalogue all the groups working to improve women's position or all the issues addressed. Recent listings indicate the diversity. A women's science and technology directory issued at a San Diego State University conference lists 207 organizations, including women's caucuses in professional science associations; the Women, Food and Population program; the Association of Feminist Consultants; the Electrical Women's Round Table; Executive Women International; the U.A.W. Women's Committee; Women in Apprenticeship Programs; Feminist Resources on Energy and Ecology; and Cinewomen. The Feminist Free University, run by San Diego's Center for Women's Studies and Services, recently offered courses in automechanics, the evolution of women, creative-solutions rap groups, public speaking, the single-mother experience, creative writing, the bioenergetic woman (workshop), integrating the personal and political, the feminist approach to social work, corrective English, beginning layout and graphic design, the history of American women, lifeplanning, radical feminist counseling, modern math, lesbian history, sexist justice, feminist socialism, convening and facilitating a men's group, body language (workshop), and crafts and sewing. Women's studies courses on nearly as great a diversity of topics had expanded by 1976 to 15,000 courses offered at 1,500 universities (Howe, 1977: 15).

Observers comment and feminists lament that the movement is dying or at least is no longer effective. For example: "I have become distressed by the movement's fragmentation, its widespread pessimism, introspection and dogmatism" (Bunche, 1976: 9). "As I listened I wondered, when had the proud, infant roar become a nagging, old Sisyphus, sentenced to pushing the rock up the hill, only to have it roll down on top of us" (Symington, 1981).

The movement is not dead; it is fragmented and decentralized perhaps, as it has been from the first, and it is still bickering, but it is not dead. Several changes help explain the appearance of a demise. First, the number of women involved has grown, as has the number of groups, many focusing on specific issues. Thus it is impossible to be aware of the full scope of the movement, let alone to know who the participants are. The public is even less aware of the great scope of feminist activity in many separate organizations. Second, expectations of an immediate and general revolution affecting women's status have faded, and most activists now recognize that women's problems cannot be solved sweepingly. Solutions are known to involve analyses, pressure, educating, legislation, enforcement, and constant monitoring in thousands of specific issue areas. Third, the demise of the movement is further suggested by lack of media attention. There are fewer media "events," and activities like lobbying or textbook revision are not newsworthy. When the media do cover feminism, they often portray division, as in coverage of the 1975 and 1980 International Women's Year conferences. Finally, many feminists have changed their style to fit the realities of dealing with "the system," and thus may appear less "activist." A long-time San Diego feminist commented, "I am more ideologically radical now than ever, but I appear less radical. I accomplish more when I am less overtly aggressive."

Organizational Issues. The women's movement, like any movement seeking broad, revolutionary changes, faces ideological and organizational problems when the original goals are not quickly realized. Those who then decide to work for goals within the present system are accused of "selling out," especially if government funding is accepted. Bunch (1976: 10) argues that the "problem is that in building feminist strategies around reform goals dependent on existing political and economic structures, feminists often come not only to accept the limitations of form, but also to defend existing institutions instead of continuing to work toward feminist alternatives. . . . Longer range questions [are] put aside in the struggle to survive."

Feminists working for change within the system also often experience problems due to organizational and philosophical commitments characteristic of at least part of the women's movement as it now exists. As concern with problem-solving increasingly takes precedence over problem identification, feminists must decide how to reconcile the desire for organizational democracy with the need for strong organization to fight national and even local problems. A similar contradiction between ideology and organizational needs is illustrated by the failure of a feminist credit union. The women working for this program were committed to helping other, especially poor and minority, women. Their difficulty saying "no" and their belief in the women who borrowed, however, proved incompatible with business reality.

There is also concern over the loss to the movement of individuals who burn out and or drop out. Some women—especially among those active in the initial stages of the movement who gave more time and energy than would seem possible to a revolution that did not occur on time,—have burned out and are no longer active participants. More severely criticized, perhaps, are women who have achieved personal success within the system and are accused of dropping out of the movement to consolidate their own positions. Gordon (1980: 54) points out that they not only participate less, but deny "economic reality in their belief in individual success; supporting the ethic of individual success assures that the distribution of wealth and power remains unequal." Some of these women, however, may become more feminist, at least at work, with job security. As a university dean said, "I am more feminist again now that I have this position. Most of the other feminists on campus are struggling for tenure or promotion."

Relations with Poor and Minority Women. From the beginning, the U.S. women's movement has failed to appeal to poor and minority women, in spite of concerted efforts to deal with problems of particular relevance to poor women. Organized activity on behalf of women's issues (among others) is not unknown among lower-income women (Brightman, 1978). There are minority feminist organizations such as the National Black Feminist Organization as well as some minority women in "mainstream" feminist organizations. But many minority women fear feminist gains will be at the expense of jobs for minority men or that middle-class feminists will only hire sisters of color to free themselves. Many also reject association with a movement thought to be anti-male, for fear of dividing the minority community.

Feminist theoretical analyses and proposed solutions are often seen as inappropriate by lower-income women (Fisher, 1977). Legislation and government programs are frequently proposed to deal with problems, yet lower-income women do not have much faith in either; programs for rape or battered women involving police and courts are also viewed with suspicion. Demands for access to male jobs are not so appealing to women whose men work at hard, dirty, repetitive, low-status jobs with little control, security, or pay. Also ignored is the fact that many working-class women have to work at unsatisfying, poorly paid jobs and would prefer to stay home. Those women resent feminist rejection of the positive side of the wife and mother roles, and find the protrayal of women as passive, weak, and dependent inconsistent with their own experience. Socialist feminists presumably redress the class bias of radical and reformist feminists, but here, too, lower-class women are alienated. The theory is too abstract and terminologically obscure; it fails to provide concrete direction. Socialists, too, are seen as a primarily white interest group.

Problems of Success. The women's movement has had many successes and has had an impact on American society. But successes have also posed new problems for the movement, either because of the responses to success or because of the unanticipated consequences of what initially appeared to be successes.

"The problem now," a male colleague commented, "is that feminism is as American as motherhood." Acceptance of women's equality in theory, plus increasing numbers of women working, affirmative action, and gains in women's financial independence, give many the impression that the battle for women's rights has been won. Thus, many of today's young women, confident of their ability to succeed in any field and unaware of the depth of change still needed, are not participating in the movement.

Another effect of the general acceptance of the feminist stand on some issues is that new and more fundamental issues are raised that create new resistance. One example is the move from the no longer controversial "equal pay for equal work" to "equal pay for work of comparable worth."[2] The difficulty of defining this concept causes some resistance, but even more frightening to many, it may not stop at women; college professors may compare themselves to bus drivers, and so on. Another example is the increased emphasis on the need to redefine male as well as female roles in order to achieve equity for women. This means redefining male domestic roles as well as female public and domestic roles, and that may, literally, be hitting too close to home.

The apparent success of feminists in challenging traditional gender-role norms has fueled antifeminist movements. Happiness of Women (HOW), which extolls traditional femininity, is one example. Another is the National Right to Life Committee, which focuses primarily on making abortion illegal but also advocates traditional female roles. The latter in particular has several strategic advantages over feminist groups. Primarily, though not exclusively, church-based, it has access to money, organizational support, and vast reserves of man and woman power at its command when necessary. The women are also more likely to be full-time housewives and have more time than today's feminists (English, 1981).

Emphasis on individual successes and many "firsts" (e.g., the first woman Senator not succeeding her husband, the first woman contractor, and so on) masks the fact that these advances represent slow or restricted change, if they affect the larger picture at all. And often these success stories reflect initial achievements but do not give the broader or long-term picture. In many traditionally male fields, women's gains have been mainly in limited areas, such as obstetrics-gynecology, family law or affirmative action, or, in management, personnel. In government, although the number of female public officeholders has been increasing, by 1979 only about 10 percent of U.S. elected officials were women (Women in Public Office, 1979). At the present rate of increase, it will be 125 years before women are equally represented in Congress (National NOW Times, 1980-1981: 3). One study, which examined women in top-level jobs, is discouraging; ten years later, few survivors were found (Kagan, 1980). The researcher's explanation was the decline in efforts by organized women. Another explanation is that the opening of new occupations has not been matched by necessary related changes, such as adequate child care, parental leaves, or flextime. Or these women may have been responding to poor treatment on the job.

Not infrequently, successes have unanticipated consequences that are not consistent with feminist goals and are discouraging to activists. Several examples will illustrate this source of frustration. The passage of no-fault divorce laws, expected to increase equality, meant husbands walked out more frequently because it became easier to evade the burden of supporting two families. "Equality was our aim, but women didn't have equality yet and in the transition to it divorced women suffered" (Friedan, 1977: 409). Title VII, prohibiting discrimination on the basis of sex, covers all women, but legal proceedings are often required for compliance. Many women, however, are reluctant to press discrimination charges. Those who do and turn to EEOC find its backlog of cases is so great that few cases are heard; furthermore, EEOC has no enforcement power over cases it hears and finds in favor of the woman. While numerous positions, boards, and the like have been established to deal with women's issues, there is no guarantee they will be filled by feminists. For example, Beverly LaHaye, on the San Diego County Commission on the Status of Women, is the openly antifeminist wife of an influential right-wing minister. (Los Angeles Times, 1981). Sometimes men benefit more than women from the elimination of sex typing in jobs: During ATT's three years of affirmative action, 16,300 men took formerly female positions and only 9,400 women took male jobs (Hacker, 1979: 539).

The movement's difficulty in relation to the above good news-bad news pattern is twofold. The public rarely hears any but the success stories and consequently many do feel battles rather than just skirmishes are being won. But the activists are too aware of the other side, and some do get discouraged and burn out.

Economic and Political Challenges. The current movement originated in a period of economic growth; since then the U.S. economy has grown weaker and jobs scarcer. This may result in a demand, on one hand, that women leave jobs for men who support families. On the other, it already appears to have made many women put job interests ahead of feminist concerns, keeping quiet to keep jobs. Women newly integrated into skilled craft occupations appreciate the movement's role in opening these jobs and are sympathetic to feminist issues, but since keeping jobs and getting promoted depend on "the boys," they avoid feminist stands. (Walshok, 1981). Women's economic position is further threatened by technological change, for computers are particularly suited to the kind of work most women do, office work.[3] The vulnerability of women to technological change was revealed in the course of NOW's civil rights action against the American Telegraph and Telephone company. "Planned technological change," NOW learned, "would eliminate more jobs for women than affirmative action would provide" (Hacker, 1979: 539).

The other swing that momentarily threatens the movement's strength and accomplishments is the apparent political shift to the right. Victorious Republicans campaigned on a platform that was anti-ERA, for the Pro-life Amendment (to make abortion illegal), and opposed to affirmative action timetables and goals. More conservative officeholders not only make feminist legislation more difficult, but, if the 1980 elections do signify a shift in public opinion, resistance to further improvement in women's status will increase and could threaten to reverse earlier gains.

IMPACT OF THE WOMEN'S MOVEMENT

In spite of economic and political reversals, it is unlikely that all the movement's accomplishments will be erased. San Diego feminists generally agree that many views feminists advocated in the late 1960s are now widely accepted. Evidence of changing attitudes toward women and reflections of women's changed position are easily found. Numerous new publications are oriented toward professional and working women. Advertisements are aimed at and depict working women, and traditional women's publications include topics quite inconsistent with their earlier reputations. *Vogue,* for instance, has covered car maintenance, investing money, and returning to college, in addition to fashion features.

OPINION, ECONOMIC, AND DEMOGRAPHIC CHANGES

Public opinion polls show changes in the direction feminists seek, but also show the tenacity of many traditional attitudes and behaviors. Demographic, educational, and economic data reveal a continuation of trends reported in the 1950s and 1960s, which seem to reflect both the impact of the women's movement and a basis of support for the movement. Again, while larger numbers of women are getting higher education and going to work, the overall pattern continues to be one of segregation, as polls suggest both males and females expect.

The public in 1980 is more supportive of feminist positions and efforts to change women's status than a decade ago.[4] Male and female opinions are very close on most points, while younger respondents of both sexes are more supportive of the feminist position. In the mid-1970s, 85 percent felt women were better off than five years earlier and gave women's groups some credit for that improvement (Gallup, 1976: 24).[5] However, the movement is also blamed by 44 percent for family life breaking down. The least educated women especially believe this (Public Opinion, 1979a: 38).

While there is general approval of married women working,[6] and nearly half (48 percent) feel marriage is best when husband and wife both work and share household tasks (Public Opinion, 1980: 24), traditional values still define the wife-mother role. Most say women should not work, unless financially necessary, while children are young; children are thought to suffer when mothers work.[7] When women do work, the husband's job comes first and the wife is held responsible for a clean house, in the public view.[8] Polls also suggest that when women do work they are expected to remain in women's jobs, though this is slowly breaking down. More than half still think women make better nurses and secretaries and men better firemen, police, and automechanics (Gallup Poll 1976: 38-39). And most, given a choice of new boss, prefer to work for a man.[9]

Educational data show continuing increases in women's participation. By 1980 53 percent of the undergraduate and graduate students in California's public universities and colleges were women (California Post-Secondary Education Commission, 1980: 35-37). In 1978 women earned nearly half the B.A. (46 percent) and M.A. (47 percent) degrees, and one-fourth the Ph.D.s (U.S. Department of Commerce, 1978: 35). Women's move into traditionally male fields of study continued but still accounts for very small proportions.[10] One of the more interesting educational trends has been the doubling of women over 35 in postsecondary educational institutions, mainly in universities and colleges, between 1972 and 1978 (Young, 1979). Most of these women had not been active in the women's movement, but 69 percent credited the movement for raising their ambitions (Astin, 1976).

Women's studies continue to be popular; enrollment in San Diego State University's women's studies courses, for example, is 1000 per year. Students report that courses have a powerful impact on their lives and education (Porter and Eileenchild, 1980), but, as the chair of SDSU's department points out, this impact is less likely to be translated into movement participation than it would have been a decade ago.

Occupational and economic statistics also continue the 1960s pattern, with the labor force including 43 percent of mothers with preschool children (U.S. Department of Labor, 1980: 21). Occupational segregation and low income still resist change.[11] Though more women are entering professional and technical occupations, 52 percent in this category are still precollege teachers or nurses, down from 60 percent in 1970 (U.S. Department of Labor, 1980: 1). Likewise, women's low income, reflecting low-paying jobs, remains at about 60 percent that of men; white women, on the average, still earn less than Black or Hispanic men.[12] These patterns persist, in part because of public opinion, including women's own stereotypes, about women's work.

Demographic data from the 1970s are no more surprising than the above, with the number of single women and female-headed households continuing to increase.[13] Postponing or avoiding marriage or even divorce may reflect, in part, a perception that women can be financially independent. As more women support themselves and their children, however, they are more likely to compare their income with others who are sole sources of support, i.e., men, rather than with women, and may become more interested in the issue of better-paying jobs for women.

Consistent with increases in numbers of working women and single women—as well, undoubtedly, as the economic decline—fertility has continued to drop.[14] However, this trend has recently reversed itself for older women. The number of first births for women over 30 increased by 37 percent in recent years, mainly among urban professional women (Newsweek, 1981). This may reflect some indirect influence of the women's movement, for this is the category of women most likely to have given priority to establishing their own careers and positions.

IMPACT ON OTHER ORGANIZATIONS

The influence of the movement, directly or indirectly, is seen in the activities of women who have not generally been active in feminist groups. While women have always been involved in a variety of women's "networks," in the early 1980s new kinds of networks are being formed, especially among successful women, in male fields such as business and politics, where professional contacts are important for success. Many have been lone achievers, only recently aware of the potential benefit from a women's network. It is hoped that a women's network would function like the informal "old boys" networks from which women are still largely excluded (Kleiman, 1980).

Women in less elite occupations, as well as women outside the paid labor force, are also organizing to improve their position. In some cases (e.g., the Coalition of Labor Union Women and San Diego's United Domestic Workers of America), this is in the union tradition and often reflects a frustration with unions' lack of attention to women's issues or their failure to organize women in low-status occupations (see Hubbell, 1980; Sexton, 1974). Female office workers are forming organizations, such as the National Association for Office Workers and 9-5, to improve wages and working conditions. Others, like Brooklyn members of the National Congress of Neighborhood Women, are organizing to improve their communities (Brightman, 1978). While many such women disavow any connection with feminism, these newer organizations are fighting for principles familiar to feminists. A number of the Brooklyn group's activities look much like those of any feminist center, including battered women's centers and advocacy programs in health care.

The long-established women's volunteer organizations have also been affected by the women's movement, as we can see in San Diego. At a practical level, organizations like the League of Women Voters and the Junior League are adapting their structures to the reality that 50 percent or more of their members now work for pay. Both are reorganizing meeting schedules and projects. The League of Women Voters has always been involved in issues that directly concern women, such as maternal and child welfare, along with others, such as energy and elections. It now officially supports the ERA and events sponsored by feminist groups at the local level, but does not consider itself a women's movement organization. The Junior League, in contrast, which has also been involved in services to children, has never had feminist connections and does not take stands on feminist issues such as ERA. In its training programs, however, which include career planning and women and changing roles, many members are beginning to develop new images of themselves. Many are redefining their roles in the community and home in a way that reflects the independence feminists advocate, but without challenging the system regarding women's status generally.

SUMMARY

U.S. women's dissatisfaction increased in the 1960s, when many felt conditions for women were improving. Realization that increased numbers of women participating in the public sphere did not change the status of women compared to that of men—and that changes in women's traditional role expectations, and therefore in their patterns of participation, were thwarted—created frustration leading to the current movement. While the movement has had victories and some changes have occurred in specific areas, feminists are aware that progress on one front does not mean liberation or even equal rights. They are aware of the need to move on to new issues while continuing to watch for challenges or reversals in areas of earlier success (e.g., abortion rights). As feminists make small gains they are also aware that, overall, there has been relatively little change; each new "victory" makes more apparent the depth of cultural conditioning underlying overt discrimination. Thus we see increasing recognition that women's roles cannot be changed without concomitant changes in men's roles. Women cannot be integrated into male economic roles, for example, unless men are also integrated into traditionally female roles. This requires men and women to change ideas about appropriate gender behavior; for example, nurturing must become masculine as well as feminine. Simultaneously, the value and compensation attached to "female" domestic and occupational roles must be increased so men as well as women will fill them.

Many feminists also appear to be changing their view of personal relations with men, placing greater emphasis on the importance of husband-wife relations in particular. In the early phases of the movement, Friedan generally ignored changing familial roles as necessary for changing women's status; her 1977 book devotes considerable attention to the nature and importance of male-female relations. Many of the more radical feminists initially talked of rejecting close relations with men. Robin Morgan, who pretended "contempt for monogamy," now emphasizes the importance of male-female relationships when redefined. Morgan now can "confess my pride at an ongoing committed relationship with the husband I love and have loved all along, whose transformation by feminism I have watched over and struggled with and marveled at" (Morgan, 1977: 16). The new awareness places less emphasis on independence, but stresses interdependence with equity in which no participant is generally subordinate.

At the basis of women's roles and responses to them is the ubiquity of patriarchy. The more we understand of women's position in all cultures and periods, the more we are aware that "development" has not significantly altered women's subordination. The clearer this becomes the more we are aware that there is patriarchy in the United States. It is a modernized patriarchy, less oppressive and more subtle, but patriarchy nonetheless. As it is manifest in myriad ways, it requires the multifaceted attack that characterizes the current movement.

NOTES

1. Minuscule increases were seen in some traditionally male fields: Lawyers who were women increased from 2.4 percent to 4.7 percent; women physicians from 7 percent to 9 percent (U.S. Department of Labor, 1975: 93). Clearly, these changes were not significant enought to affect women's general occupational pattern.

2. General acceptance of equal pay for equal work is widely cited as an accomplishment for the current movement. Opinion polls, however, show that in 1942 92 percent of women and 78 percent men already accepted the concept; by 1973 96 percent women and 94 percent of men supported the idea (Public Opinion, 1979a: 36).

3 This had not happened between 1970 and 1979; the number of female bank tellers, bookkeepers, and secretary-typists increased (U.S. Department of Labor, 1980).

4. Efforts to strengthen women's status were supported by 42 percent in 1970 and 65 percent in 1978 (Public Opinion, 1980: 33).

5. Women's increased satisfaction is also seen in the fact that 87 percent of women in the mid-1970s chose to be women if reborn (Gallup, 1976: 31).

6. Seventy-two percent approve women working if husband is capable of support, compared to 60 percent in 1970 and 24 percent in 1945 (Public Opinion, 1980: 24).

7. Fifty-seven percent of female respondents strongly believe women with young children should not work unless it is financially necessary (Public Opinion, 1979b: 16); 69 percent felt children suffer when the mother works (Public Opinion 1979a: 36). However, in 1980, only 40 percent said "working women make worse mothers," while 48 percent split evenly between "working women make better mothers" and "it makes no difference if a mother works" (Public Opinion, 1980: 25).

8. In 1977 66 percent said the couple should not move if the wife is offered promotion elsewhere (Public Opinion, 1979a: 37); 90 percent of married employed women would give up their own careers and relocate if essential to accommodate a husband's career, but only 22 percent feel their husband would do the same (Public Opinion, 1980: 25). In 1978 78 percent believed a wife should put husband and children ahead of her own career (Public Opinion, 1979a: 36). Fifty-two percent hold the wife responsible for keeping the house clean, even if she works as hard as the husband (Public Opinion, 1979a: 36).

9. Sixty percent of women and 63 percent of men prefer to work for a man, given the choice (Gallup, 1976: 45).

10. Between 1971 and 1976 the percentage of degrees awarded women went from 9 to 20 percent in business, from 14 to 20 percent in computer science, and from 1 to 3 percent in engineering (Rotella, 1980), though one engineering school reported to Horst (1980, conversation) that it had 30 percent women in 1980.

11. In 1979 55 percent of employed women did clerical and service work, and women were 98.6 percent of all secretary-typists, 97.6 percent of private household workers, 80 percent of all clerical workers, and 59 percent of all service (non-private, household) workers (U.S. Department of Labor, 1980).

12. In 1979 median weekly earnings were: white men, $306; Black men, $233; Hispanic men, $226; white women, $187; Black women, $174; Hispanic women, $156 (U.S. Department of Labor, 1980: 50).

13. Between 1970 and 1978 the number of not yet married women increased 111 percent; the number of divorced but not remarried, 170 percent (U.S. Department of Commerce, 1978: 2). Female-headed families increased 51 percent between 1970 and 1980 (San Diego Evening Tribune, 1980).

14. In 1970 the mean number of children per woman was 1.9; in 1978, 1.6 (U.S. Department of Commerce, 1978: 2). Birth expectation of currently married 18-29-year-olds stabilized in the 1970s at slightly more than 2 per woman. A larger number in 1978 than in 1971 expected 0-2 children (U.S. Department of Commerce, 1978: 30).

REFERENCES

ASTIN, H. S. (1976) "Continuing education and the development of the adult woman." The Counseling Psychologist 6, 1:55-60.

BRIGHTMAN, C. (1978) "The women of Williamsburg." Working Papers (Jan/Feb): 50-63.

BUNCH, C. (1976) "Beyond either/or: feminist options." Quest 3: 2-17.

California Post-Secondary Education Commission (1980) Post Secondary Education in California: Information Digest. Sacramento: Author.

CARDEN, M. L. (1974) The New Feminist Movement. New York: Russell Sage Foundation.

CHAFE, W. H. (1972) The American Woman: Her Changing Social, Economic and Political role, 1920-1970. New York: Oxford University Press.

DIXON, M. (1970) "On women's liberation." Radical America (February): 27.

———(1971) "Why women's liberation?" pp. 419-432 in E. Adams and M. L. Briscoe (eds.) Up Against the Wall, Mother. Encino, CA: Glencoe.

ENGLISH, D. (1981) "The war against choice: inside the anti-abortion movement." Mother Jones 6, 11: 169-176.

EVANS, S. (1979) Personal Politics. New York: Knopf.

FERRISS, A. (1971) Indicators of Trends in the Status of American Women. New York: Russell Sage Foundation.

FISHER, B. (1977) "Race and class: beyond personal politics." Quest 3, 4: 2-14.

FREEMAN, J. (1975) The Politics of Women's Liberation. New York: David McKay.

———(1979) "Resource mobilization and strategy: a model for analyzing social movement organization actions," pp. 167-189 in M. N. Zald and J. D. McCarthy (eds.) The Dynamics of Social Movements. Englewood Cliffs, NJ: Prentice-Hall.

FRIEDAN, B. (1963) The Feminine Mystique. New York: Dell.

———(1967) Report of the President. NOW Second National Conference, Washington, DC.

———(1977) It Changed My Life. New York: Dell.

Gallup Opinion Index (1976) Women in America. Report 128, March.

GORDON, S. (1980) "Marketing the working woman." Working Papers for a New Society 7, 3: 52-54.

HACKER, S. (1979) "Sex stratification, technology and organizational change: longitudinal case study of ATT." Social Problems 226, 5: 539-557.

HOLE, J. and E. LEVINE (1973) Rebirth of Feminism. New York: Quadrangle Books.

HOWE, F. (1977) Seven Years Later: Women's Studies Programs in 1976. Report of the National Advisory Council on Women's Educational Programs.

HUBBELL, S. (1980) "The state of the unions for women." Working Woman (June): 62+.

KAGAN, J. "How management hurts women: an interview with Linda Keller Brown." Working Woman (December): 75+.

KLEIMAN, C. (1980) Women's Networks. New York: Lippincott and Crowell.

LANDECKER, W. (1963) "Class crystalization and class consciousness." American Sociological Review 28: 219-229.

Los Angeles Times (1981) "Tim LaHaye: waging war against humanism." February 22, San Diego County Section: 1+.

MORGAN, R. (1970) Sisterhood Is Powerful. New York: Vintage.

———(1977) Going Too Far. New York: Random House.

National NOW Times (1980-1981) "How women candidates fared at the polls." 8, 12-1: 3.

Newsweek (1981) "At long last motherhood." March 16: 86.

OPPENHEIMER, V. K. (1973) "Demographic influence on female employment and the status of women," pp. 187-199 in J. Huber (ed.) Changing Women in a Changing Society. Chicago: University of Chicago Press.

PORTER, N. M. and M. T. EILEENCHILD (1980) Effectiveness of Women's Studies Teaching. National Institute of Education Women's Studies Monograph Series.

Public Opinion (1979a) January/February.

———(1979b) October/November.

———(1980) December/January.

Redstockings (1970) "Redstockings Manifesto," pp. 533-535 in R. Morgan [ed.] (1970) Sisterhood Is Powerful. New York: Vintage.

ROTELLA, E. J. (1980) "Women's roles in economic life," pp. 329-346 in S. Ruth (ed.) Issues in Feminism. Boston: Houghton Mifflin.

San Diego Evening Tribune (1980) "More women are heading families." December 3: A-26.

SARACHILD, K. (1969) "A program for feminist 'consciousness raising.'" Notes From the Second Year: Women's Liberation—Major Writings of the Radical Feminists: 78+.

SEXTON, P. C. (1974) "Workers (female) arise." Dissent (Summer): 380-395.

SYMINGTON, N. (1981) "The questing beast." Newsline (February 25): 4.

U.S. Department of Commerce, Bureau of the Census (1978) Statistical Portrait of Women in the United States. Current Population Reports Special Studies, Series P-23N100.

U.S. Department of Labor, Bureau of Labor Statistics (1980) Perspectives on Working Women: A Databook Bulletin 2080 (October).

———Employment Standards Administration, Women's Bureau (1975) Handbook on Women Workers, Bulletin 297.d(1969) Handbook on Women Workers. Washington DC: Government Printing Office.

WALSHOK, M. (1981) Blue Collar Women: Pioneers on the Male Frontier. Garden City, NY: Doubleday.

Women in Public Office (1979) in Women: A Documentary of Progress During the Administration of Jimmy Carter 1977 to 1981. From the Office of Sarah Weddington,

Assistant to the President, The White House (B. Haugen, ed.). Washington DC: Government Printing Office.

Women Today (1971) 1, 14.

Working Woman (1980) "New survey of the 70's: women work more, better, and enjoy." 5(July): 27-29.

———(1981) "On the job: equal pay for work of comparable value." (January): 10.

YOUNG, A. M. (1979) "Back to school at 35 and over." Monthly Labor Review (August): 53-55.

PART V
CONCLUSION

13

THE FUTURE FOR WOMEN AND DEVELOPMENT

NAOMI BLACK

> In Mexico, the issue of integrating women in development seemed clear. Now after five years, I'm not so certain as I was [because] as far as I'm concerned there are very few "developed" countries. . . . Do women want to be integrated into "patriarchal development"? The goal of a feminist development strategy would be . . . to allow women to make decisions and to shape the societies in which they lived . . . [Peggy Antrobus, Jamaica, quoted in *Forum 80*, July 16, 1980].

These remarks were made at an unofficial meeting connected with the United Nations' second world conference on women, held in Copenhagen in 1980; they refer to the earlier Mexico City meetings held for International Women's Year. The statement returns to the topic of the beginning section of this book, which is also the topic of this conclusion: the possibilities for an adequate theory of development. Like Peggy Antrobus, I shall focus on the recent United Nations conferences on women. At the official meetings attended by national representatives, the currently accepted views about the relationship between women and development were authoritatively stated. At the accompanying unofficial meetings, alternative feminist views were articulated, though rarely recognized. The chapters of *Women and World Change* supply evidence to support the feminist interpretation.

One lesson of this collection of essays is, of course, the wide diversity of settings within which women, like men, live out their lives.

Even within the smallest national unit there are divisions of caste and class, of ethnicity and religion, all of which shape the distinctive form taken by divisions of age and status within families. Yet the chapters demonstrate that such dissimilarities of situation produce at least three shared characteristics for women: first, persistent disadvantage in treatment and well-being; second, minimal access to authority and influence on planning for change; and third, dependence upon other women. That is, women share men's hardships of situation, but with added handicaps, because under present conditions men have privileged access to limited resources. Direction of change remains essentially a male monopoly. As a result, women need the support of other women in a way that men do not need the support of other men. The first two points are by now commonplaces in the analysis of the situation of women; the third is less so. The three points together have important implications for development, and for development theory.

This volume has provided additional documentation of the continuing disadvantage and lack of influence on the part of women even under conditions where development seems relatively well advanced. Levels of development and basic dissimilarities of political, social, and economic systems do not seem to make much difference. As Ann Cottrell shows, even policies ostensibly directed at improving the situation of women, such as equal opportunities legislation in that advanced industrial society, the United States, often have other purposes and consequences than the welfare of women. Similarly, Mary Ruggie demonstrates how two countries generally thought of as outstanding in their concern for women, Britain and Sweden, in fact have women as only a secondary consideration, even in policies for areas such as day care; the result is facilities at a level that these countries' own guidelines identify as inadequate. In less developed countries, there continues to be uniform reliance on the unpaid or underpaid services provided by women.

In a wide range of settings, female domestic labor provides the necessary support for the male workforce. As Janet Salaff shows, Singapore's industrial policy has been able to leave certain key social services to women in the informal sector; the city-state is also able to be an attractive location for investment because of women's willingness to work for uneconomic salaries. Lynn Bolles demonstrates a similar pattern in Jamaica. In both of these, as even in the developed societies, the underpaid labor of women workers cushions the unemployment resulting from shifting phases of economic development. In the least developed nations, subsistence agriculture, largely carried on by women, still invisibly provides the food supply that keeps famine from being endemic on a worldwide scale. However, as Rae Blumberg and Katherine Newman show, the movement toward cash crops and agribusiness proceeds in ignorance of the role women play in agriculture; this ignorance has had a disastrous effect on basic nutrition and on the situation of women.

The chapters also show the essential irrelevance of ideologies. Development consistently means the "double shift" for women, who find full-time paid labor added to the continuing responsibility for homemaking and child care. Barbara Jancar gives a detailed account of how the double shift has persisted in planned economies since the time of the Revolution. Other contributors show the same pattern: Cottrell for the capitalist United States, Ruggie for socialist or semi-socialist Sweden and Britain, and Nanciellen Davis for a francophone Catholic community in Canada. In a long book we were not able to include material about women in the Moslem world, but the work of scholars such as Deniz Kandiyoti (1980) shows something similar developing in those societies, which still have the strongest ideological commitment to confining women to the home.

The disadvantage and powerlessness of women is a familiar enough topic. I have not commented much here on the ways in which development seems actually to have worsened the situation of women, though the chapters by Newman and Blumberg document it at length in relation to agriculture and land tenure. Rather, the theme is the relative lack of change in the situation of women—the continuities and commonalities of women's situation over time and place. Most important of these is the dependence of women upon each other. I have in mind here more than just the role of formal and informal women's organizations, though I have been struck by how common such groups are in almost all societies and by how little research attention they get. I would include also the influence of individual women on one another's opportunities, both within families and in different spheres of action. Women's autonomy on an individual or a group basis is never a centrally important cause for men. Women's efforts therefore remain crucial for any change in their situation.

In a society where women are not cloistered and in fact are more steadily employed than men, Bolles shows the dependence of Jamaican industrial women workers on the homemaking services of their younger female relatives. Salaff and Jancar show similar dependence in Singapore, China, and the Soviet bloc, and Salaff's account stresses the importance of older women as role models and encouragers. In other articles we see how family and community linkages among women can become informal consultative and action groups that articulate women's specific goals; Susan Bourque and Kay Warren document this process among Andean women of Peru. Another example is provided by my account of a social Catholic women's organization in France that developed a training program for the participation of women in politics. These articles suggest that male indifference to women's issues is worldwide. Women can rely only on their own responses. Barbara Ramusack reinforces the point with her account of the connections between the Indian and British women's movements in campaigns for the amendment of the laws regulating marriage in India. Her chapter should discourage any sentimentality about sisterhood or about the difficulties involved in collaboration across differences of culture, economy, and nationality. At the same time, like this book as a whole, Ramusack's chapter directs our attention to the shared situation and interests of women, and to the areas in which they seem to share a desire for change—a desire not given much prominence by their men. A limited but still real degree of practical autonomy may grow out of women's individual or collective response to shared disadvantage and to male monopoly of power.

When I began to study the relationship between women and development, I thought of women's mutual dependence as at most a way of coping with the additional burdens imposed by change. I now believe that such cooperation is more significant. It seems possible that new directions for development and for theories about development can be found in the implicit programs of these responses. The shared experience of women has produced viewpoints, practices, and policies that are relevant to the problems the notion of development is supposed to address. The evidence of this volume is that it is possible after all to work out a satisfactory theory of development—which will be the theory of development with feminist equity.

In the first chapter of this book, Thelma McCormack presented an analysis of the failure of various forms of development theory to address adequately the situation of women. Such theory seems to have been unable to rise above the historical evidence of the continuing subordination of the female half of humanity. The outcome is, as McCormack shows, an unjust theory that takes no account of the legitimate claims of women. I would argue here that the result is also an inadequate theory, ineffective precisely because it takes no account of the possibly relevant portions of women's distinctive experience. A "just" theory would aim at articulating a possible situation of well-being that includes women as equals. Such a theory could then incorporate the more specific goals and perspectives of women. It could then be effective in a way impossible for the limited theories with which the theorists of development must work today. Development with feminist equity would thus be more than integration of women into development by recognizing their roles as resources and recipients and their claims to equal benefits. That would be *equity*, and it is the least that can be asked. *Feminist equity*, more difficult to achieve, would entail a rethinking of the processes and priorities for change. The outcome would be development with equity for women.

In terms of development theory, the greatest change in the postwar years has been the widespread acceptance by governments of the need for deliberate intervention into the course of change. But notions of equity, let alone feminist equity as we understand it here, have had little impact. Instead, governmental response to demonstrated inadequacies of development theory has taken the form of a shift to the international level. This is not surprising in an increasingly interdependent world. Although national governments continue to be the main initiators and agents of policy, we can expect expanding coordination, even cooperation among them. As a result, explanations—theories—seem likely to be increasingly global. Accordingly, I shall turn to the international scene for a final examination of the current prospects for a theory of development with feminist equity. There we shall see the usual discouraging pattern continuing—but also some grounds for hope.

THE UNITED NATIONS' OFFICIAL CONFERENCES ABOUT WOMEN

The last few years have seen what looks like a remarkable recognition of women within the United Nations system. 1975 was designated as International Women's Year (IWY), and 1975-1985 as the International Decade for Women. A resolution and then an international treaty outlawing discrimination against women were approved. An international research and training institute (INSTRAW) has been set up, along with a voluntary fund for the Decade. The most visible activities have been the two large international conferences held under United Nations auspices: the world Conference of the International Women's Year held at Mexico City from June 19 to July 2, 1975, and the World Conference of the United Nations Decade for Women, usually referred to as the Mid-Decade Conference, held at Copenhagen, July 14 to 30, 1980. The Mid-Decade Conference requested that another meeting be held at the end of the decade; it is not clear whether this will happen.

These two "women's" conferences belong to the series of United Nations technical conferences that began with the World Conference on the Environment held in Stockholm in 1972. Their topics are basic human problems such as population, food, water, and desertification. They are generally thought of as devoted to shared "functional" issues of worldwide concern, and are therefore expected to avoid the major political conflicts that divide the world. The IWY and Mid-Decade conferences are included in this sequence because of the close connections that are felt to exist between the situation of women and the problems under consideration (Ferraru, 1979). All these conferences are necessarily related to the issue of development. In the case of the women's meetings the connection was made explicit by placing the year and decade of women in the period of the United Nations' Decade of Development, 1970-1980. The resolution proclaiming IWY included "the integration of women in the total development effort" among the three purposes of the year. The other two purposes were more traditional: "promoting equality between men and women" and "increasing the contribution of women to the strengthening of world peace" (United Nations, 1976: 2). Development became the central issue of the two conferences in question.

The Mexico City and Copenhagen conferences each produced a substantial report, including long lists of specific recommendations. They include extensive collections of possible policies related to women in the context of economic growth. The lists are randomly arranged and incoherent, diluted by items that have little or nothing to do with the situation of women. Enforcement is entrusted to national governments, assisted only by the weak and isolated international institute, INSTRAW. At best, these are consciousness-raising provisions. Not surprisingly, the 1980 conference, whose major purpose was to monitor possible change since the 1975 meeting, reported little improvement and even some regression in the situation of women over the intervening five years.

Of more interest here, however, are the general statements of principle and interpretation. These reports are official United Nations documents, hammered out in each case over a long series of meetings and approved by the substantial majority of the world's governments. Those nations that did not support the statements made it clear that they did so because of specific sections that were against national policy, not because of disagreement with the basic logic of the arguments made. For example, the United States would not approve declarations including statements that equated Zionism with racism, or that supported noncompensated nationalization of foreign investments. Many nations also registered reservations about particular sections, in order to retain control over areas seen as strategically or culturally important, such as population policy. In general, the debates and reports show agreement about the relationship between women and development. The "official" interpretation of this crucially important relationship can be demonstrated in the reports of the two conferences. This interpretation is currently shared by those responsible for development planning both nationally and internationally.

To begin with, this official position now recognizes the worldwide disadvantage of women:

> While they represent 50 per cent of the world adult population and one third of the official labor force, they perform nearly two thirds of all working hours, receive only one tenth of the world income and own less than 1 per cent of the world property [United Nations, 1980: 8].

The implicit comparison is in terms of the whole of the world's population. Few speakers at either conference were willing to recognize that similar disadvantages existed within their own national units. The argument about causes of inequality supports this global view:

> The issue of inequality as it affects the vast majority of women of the world is closely related to the problem of underdevelopment which exists mainly as a result of unjust economic relations. . . . [It] stems to a very large extent from mass poverty and general backwardness of the majority of the world's population caused by underdevelopment [United Nations, 1980: 4-5].

The causes of these "unjust economic relations" are repeatedly identified; they are worldwide structures of exploitation, summed up as a combination of imperialism, colonialism, and racism.[1] The primary policy goal in relation to the situation of women is therefore to end underdevelopment by ending the unjust conditions responsible for it. In programmatic terms, this goal amounts to support for the various segments of the New International Economic Order, a specific policy for redistributing wealth and power from developed to developing nations; the NIEO has been described in detail by a coalition of Third World countries working together in United Nations and other meetings since the 1960s. Imperialism, colonialism, racism, and the like describe the principles of the present unacceptable order. Development, implying peace, prosperity, equality, and justice, sums up the structure of the desired future system.

The NIEO is still far from general acceptance. The developed nations in particular dispute the implications of parts of the analysis. But even those states that are less than enthusiastic about the specific provisions of the NIEO tend to accept that part of the argument that links poverty to underdevelopment—and the disadvantaged situation of women to both. Thus, even developed nations, capitalist or noncapitalist, accept the view that development is the central priority in relation to women. They accept the argument that the situation of women is a secondary consequence of world conditions. The 1975

Declaration of Mexico is explicit about the primacy of overall change: "Individual human rights can be realized only within a framework of total development" (United Nations, 1976: 4). Some few delegates at the conferences disagreed with this point of view, most notably representatives of New Zealand and Australia. In response to their sustained efforts, the following minimal concession was added in the 1980 report: "The unfavorable status of women is aggravated in many countries, developed and developing, by *de facto* discrimination on the grounds of sex." A footnote adds, "In a group of countries [this is] called sexism" (United Nations, 1980: 7).

The conference delegates, by and large, disliked the term "sexism," which they considered barbarous and insulting. Their incorporation of it into the report reduced it to something trivial, easily handled under conditions of full development—a few legal changes, a little education, a moderate amount of goodwill. Soviet bloc spokesmen even denied the very existence of discrimination in their societies. Yet, the worldwide statistics of women's disadvantage suggest the existence of a structure equivalent in importance to the racism, imperialism, and colonialism cited in the two conference reports. If racism, imperialism, and colonialism are more than "*de facto* discrimination," why not also the persistent domination and exploitation of women by men? However, although the 1975 conference included apartheid and Zionism among the structural causes of underdevelopment and therefore of inequality, sexism was not mentioned at all in that report, and in 1980 it achieved only the derisory footnote cited above.

In such a context, the official goal of the IWY conference is not particularly encouraging when it offers women the prospect of "the creation of a just society where women, men, and children can live in dignity, freedom, justice and prosperity" (United Nations, 1976: 7). "Justice," the key term, has already been formulated in such a way that the situation of women is considered only indirectly, and without consulting them. The 1980 conference, which found little progress since 1975, reported the least in the area of women's authoritative participation in planning and decision-making, even within international organizations including the United Nations itself. The 1980 report responded to this problem by reformulating the goals of the Decade for Women. A typical statement is the following: "equality of rights, responsibilities, and opportunities for the participations of women in development, both as beneficiaries and as active agents" (United Nations, 1980: 4). Equity demands no less. Implementation will depend, however, upon the understanding of the causes of inequality. Here development remains central. The deep structure of gender relationships continues to be invisible. It is assumed that women will serve their own cause by participating in development, for it is underdevelopment that explains their disadvantage. Sexism has not yet been recognized as a fundamental explanation of how societies are organized.

What has happened is that the international system has finally noticed the potential instrumental role of women in development. There are related prudential reasons for paying direct attention to the impact of change on the female half of the population. "Population" is one of the key terms, for even planners are beginning to realize that women play an important role in reproduction. In general, there is growing awareness that women's resistance or indifference can cripple promising projects, and that ignorance about women's activities has caused planners to overlook significant sources of labor, food, and even creativity. Women's organizations are now sometimes noticed as useful devices for cooptation. Such aspects of the situation of women as education and labor force participation are now recognized as useful if crude indicators of the level of a state's development. The official line expressed at the conferences thus sees the incorporation of women into development as necessary. But anything unsatisfactory about the situation of women continues to be interpreted as one of the consequences of the failures of development.

Certainly there is widespread agreement about one point: Until now, development has been at best partially successful in some places, close to a failure in others. The overall level of human well-being has not increased globally, the gaps in well-being between nations and classes have if anything increased, and it is not even possible any more to argue for a continuing process of improvement. The technologies of which so much was expected have been restricted in impact and have had unanticipated negative by-products, as with the "green revolution" of high-yield foodstuffs, the contraceptive pill, and the domestic use of nuclear power. The hoped-for industrialization has only rarely occurred, and its beginnings have not been associated with improvements in living conditions for the majority of the population. The activities of the less developed nations' Group of 77 are essentially a response to such disappointments; they explain them by the poorer nations' lack of access to necessary resources. The NIEO spells out how to change the balance of advantage to favor the less-developed nations. It is in this context that women become important as a neglected resource.[2]

A feminist would make a rather different argument and claim that the failure of development is a consequence of the situation of women. This is not to say that the elimination of sexism would guarantee success in development. However, the pervasive complex of attitudes and institutions that keeps women subordinate must take part of the blame for the continuing lack of success. "Integration of women in development," as in the IWY goals, will not in itself be enough to alter the situation, for it does not imply acceptance of women as equals in the sense of taking seriously their distinctive experience and values. When feminists talk of sexism, they do not refer to incidental or contingent discrimination but to masculine control of values, access, and allocation of resources. Sexism thus explains in part the persistence of underdevelopment even under conditions where structures such as imperialism, racism, or colonialism have lesser or diminishing impact, as in the planned economies of the Soviet bloc and the unplanned systems of Western Europe and the United States.

Such a feminist interpretation can be found at the meetings that accompanied the United Nations' IWY and Mid-Decade conferences, the 1975 Tribune and the 1980 Forum. This "unofficial" version of the relationship between women and development is clearly feminist, although often articulated by women who reject such a designation.

THE UNOFFICIAL CONFERENCES ABOUT WOMEN

The United Nations' large technical conferences have tended to be accompanied by unofficial meetings organized by the international nongovernmental organizations concerned with the subject matter of the main sessions. They are attended by representatives of these private voluntary organizations and also by interested individuals; in some cases governments or would-be governments subsidize delegations. The link to the main conferences is these international nongovernmental organizations, which have been granted observer or consultative standing by organs of the United Nations. Such groups are allowed a limited role at the official sessions, and provide a channel by which participants in the unofficial companion meetings may be able to communicate views. At best, the impact of the unofficial sessions is indirect; their importance is most likely to be in any message that the media convey to a worldwide public. The press paid more attention than usual to the IWY Tribune (1975) and the Mid-Decade Forum (1980) that accompanied the United Nations' official conferences on women. Statements made at the Tribune and the Forum were used as a basis for generalizations about the beliefs of the world's women. I shall use them the same way, but rather more carefully.[3]

Those who attended the women's conferences agree that press coverage, particularly of the unofficial sessions, was sensationalist and unperceptive. Much attention was paid to disagreements among the women present and to the organized disruptions staged by groups such as the PLO. Disturbances were ascribed to a "characteristically female" lack of solidarity among women, in spite of efforts at special briefings for journalists—briefings that saw as much disruption and conflict among a group that was almost all male. The disagreements were also generally interpreted to mean that development should indeed take priority over what were stigmatized as the selfish concerns of "feminists" from rich countries.

Even more sympathetic academic analysts saw a basic split between women of the developed and the developing world. In a generally perceptive account, for instance, Jennifer Seymour Whitaker of *Foreign Affairs* saw a serious incompatibility between the Western women's concern to compete with men for control of power and the Third World focus on material improvement in the condition of life (Whitaker, 1975: 174, 176). Hanna Papanek (1975: 220-222) found a contrast between concern for symbols of personal status and concern for major social and economic change, and also between formulations of women as individuals and women in the context of families. There was a tendency to contrast two groups of women: first, the limited feminist women who were believed to give priority to changing the situation of women and therefore to accept existing social, economic, and political structures; second, those women who thought that a general transformation of the existing structures was necessary if the situation of women was to be changed. The latter was thought to be the position of the women of the developing world, who showed in this way that they agreed with their leaders and with the official position, giving priority to development. One of the most widely quoted statements of the two sets of conferences was one that went roughly as follows: "To talk feminism to a woman who has no water, no food, and no home is nonsense." The impression given by reports of the meetings was clear: At these conferences no viable feminist alternative had been presented to the official views, and the women most concerned had recognized the fact.

Such assessments of the views of women about development had two distinct bases, which published reports did not always distinguish. One was women who were part of the official delegations. Very few of these women had sufficient independent political standing to be able even to speak as individuals; all had to vote as directed, supporting their countries' policies and the official interpretations.[4] Most commentators understood very well the dependent situation of such women; the press's reports of the conferences were damaging because they seemed to show women at the IWY Tribune and the Mid-Decade Forum also supporting the official view with the "real" voice of the women of the world.

The Tribune and the Forum were organized and run by representatives of the long-established voluntary international women's organizations, whose history of combined political efforts in international organization antedate the founding of the League of Nations (Whittick, 1979; International Council of Women, 1966). In the past, these groups had the major responsibility for making the League formally nondiscriminatory with respect to the hiring of women, and for the establishment within the United Nations of their Commission on the Status of Women. They also deserve considerable credit for the proclamation of International Women's Year, and contributed to the preparation for its conferences when the skimpy provision of funds and personnel proved troublesome (Sebo, 1976). At Mexico City these organizations were involved in arranging both a preliminary Journalists' Encounter and an academic seminar on women and development along with the Tribune (Tinker and Bo Bramsen, 1976). Therefore, the Tribune and the Forum really did represent the international voluntary aspects of the women's movement, the part that might be expected to provide some spontaneous and authentic communication of women's views. And observers reported, in effect, that even at the Tribune and the Forum Third World women mirrored their governments' views, sharing the official analyses and priorities. Those present, mainly the American feminists, who did not see development as primary were reported as either sharing their own governments' exploitative priorities or expressing their inability to empathize with the truly deprived.

Such an interpretation is possible only on the basis of a very unselective view of the unofficial delegates, one that overlooks the extent to which many were in fact funded or briefed by governments or other official groups. Even naive delegates noticed the unfailing praise of local conditions by many speakers and the lavish resources available to some who identified themselves only as "citizens of the world." A search for the authentic viewpoint of women can best rely on what was actually said. It is necessary to look for evidence of a perspective different from that present at the official meetings. Such evidence in fact exists, and it gives a very different picture of what was important at the unofficial meetings.

There can be no doubt that women from the developed nations came to these international meetings, particularly the first one, naively expecting an easy, sisterly agreement about goals with women of the other nations. They were jolted to learn how central national conditions were for women in other countries, particularly those suffering from gross exploitation either internally or externally. Women from North America, for instance, had not realized how life under apartheid meant that a change of regime had to take priority over all other considerations. They might have found this easier to understand if they had remembered how the trauma of the Vietnam War had dominated life in the United States. Such monopolization of resources and energy needs to be ended before any creative change is possible. Most of the obsessive, potentially explosive situations grouped under the rubrics of imperialism, colonialism, and racism are actually issues of autonomous control of resources and policy, that is, of development. This is why they are of highest priority. The unofficial women did not disagree about the necessity for removing the crucial impediments and making development possible. Where they disagreed was about how best then to develop—and their disagreement was not among themselves, but with the official views.

The process of development has the goal of appropriate and sufficient food, shelter, education, jobs, and social services for all. Once resources are available, the important disputes are about how to translate such vague goals into specific policies. *This* is the point at which the unofficial delegates diverged from and disagreed with the official ones. Consistently, the unofficial delegates focused on policies related to the needs and preferences of women and children. They repeatedly insisted, furthermore, on the need for women "to own our own lives." These are the words of an Indian woman speaking in 1980 to a session on rural women. "It is not enough to be represented by benevolent men, or even feminist men," she insisted (Forum 80, July 16, 1980).

The themes that were virtually absent at the official sessions and frequent at the unofficial ones are the following: a priority for women's concerns as having an independent, self-evident validity, and a claim that women act to formulate their own response to development and to other issues. By implication, the subordination of women's problems, women's preferences, and women's voices becomes one of those worldwide conditions that impede the proper use of resources for development. Seeing women's goals and participation as merely instrumental for male-defined and -controlled purposes has interfered with development, even under conditions when such constraints on resources as racism, imperialism, and colonialism no longer do so. Western women had wanted to make explicit the dependence of development on the elimination of sexism, and they were disappointed when their rhetoric was rejected. Non-

Western women, refusing the vocabulary of women's liberation, nevertheless made the same point in their refusal of a secondary and instrumental role for women's beliefs and their contributions.

The official position belatedly had given women some status as resources themselves. Their needs would now have priority to the extent that such consideration was useful in terms of overall economic development. To the Third World, for instance, the women's conferences were useful as a new set of forums in the battle for the NIEO. Certain specific policies related to women, such as education and contraception, would now temporarily be moved higher on the list of usefulness. But this meant little or nothing about consulting women concerning general problems of allocation of resources, or even about the use of the newly discovered resources of the women themselves. Unofficial women, by contrast, were asking for a whole new shape to the agendas and for a different set of people—female—to make certain of the key decisions. This would mean the end of sexism; it identifies sexism as the unrecognized structural condition barring development.

The unofficial view might be thought of as a concealed feminist stance. It can be seen in statements made by Third World women in a variety of unofficial contexts. For instance, Zoreh Tabatieh of Iran reported as follows about the deliberations of the Group of 77 delegates who drew up the Declaration of Mexico:

> We wanted it to represent some sort of spirit or declaration of the Group of 77. *There were very few women there,* and *those who were tried, by hook or by crook, to make sure whatever was in it reflected women* [United Nations, 1975a: 27-28; emphasis added].

That is, the overarching international goals are accepted, but once those have been achieved, there are separate important goals, related to development, that women value and that women articulate. We can see something similar in statements by Jamaican Lucile Mair, active at the 1975 conferences and Secretary-General of the 1980 Mid-Decade Conference. She tended to be very impatient with the North American feminists, particularly when they complained that the conferences had been contaminated by politics through the intrusion of the stereotyped issues of world dispute. The 1975 Declaration of Mexico, she said impatiently and correctly, had not "aggravated any tensions among women as women" (United Nations, 1975a: 6). Certainly it was not as women that Americans and Jamaicans disagreed about claims to ownership of natural resources. Lucile Mair seemed typical of Third World women when she scolded feminists for paying insufficient attention to the inequalities between women in countries at different levels of development:

> We would like to see the position of women in developed and developing countries on a level with men, but equally important, if not more important, we would like to see the conditions of these women brought closer together so that the appalling level of living of women in developing countries could be brought closer to that in developed countries [United Nations, 1975a: 6].

This looks like the familiar official focus on resources. But when we look at the uses of those resources, it turns out that Lucile Mair has a view close to that of the unofficial women, and very remote from that of the official men:

> *Women have a common agenda and are linked by a common biology. . . .* Women have to be part of the processes of war and peace. All women are affected by political conflicts and by the expenditure of vast sums on armaments that could go towards education, health, and jobs. [Forum 80, July 15, 1980; emphasis added].

This is once again an argument for a changed agenda that will be defined by women. The same argument can be found in a statement by a North American activist. This is from a report made to the National Council of Jewish Women:

> Workshops, sponsored by non-governmental organizations, should have provided ample opportunity for dialogue on the subject of women's issues. The workshops on adolescent pregnancy, child care, nutrition, equality in marriage and family life, women and credit, growing older, female circumcision, and family violence, were probably well attended. *But*, as an American and a Jew, I could not participate in them.

The tone of regret is unmistakable. She continues:

> I was needed to attend workshops on more volatile subjects [National Council of Jewish Women, 1980].

She spent her time in contest with representatives and supporters of the PLO. The situation of the nation of Israel was for her as for them more important than any other topic, including those related to allocation of resources for development. But after the crucial issues came the ones which would be dominant in the happy future when she was no longer prevented from paying attention. They are items from the women's agenda to which Lucile Mair referred, an agenda articulated by women yet affecting everyone. They are not items that appear with any prominence, if at all, on the lists of topics associated with official views about development.

The unofficial view may be summed up by a statement made by an English feminist who thought the unofficial delegates, to the extent that they were really unofficial, largely in agreement. Dale Spender (1980) wrote,

> When comments such as "to talk feminism to a woman who has no water, no food, and no home is nonsense" become the "quote of the day" and are blazoned across the newspapers *without anyone seriously asking why it is that women have no water, no food, no freedom of movement, no autonomy*, one wonders if there is any hope. But then, when so many women get together as they did at Forum and talk so seriously about peace and a refusal to become involved in men's wars, I feel some grounds for optimism.

The wars against imperialism, racism, and colonialism were not seen as men's wars. But afterwards—afterwards the feminist plan for post-war was very different.

CONCLUSION: LES FEMMES VONT ENTRAINER LES HOMMES

It had been hoped to end this book with a neat and specific list of policy changes that would be desirable, justified by an emerging theory of development with feminist equity. I end instead with an appeal for a new perspective. The necessary research has been started and could, given funding, provide the needed data on what the invisible half of humanity is doing and could do. That research could bring into view the vast networks of women's organized and more informal systems of mutual support. The goals implicit and explicit in these systems provide the policies that are missing from development as we know it. But more important, missing is a mode of understanding that will shift women from a resource to a central feature of public life. To see women as instrumental is to continue the subordination that sexism means. The gap between the official and the unofficial views of the relationship between women and development is discouraging; the new feminist scholarship represented here seems to have had almost no impact. If the official view continues to be dominant, the so-called integration of women in development is likely to make little difference either for the situation of women or for the faltering processes usually called development.

It is important not to be misled by the now common inclusion of women as resources in plans for development. Such limited, instrumental integration will not have great impact. It will certainly not have the systems-transforming consequences that might be hoped for. We may take an example from the most recent World Development Report of the World Bank, as the epitome of official views on the theory of development. Women are now mentioned throughout the Bank's analysis, and the one reform most strongly urged is primary education for girls. This may be the best investment a developing country can make; although many women will not enter the paid labor force, their education will pay off in increased use of contraception, improved family nutrition, and decreased infant mortality. This same Bank report stresses the importance of contraception in planning for growth, and the crucial role of popular consultation. Yet there is something quite surprising in a featured account of a successful experiment in family planning. This is the case of the "banjars of Bali," which are village councils attended monthly by adult males. Here a public commitment is made by men to use contraception. The chiefs of the villages with the highest reported pledges are rewarded. Result: 49 percent of eligible couples are said to be participating, and "the average number of children a Balinese woman could expect . . . [has] fallen from 5.8 in mid-1969 to 3.8 in 1976" (World Bank, 1980: 80). What is missing is any involvement on the part of the women involved, and any consideration of family or fertility *control* as contrasted to simple reduction. Assuming the figures may be trusted, 49% use is high, but still low compared to potentiality; one is entitled to wonder, in any case, if the program will continue once the incentives for the men are removed. Recent research links sustained fertility reduction less to economic incentives than to changes in family relationships transmitted mainly by women (Degler, 1980). Other evidence suggests that women's organizations are the most effective agents for change in women's behavior (Caplan and Bujra, 1979). The impact of programs such as the "banjars of Bali" seems likely to be merely a temporary reduction of births; apart from the milder version of inducements, it resembles nothing so much as the ill-fated sterilization programs attempted in India. A society is perpetuated in which reproduction is seen as essentially uncontrollable, and the role of women is limited to that of a biological machine. Individual women and families will reap short-term benefits, but the overall processes will not change.

Such instrumental views of the role of women produce praise of something like the Malaysian women's "Rice Noodles Cottage Industry" featured on a poster prepared by INSTRAW. This new industry represents the women's "yearning to complement the activities of their farmer-husbands" and is "only done to fill the time released from cultivating paddy and tapping rubber." That is, noodle production is added to normal housekeeping and farming, and on occasion includes working until midnight after normal chores are completed. This double shift is described by INSTRAW as having "occupied their time meaningfully." The new activity does indeed add to "family income," and thereby adds new value for the GNP. But it does not respond to the demand that women have impact on development plans, for it perpetuates a traditional cottage industry that is at best a stopgap measure for supplementing insufficient income in the main cash sectors of the economy. Nor does it support or recognize women's noncash contributions to the economy, for it ignores the continuing agricultural and household work of women, while adding another fatiguing cash-producing burden (INSTRAW, 1980). It represents an integration of women in development in a way that gives little help to women and none to development.

Yet alongside these continuing mainstream interpretations there are tantalizing suggestions of something closer to the approach that needs to be promoted. Even the World Bank is now talking of "human needs," although still as a proximate goal for economic strength and growth. The mode of analysis known as the "global problematic" focuses on holistic interpretations of worldwide social change. As John Ruggie points out, the global problematic has been developing in the context of the United Nations' functional conferences and particularly the unofficial sessions accompanying them (Ruggie, 1980). In 1979 the well-known scholar Richard Barnet presented in the *New Yorker* magazine, and thus to a substantial official audience, an argument that had a resemblance to the one being made here. Barnet's discussion, without being feminist, included discussion of the situation of women at all the appropriate points, in relation, for example, to subsistence agriculture, to migration, to education, and to population policy. He concluded, "Our educational system inoculates us against empathy. The survival values that our society prizes are individualist. We are trained to be cerebral, thick-skinned, and obsessed with ourselves. These are not the survival values of a world of scarcity." Nor are they the female values. Barnet (1979:114) adds, "The task of politics in an age of scarcity is to create institutions that enable people to do what they know they must." The formulation ends with an almost despairing question, searching for the necessary missing values and institutions. Barnet is thus aware of the absence of solutions in the current official formulations, but he does not yet know where to look for them.

A member of the group that works on development policy, an official of the United Nations Development Program, gave an unofficial response—unofficial in the double sense that she was not speaking on behalf of her employer, and she was accepting an "unofficial" or feminist version of the role women ought to play in development. In a 1976 article first presented at a seminar preceding the IWY conference, Ulla Olin made much the same argument as Barnet about development needs in the realm of values and institutions. She concluded, however, by recommending the model of an existing institution that

> shelters, protects, and nurtures *all* its members; it is also a place of constant competition and rivalry, with compromises and sharing as its basic ingredients in resolutions of conflicts; it demands sacrifices and gives rewards.

She was writing about the family. Working from its example and base,

> there would seem to be scope for much needed social innovation, in which women would have an opportunity to contribute their share *as women* [Olin, 1976: 129].

The family is the source of the values, the specific goals, and the organizations of female cooperation. Specific female experience thus becomes the missing element in the necessary improved model of development.

After the IWY conference, in the fall of 1975, a Journalists' Encounter was organized in New York by the United Nations. The three featured speakers were Danilo Dolci, Mme. Caroline Diop (of Senegal), and the well-known American feminist Gloria Steinem. Dolci spoke, much as Richard Barnet was to speak, of the world's need for a new, nonviolent culture and ethical development on the individual level. It was the standard viewpoint of the humane Western man who assimilates the human situation to the male one, refuses to admit any structural disadvantages or specific values for women, and attributes women's subordination to the imperfections of the world. Unlike Barnet, Dolci was relatively unresponsive to women's situations. Mme. Diop made a conventional Third World statement of the need to end imperialism, racism, and colonialism, and to produce the NIEO. To this, however, she added a powerful plea for the abolition of polygamy. Gloria Steinem gave, finally, a radical feminist argument that presented feminism as "the only path to humanism." The feminists' goal is a society where equality ends ascribed inferiority and makes possible the end of violence. Her feminist example was the movement from the concept of population control to the concept of reproductive freedom (United Nations, 1975b). Not many people are yet very responsive to Steinem's argument, which is very close to the one made here. Yet even Dolci's argument, like Barnet's, can be used to lead to it. In what Mme. Diop said there is the most encouragement to be found, however. To the unavoidable arguments of her national unit's political situation, she adds a women's argument, one no man would make in such a context. Denial of polygamy is equivalent to the denial of the double standard, of male sexual domination, and of existing male African views about sexuality and reproduction. An Africa where all shared her views would be a continent transformed, and one closer to being a developed continent. It should be added that Mme. Diop in fact speaks not just for herself but for an increasingly influential network of women's organizations, whose standing she reflects by her prominence. If it is discouraging how little impact she and those she represents have yet had, still there are grounds for hope in the emergence of the programs and the structures of feminism.

A report on rural women in Upper Volta supplies a slogan for future development—development that is not possible without the feminist equity that means the end of the structural constraint of sexism. Recounting development projects far more impressive than the Rice Noodles Cottage Industry, the journal *Construire Ensemble* concludes, "Les femmes ont entrainé les hommes"—the women led the men (Centre d'études économiques et sociales d'Afrique occidentale, 1980). It is no accident that Upper Volta is a country rich in traditional women's organizations. A change of two letters produced, "Les femmes vont entrainer les hommes"—the women are going to lead the men. When that happens, development will be possible.

NOTES

1. The list of structures of oppression is usually longer, and likely to include neocolonialism as well as specific examples like apartheid and Zionism. Given the difficulties of definition, I am using "imperialism" to stand for structures of economic exploitation, "colonialism" to stand for forceful foreign occupation of territories, and "racism" to mean domination of one ethnic group by another.

2. The past failure to utilize women as a resource is sometimes seen as a more direct consequence of imperialism. Anti-imperialism then includes rejection of the emancipation of women because it was a result of cultural imperialism.

3. Accounts of the conferences, official and unofficial, can be found in the United Nations documents, including the unofficial Meeting in Mexico (United Nations, 1975b); in a wide range of personal accounts made to constituent nongovernmental groups; in the few academic articles cited; and in the newspapers published for the Tribune and the Forum: *Xilonen* (1975) and *Forum 80* (1980). The latter, which was run by men, was criticized by participants at the Forum, but the other reports seem to indicate that it gave an accurate account of at least some of the relevant activity; at a large, diverse, and loosely organized set of meetings, no complete account is possible. I have made no attempt to give a full bibliography for the meetings here.

4. The majority of the delegates to these conferences were women, and some delegations even had women as their official leaders. In practice, decisions had to follow instructions given by the (male) government and by those males among the delegates who had actual power.

REFERENCES

BARNET, R. (1979) "The world's resources III: human energy." New Yorker (April 7): 46-115. (Reprinted in expanded form in 1980 as The Lean Years: Politics in the Age of Scarcity. New York: Simon & Schuster.)

CAPLAN, P. and J. BUJRA (1979) Women United, Women Divided: Comparative Studies of Ten Contemporary Cultures. Bloomington: Indiana University Press.

Centre d'études économiques et sociales d'Afrique occidentale (1980) "La parole aux femmes rurales." Construire Ensemble, 1/2.

DEGLER, C. (1980) At Odds: Women and the Family in America from the Revolution to the Present. New York: Oxford University Press.

FERRARU, A. (1979) "From UNCHE to UNCSTD: aggregate data on nongovernmental organizations with observer status at UN-sponsored conferences." Presented at the annual meeting of the International Studies Association, Toronto, Canada, March.

INSTRAW (1980) "Emerging women." Poster prepared for the United Nations' International Training and Research Institute for the Advancement of Women.

International Council of Women (1966) Women in a Changing World: The Dynamic Story of the ICW. London: Routledge & Kegan Paul.

KANDIYOTI, D. (1980) "Women's work: a critical appraisal within the context of rural transformation in Turkey." (unpublished)

National Council of Jewish Women (1980) "Reflections on Copenhagen." Journal of the National Council of Jewish Women (Winter): 5-7.

OLIN, U. (1976) "A case for women as co-managers: the family as a general model of human social organization," pp. 105-128 in I. Tinker and M. B. Bramsen (eds.) Women and World Development. Washington: DC: Overseas Development Council.

PAPANEK, H. (1975) "The work of women: postscript from Mexico City." Signs 1, 1: 215-226.

RUGGIE, J. (1980) "On the problem of 'the global problematic': what role for international organizations?" Alternatives 5, 4: 517-550.

SEBO, K. (1976) "The women's movement as a transnational phenomenon." Presented at the annual meeting of the International Studies Association, Toronto, Canada, February.

SPENDER, D. (1980) "Report on the 'alternative' Copenhagen conference." WRRC Newsletter 5 (July).

TINKER, I. and M. B. BRAMSEN [eds.] (1976) Women and World Development. Washington, DC: Overseas Development Council.

United Nations (1975a) Meeting in Mexico. New York: Centre for Economic and Social Information, International Women's Year Secretariat.

——— (1975b) IWY Bulletin No. 6. New York: Department of Economic and Social Affairs, Centre for Social Development and Humanitarian Affairs, Branch for the Promotion of Equality of Men and Women.

——— (1976) Report of the World Conference of the International Women's Year. New York: E/CONF. 66/34.

——— (1980) Report of the World Conference of the United Nations Decade for Women. New York: A/CONF. 94/35.

WHITAKER, J. (1975) "Women of the world: report from Mexico City." Foreign Affairs 54, 1: 173-181.

WHITTICK, A. (1979) Woman into Citizen: The World Movement towards the Emancipation of Women in the Twentieth Century with Accounts of the Contributions of the International Alliance of Women, the League of Nations and the Relevant Organizations of the United Nations. London: Atheneum with Frederick Mueller.

World Bank (1980) World Development Report. New York: Oxford University Press.

THE CONTRIBUTORS

NAOMI BLACK is Associate Professor of Political Science at York University, Toronto. Her current research is on traditional women's organizations in Britain, France, the United States, and Canada.

ANN BAKER COTTRELL is Professor of Sociology at San Diego State University. Her research interests include cross-national marriages and women's movements.

RAE LESSER BLUMBERG is Associate Professor of Sociology at the University of California, San Diego. Her research focuses on sociology of economic development—including the emerging field of "women in development"—and socioeconomic and sexual stratification.

A. LYNN BOLLES is Director of the Afro-American Studies Program and Assistant Professor of Anthropology at Bowdoin College, Maine. Her areas of interest include peoples of African descent in the Americas, economic and urban anthropology and women's studies. She is currently studying black communities of coastal Maine.

SUSAN C. BOURQUE is Professor of Government at Smith College. Her research has been on peasant movements, rural development, women and social change, and contemporary national policy in Peru.

NANCIELLEN DAVIS is in the Department of Sociology, Mount Saint Vincent University, Halifax. She has continued her research on Acadians and women and the family, and has recently begun a comparative study of household and family in a bicultural area of nineteenth-century New Brunswick, Canada.

BARBARA JANCAR is Professor of Political Science at the State University of New York, Brockport. She has done research and published in the areas of community health policy, modernization and dissent, religious dissent in the Soviet Union, and women in the USSR and Eastern Europe.

India 25 44 63 (40) 71 74-5

Agency 69 70 73-74 75-76 78